MEXICO
TRAVEL GUIDE

**By the Editors of Sunset Books
and Sunset Magazine**

LANE PUBLISHING CO. • MENLO PARK, CALIFORNIA

Supervising Editor: **Barbara J. Braasch**

Staff Editor: **Cynthia Field Spoor**

Design: **Lea Damiano Phelps**

Cartography: **Roberta Edwards**

Mariachis, *Mexico's wandering minstrels,*
serenade everywhere south of the border.

Our thanks...

to the many people and organizations that assisted
in the preparation of this travel guide. Special
appreciation goes to Editorial Minutiae Mexicana,
Bud Lewis Associates, the Mexican National Tourist
Council, and the Mexican Government Tourist
Offices, for their invaluable help in compiling and
verifying information.

Editor, Sunset Books: David E. Clark

Second printing March 1984

**Hours, admission fees, prices, telephone numbers, and
highway designations in this book are accurate as of the
time this edition went to press.**

　　**Maps have been provided in each chapter for the spe-
cial purpose of highlighting significant regions, routes,
or attractions in the area. Check automobile clubs,
insurance agencies, government tourist offices, or travel
agents as possible sources for detailed road maps of
Mexico.**

Cover: Waves scallop the sand along Zihuatanejo Bay.
Boats' bright sails add touch of color to greenery surround-
ing this west coast vacation spot. Photographed by
Carol Simowitz.

Contents

Mexico

¡Bienvenidos!

A Warm Welcome

You'll feel welcome in Mexico from your first *bienvenidos* (greetings) to your last *hasta luego* (until you return). And return you will, to experience more of this colorful country.

Pick your pleasure

Fun in the sun? Mexico offers countless resorts along its 6,000 miles of coastline. Peek into the past? View ancient ruins hacked free from the clinging jungle. Nose for nostalgia? Revel in cities impressed with a Spanish stamp; follow the route of this country's struggle for independence. Seeking shopping? This is a land of handicrafts; try village markets for browsing and buying.

From spectacular game fishing, skin diving, and just plain loafing in the sun, to boating on high plateau lakes, to tackling the jungle on horseback—the range of activities is wide. You won't have to travel far to find the contrasts of this land.

In short treks from Mexico City, the country's cosmopolitan capital, you can visit tranquil mountain spas, sparkling seacoast resorts, quaint and historically interesting towns, picturesque artists' colonies, and awe-inspiring archeological wonders.

Meet the people

Fairly early in your visit, you'll realize that Mexico's people are one of its greatest attractions; and to understand the country, you'll need to know something about its people.

Friendly, happy, gracious, and expressive, these people are both quick and gentle in personal interchanges; spontaneity and sensitivity are reflected in their faces. In music and arts, the Mexicans are more liberated and exuberant than the North Americans: bold colors and powerful forms are characteristic of both ancient and modern artists and architects.

Folk art is special

For the U.S. shopper, accustomed to a machine-made world, part of the appeal of Mexican folk art lies in its handcrafted quality. Perhaps more important, it represents a way of life that is still in touch with nature. Many of these objects could not emerge from our modern culture—Tarascan altar offerings of wheat, for example; Huichol altar depictions of animals in yarn; or Metepec visions of paradise in ceramic. Nor are we accustomed to everyday kitchen bowls, baskets, or birdcages individually designed and made by hand.

The Mexican techniques vary from primitive pottery making to refined lacquerwork, from weaving of rough-textured fabrics to intricate embroidery. Designs are nearly always geometric, often with a childlike simplicity that is deceptive because it is anything but naive. And they are generally traditional, for the motifs may have been in use for generations, if not for centuries.

Whole villages in Mexico do one kind of work. But from village to village and from region to region, you'll find astonishing diversity; Mexico's mountains have provided the long isolation that is a prime ingredient in the development of distinctive local cultures.

Your introduction to Mexico

Mexico appeals to almost everyone. We hope this book will lead you to happy discoveries in this land of variety. Consider it an introduction to the country, its people, its customs, and its atmosphere.

New in this edition is an "Essentials" section reviewing accommodations, transportation, tours, and entertainment for each of Mexico's seven areas (see pages 149–158). The "Details at a glance" feature in each chapter offers a regional overview. But your best bet before setting out on a trip to Mexico is to check with a travel agent for current information.

Maya temples at Palenque

Mexico—where yesterday, today, and mañana merge...

Leisure, West Coast style

Chiapas Indians

Acapulco's native dancers

...this welcoming land offers color, spirit, creative flair

Classic encounter at Mexico City bullring

Sea of Cortez prize

Braided tassel brooms

Colorful fiesta balloons

Multicolored plates and pots

Rock outcropping becomes craggy island when tide comes in along wide beach at Baja's tip.

Baja California

To Land's End

(For "Facts at Your Fingertips," see page 149)

Changeable Baja presents two faces to visitors. One is the stark beauty of a rugged terrain, with arroyos and barrancas crowned by cactus forests and brilliant desert flowers and punctuated by towering peaks mantled in pines. The other face is a vast winter playground for vacationers who appreciate miles of isolated beaches, fish-rich seas, and palm-shaded resorts that dot the peninsula's eastern side and southern tip.

The big news from Baja California has been the opening of the 1,659-km/1,037-mile Transpeninsular Highway (Mexico 1) extending from the U.S. border to the southern tip at Cabo San Lucas (poetically named "Land's End"). Noting that roads act as filters, Joseph Wood Krutch once wrote, "Baja California is a wonderful example of how much bad roads can do for a country." While it is true that most of Baja was once the preserve of private pilots and auto adventurers with all-terrain vehicles, the paved highway has made the whole peninsula a motor route—complete with a string of government-financed hotels, and with campgrounds in such startling locations as the Vizcaino Desert.

Baja offers no ancient cathedrals, large marketplaces, or brassy night life beyond the border. Tijuana and Mexicali—both border towns—are its largest cities. Only Ensenada and La Paz qualify as small towns; other spots are little more than villages.

But beyond the main highway lies a land of antiquity, of pastel deserts and startling green oases, of deep blue waters and crashing surf, and of supreme peace and quiet.

A peek into the past

Conquerors, colonizers, and developers have found Baja California's rugged terrain inhospitable in the extreme. Even today, a good portion of the peninsula remains uncultivated, unmined, and virtually uninhabited.

Since its discovery (when it was thought to be an island), Baja has changed little. Most of Mexican territory was rapidly explored, subjugated, and mapped by the Spaniards, but the peninsula continued to be an enigma until the end of the 17th century.

Hernando Cortes sent the first exploratory expedition to Baja in 1532, and he stayed there himself in 1535 after hearing tales about great pearl-fishing grounds. No permanent settlement resulted from his efforts, though in 1539 his last envoy, Captain Francisco de Ulloa, was the first to sail along both the Pacific Coast and the Sea of Cortes (Cortez).

Pirates and buccaneers — Sir Francis Drake among them—made it necessary for the Spanish to occupy Baja, establish defenses, and locate a safe port for galleons en route from the Philippines. It was then that the Bay of La Paz (Peace) received its name.

In 1697 a Jesuit missionary, Padre Juan Maria Salvatierra, landed on the coast of Baja to establish a chain of missions. Along with his followers he brought fruit trees, dates, and vegetables that remain today as reminders of the settlers' perseverance and toil. Dominicans and Francis-

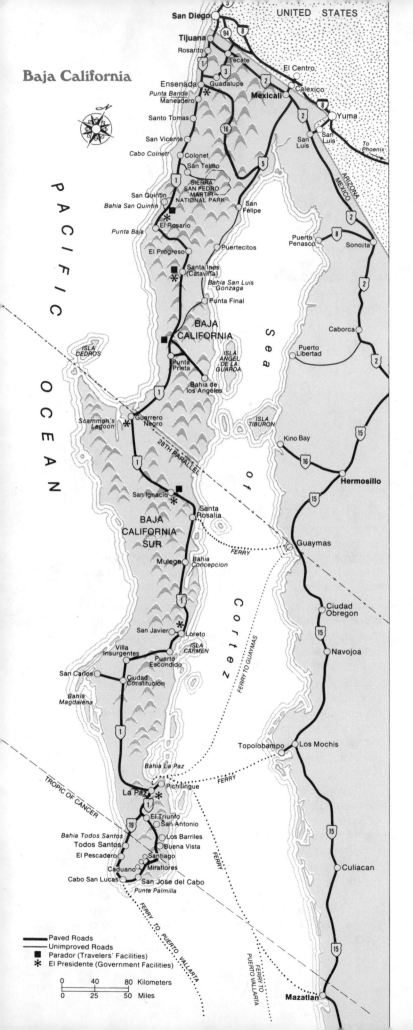

Baja California

PACIFIC OCEAN

Sea of Cortez

Paved Roads
Unimproved Roads
■ Parador (Travelers' Facilities)
* El Presidente (Government Facilities)

0   40   80 Kilometers
0   25   50 Miles

Details at a glance

How to get there

Millions of people cross the border into Baja for a day or so of shopping or sports, but until recently only the most adventurous attempted to trek down the wild peninsula. Now you can do it in your car. But if you want to avoid the time and energy commitment of driving your own car or camper, consider these alternate ways to visit Baja.

By air. Scheduled airlines serve major gulf coast settlements as far south as San Jose del Cabo, and commuter airlines cover the resorts of the Cape country. Almost every resort has its own landing strip for private planes.

A comprehensive travel service—started to provide Baja pilots with air charts and resort reservations—has recently added services for other travelers, too. For information write to Patti Senterfitt, Baja Reservation Service, 1575 Guy Street, San Diego, CA 92138, or call (714) 291-3491.

By boat. Good harbors are open for private boats, and modern car ferries crisscross the gulf between Santa Rosalia and Guaymas; between La Paz and the mainland ports of Puerto Vallarta, Mazatlan, Topolobampo, and Guaymas; and between Cabo San Lucas and Puerto Vallarta. Because ferry schedules change frequently, it's best to make your inquiries in person. Book your passage as soon as you reach your departure point. You'll need a car permit from customs to take your vehicle to the mainland, so get it first.

Tours

A growing number of outfitters and organizations lead nature expeditions to Baja—through the high desert, along the Pacific shore, on the Sea of Cortez, and among wild islands of both coasts.

Accommodations

Attractive government-owned El Presidente hotels, scattered trailer parks with hookups, and campgrounds stretch up and down Highway 1. Larger cities, Cape resorts, and guest ranches offer additional choices. For more information, see page 149.

Climate and clothes

It's best to visit Baja's high northern mountains in late spring, summer, and early autumn. From La Paz to the tip of the peninsula it is always warm and sunny—hot during the summer. Winter and spring are ideal for traveling; autumn is pleasant.

Casual attire is the note. At plush resorts you'll see women in dressy attire and men in jackets (never ties) for evening.

cans helped in the actual construction of the stone edifices (San Ignacio, rebuilt in 1786; Santa Gertrudis, built in 1796; and San Borja, built in 1801).

After more than 400 years of exploration and settlement, these fortresslike stone missions are the only marks of civilization that look at all permanent. Probably nowhere else in the habitable world is there so much land without roads and railroads, or so much shoreline without ports and power lines.

Throughout its history, Baja has been shunned by the civilized world. Baja's Indians were the poorest and most despised, and its deserts the most feared of all in Mexico. In 1847 the United States forces that conquered Alta California had an equally secure grip on Baja California, but they let it go; nobody considered Baja worth keeping.

La Frontera

For most residents of the southwestern United States, Mexico is just a few hours or, at most, a day's journey away. It is not at all unusual for a family to run down from San Diego to Baja for a spur-of-the-moment shopping spree.

La Frontera (Mexico's border) is often the first and only impression many *Norteamericanos* have of Mexico. Because of the concentration of visitors along the border, many Mexican border areas are a strange mixture of elements. Unique and atypical of the rest of Mexico, the towns and villages near the border provide a gradual transition to the Mexico that awaits those smitten with greater curiosity. Handicrafts from all over Mexico can be found here.

To Tijuana for shopping or sports

Each year Americans from the north make literally millions of border crossings over the Tijuana River into Tijuana, giving the city its title of "the most visited city in the world." From here they can catch planes or buses to points all over Mexico, or join adventurous expeditions to the interior of Baja. Most visitors come to shop and play.

New Tijuana is rising beside the river. Shops, restaurants, promenades, and a hotel are located at or near Plaza Rio Tijuana, an area formerly characterized by tumbledown shacks that periodically were washed away by the now-channeled river. Paseo de los Heroes — intended to rival Mexico City's Paseo de la Reforma—is complete with *glorietas* (traffic circles) and statues of Mexican heroes — as well as one of Abraham Lincoln. Still under construction at press time was the Cultural and Tourism Center, an architecturally innovative structure containing space for handicraft displays, a museum, a concert hall, and the spherical Omnitheater for folk entertainment from all over Mexico.

Avenida Revolucion, the traditional shopping street downtown, is another area of change, with underground wiring, offstreet parking, and new paving, buildings, street trees, and benches for people-watching. Good restaurants and bakeries add to the area's appeal.

Shopping here can be fun and truly rewarding if you know what to look for. Finds still range from the best in folk art (government-sponsored Tolan and Puebla state stores) to the gaudiest of tourist horrors — all displayed in a profusion rivaling that of Hong Kong's marketplaces. Because Tijuana enjoys free port status, some of the best buys are imports—fabrics, perfumes, and cameras.

Following Revolucion south, then east after it becomes Boulevard Agua Caliente, and continuing all the way to the new racetrack (Hipodromo de Aguacaliente), you'll discover some good Mexican folk art — tree-of-life candelabras, yarn paintings, Huichol costumes, Paracho guitars, copper ware, fabrics, tiles, and more.

Sporting events draw sizable crowds: year-round horse racing and greyhound racing at Agua Caliente Racetrack; Sunday afternoon bullfights from May through September at Plaza de Toros or the bullring-by-the-sea, Plaza Monumental; jai alai at newly repainted Fronton Palacio Friday through Wednesday evenings; and *charreadas* (Mexican-style rodeos) at any of four *charro* rings. Check the tourist information center at the border for current schedules of all sporting events.

Other attractions in Tijuana include a verdant city park that few north-of-the-border people visit. On a Sunday afternoon it teems with life, and a carnival atmosphere prevails. In summer you'll hear band concerts in the tall central pavilion donated by Tijuana's sizable Chinese colony. One of Baja's two cathedrals (Nuestra Señora de Guadalupe) is downtown at Second and Niños Heroes — on Sunday mornings the city's busiest intersection. Also on Sunday (and every other day), you can play golf on the 18-hole course at the Tijuana Country Club east of the downtown area on Agua Caliente.

Ensenada—bargains on a beautiful bay

The 107-km/66-mile drive to Ensenada takes you along a scenic coast reminiscent in part of California's cliffside stretch around Big Sur, though much more developed. From Tijuana, follow the signs for "Ensenada Cuota" (I-D), still a toll road for part of the way with a small charge for autos (slightly more for trailers and motor homes). In addition to new building developments, the sights along the way include Rosarito Beach, once the site of a famous gambling casino; Puerto Nuevo, where every house is a lobster restaurant; and Cantamar, where Southern California's hang gliders gather on cliffs and beetle-brow the beaches.

You can follow the old road (Ensenada Libre) from Tijuana past farms and dairies in the La Joya valley, reaching the coast north of Rosarito Beach. The road is slow, narrow, and curving; most motorists prefer the newer highway.

Ensenada differs widely from Tijuana, partly because of its setting on lovely Bahia de Todos Santos. A busy seaport and commercial hub, Ensenada also attracts tourists. You'll find a wide choice of many charming small hotels and restaurants; rates are generally lower than what you would pay on the U.S. side of the border. A few good restaurants also attract tourists; fresh seafood is always a good choice.

Getting around town is easy. Shops, hotels, restaurants, and sport-fishing boat rental offices line the main street — Lopez Mateos — which becomes the highway leading south to the airport (at the edge of town), to Estero Beach (resort and shops, 10 km/6 miles from Ensenada) and to La Bufadora, the famed blowhole on the coast at Punta Banda (32 km/20 miles from Ensenada). Seaward of Lopez Mateos, Lazaro Cardenas, the waterfront esplanade, leads to the civic plaza lined with 12-foot-high busts of Mexican heroes and provides access to the pier, fish markets, and marina.

Shopping is attractive for imports as well as for Mexican goods, since Ensenada, like Tijuana, is a free port. To do some comparison pricing for Mexican handicrafts, stop first at the government-owned Centro Artesanal de Ensenada, also home for the tourism office.

Lopez Mateos and the streets crossing it are the main shopping areas. Stores contain everything from fine furniture and pâpier-maché to pure junk. Look for rare black coral items.

Fishing is big — especially from April to November, and mostly for yellowtail, barracuda, albacore, white sea bass, bonito, and halibut. Bring your own boat, rent one of the many available, or join a fishing party boat. Check established catch limits, closed seasons, and license requirements. You'll find places to have your fish cleaned, filleted, iced, packed, smoked, or stored.

Other attractions include visits to the Santo Tomas Winery (weekday tours), Hussong's Cantina (a turn-of-the-century landmark), and any of the hot springs in the mountains behind town. Todos Santos Island, just opposite the shores of Ensenada, is open to adventurous visitors for hiking, fishing, and swimming. Winter surfing at Estero Beach ranges from good to excellent. At Kilometer 39 off Highway 1, a 4 to 12-foot surf breaks half a mile out.

Ensenada annually celebrates Mardi Gras (the 4 days preceding Ash Wednesday) and Cinco de Mayo, a holiday commemorating Mexico's defeat of the French in the Battle of Puebla on May 5, 1863. (May 5 is also the day on which the annual Newport-Ensenada International Yacht Race is completed.)

An upper Baja loop

With the completion of the paved road between Ensenada and San Felipe, motorists now have an unusual opportunity to cover a wide area of Baja Norte — an area including its three largest cities. The drive includes many scenic surprises and takes you through several different climates.

San Felipe, on the east coast of Baja, nestles between the Sea of Cortez and the foothills of the Sierra San Pedro Martir. It's a popular place for fishers and well known to campers.

There's good fishing all year for bottom fish such as sea trout, corvina, and baya grouper. Punta San Felipe (north of town) is a fine spot to try your luck ashore, or you can rent a boat and equipment in town. If you take your own boat, you can launch it at the village or at the cove of Punta Ensenada Blanca. Large boats take passengers for a day of fishing around Gonzaga Island (29 km/18 miles out), as well as to Punta Estrella or Punta Ensenada Blanca. Fishing boats can be chartered for trips to Bahia de los Angeles.

If you'll be fishing from a small boat, do it in the morning; the breeze that comes up around noon makes offshore boating dangerous. Also watch for the freak tides that leave shore boats high and dry — a good time to try clamming.

Mexicali, 200 km/125 miles north of San Felipe on paved Highway 5, is Baja California's largest city and the state capital — but little known, as border towns go. Though Mexicali has had a reputation for vice since U.S. prohibition days, its bawdy past is hardly evident today.

Agriculture is the backbone of Mexicali's economy, though tourism is on the rise. As part of a Mexican large-scale experimental renewal project, Mexicali's downtown was moved uptown. The shopping area was moved farther south along Calzado Lopez Mateos. New hotels, a bullring, shops, theaters, and dining spots were added.

Bullfights are held twice monthly from October through late May. Colorful charreadas also take place on winter Sundays. The city market near the border offers everything from food to folk art. Beer buffs will enjoy the tasting room at the fortresslike brewery — Baja's first.

Tecate is small, simple, and clean. Located on Highway 2 (the scenic border-hugging route between Mexicali and Tijuana), it's a pleasant place to stop. Pick up a map and visitor's guide at the tourism office south of the plaza on Callejon Libertad. Highlights include the bakery, candy store, Tecate Tile Art (handpainted tile), and local glass blower's shop in the Centro Artesenal de Tecate. Around town you'll notice piles of bricks and the kilns where they're fired. Tecate is also the home of the Tecate brewery; this imposing structure is worth a look, if only from the outside. The Market on Wheels — a flea market — sets up at various sites during the weekend in the area near the Mother's Monument on Highway 2 on the west side of town.

For a change of pace, try a complete physical renovation at Rancho La Puerta, a famed health spa. Here guests enjoy organic repasts, swimming classes, early morning jogging, yoga, jazz calisthenics, massages, facials, herbal wraps, and much more. In the mountains a few miles southeast of Tecate lies Rancho Santa Veronica, a bull ranch and tennis resort where you can learn to cape a frisky calf.

Flopping fish *fill net hauled in by energetic scoopers at San Felipe. From shore or boat, fishing is good all year.*

A short paved road connects Tecate with California State Highway 94 across the border. South of Tecate, Highway 3 heads up and over the mountains, joining Highway 1 about 24 km/15 miles north of Ensenada. A Russian religious sect settled the village of Guadalupe along the way.

Northern Baja highlights

If you plan to drive down the peninsula, use Ensenada as a springboard. From here it's 571 km/357 miles to Guerrero Negro at the boundary of the states of Baja California and Baja California Sur — an easy 2-day (or grueling 1-day) drive. You'll probably be tempted by several attractive detours along the way. A few miles below Ensenada is the check point of Maneadero for validation of tourist cards — the first place you'll use them in northern Baja.

Scenery along this stretch of Baja varies widely, from Pacific coastal views to green farming valleys to towering peaks. The high desert is alive with tall, tapering *cirio* (boojum), grooved *cardons* (cactus), graceful *ocotillo,* and tortured elephant trees.

From the sea to the mountains

Long visualized by most travelers as a vast, cactus-studded wasteland between border towns and distant fishing resorts, Baja contains some startling surprises. It is only a few hours' drive from the border to some virtually unexplored vacation retreats in the Sierra San Pedro Martir National Park, where peaks rise to their highest on the peninsula in Baja's first national park. About a century ago a few prospectors tried their hands at gold panning.

The easiest way to reach these mountains is by way of Highway 1, turning off at San Telmo (134 km/84 miles south of Ensenada). From here a graded road — passable to standard cars in good weather — leads into the foothills to two ranches offering guest facilities. Beyond, you'll need a four-wheel-drive vehicle for the steep, ever-climbing road that terminates deep in the mountains at the Mexican observatory. From this spot you are rewarded with spectacular views of the Pacific Ocean to the west and the gulf to the east. Directly below lie the barren plains of the San Felipe Desert; looking southeast, you'll see the precipitous, double-peaked Picacho del Diablo (10,126 feet) — the highest point in Baja.

(Continued on next page)

...Continued from page 15

Inlets and coves *of Bahia Concepcion offer secluded camping, good boating and swimming.*

Though the piñon and ponderosa country is ideal for camping, you must take your own food, water, and supplies; the park has no developed areas. For this reason you may prefer to make one of the following foothill ranches your home base for exploration. Reservations are advisable; both have dirt landing strips for private planes.

Meling Ranch, one of Baja's oldest cattle ranches, still looks much as it might have at the turn of the century — with the exception of modern guest accommodations that include a family-style dining room and stream-fed swimming pool. Horses and guides are available for pack trips.

Mike's Sky Ranch (also accessible from the road between Ensenada and San Felipe) is a more sophisticated resort, offering four-wheel-drive vehicles instead of horses for high-country trips. Campers will find developed sites along the San Rafael River below the ranch.

San Quintin—beach of 11,000 virgins

One historical account credits Cabrillo with naming this region in 1542. History doesn't add much about his obviously warm reception, but the name lends a colorful note to the area. A popular tourist destination despite the frequent coastal fogs, San Quintin attracts visitors who come to fish (especially for surf-perch), observe waterfowl, or enjoy the wide sweep of sandy beaches. Bird watchers stop here because the marshes are a major resting area along the Pacific Flyway. Near El Molino Viejo (old mill) and in the weathered cemetery, you'll see reminders of an English attempt at colonization in the late 1800s.

The high desert

Before Highway 1 was built, El Rosario (south of San Quintin) was the jumping-off spot to the rugged heart of Baja. Now the paved road cuts sharply east and up onto the edge of Baja's high central desert, where you'll catch your first glimpse of cirio and cardons.

If you have a four-wheel-drive vehicle, turn off at El Progreso to view the ruins of Mission San Fernando, the only Baja mission founded by Father Junipero Serra.

For desert lovers, the following 166 km/104 miles can be the most fascinating part of the trip. The high desert is best glimpsed after winter rains, when the desolate land blooms with kaleidoscopic color. Santa Ines (Cataviña) is right in the midst of the most spectacular part of the boulder-strewn desert. Accommodations include the rustic Rancho Santa Ines — once a pit stop for the Baja 1000 Road Race.

Bahia de los Angeles—on the Sea of Cortez

From the parador at Punta Prieta, a 67 km/42 mile paved road leads across the narrowest part of the peninsula to Bahia de los Angeles on the Gulf of California.

This incredibly beautiful bay is usually the first goal of people who pilot their own boats and aircraft down the gulf side of the peninsula or across the gulf by way of the steppingstone islands of "The Midriff." Some visitors make the bay their objective by car or camper. Traffic on the road is light at present, but growing steadily, causing a littering problem at this once pristine spot.

The mountainous length of Guardian Angel Island rises only a quarter of the way across the bay, forming — and protecting — a coastal channel that's filled with fish. There are yellowtail, cabrilla, and grouper all year, with dorado as well during the summer and early fall. Large schools of porpoises and whales move through the channel within sight of land. Once a productive turtle fishing region, the channel has been badly depleted by overharvesting. Shrimp boats spend some nights anchored only 100 yards from the soft, sandy beach.

Campers have a wide choice of sites, but there are only two lodges at present. Limited trailer facilities are available. To inquire in advance about fishing conditions and boat rentals or charters, write to Villa Vita Resort Hotel, 2904 Pacific Highway, San Diego, CA 92101, or Casa Diaz, Bahia de los Angeles, Apartado Postal 579, Ensenada, B.C., Mexico.

Guerrero Negro—salt and whales

On the 28th Parallel (dividing the state of Baja California from the state of Baja California Sur) sits Guerrero Negro, a rather bleak spot on the Pacific where the main business is salt production in the ponds bordering Scammon's Lagoon. You can't miss it because as you approach from the north you'll see, stabbing the sky, two massive fins — *Monumento Azteca*, a seven-story-high abstract study in steel. Guerrero Negro's facilities include a hotel, motels, and a good seafood restaurant, as well as a trailer park and gas station.

From November through February, hundreds of California gray whales head for Scammon's Lagoon to breed and train their young. Right after them come the tourists. For a whale-watching, follow signs that take you to the best viewing spots; carry binoculars and go early in the morning.

Central Baja highlights

An increasing number of sports-minded vacationers, lured by good weather, water, scenery, and comparatively low-priced resorts, are arriving at Loreto and Mulege (moo-la-hay) by plane and road. There, you're on the Sea of Cortez, which has some of the best fishing in the world. In the summer you can have your pick of marlin, sailfish, roosterfish, and grouper; smaller fish are available all year.

Southbound drivers reach the first interruption in desert harshness along the road south of the inland turn at El Rosario.

Mellow dates in San Ignacio

Date palms introduced by Jesuit colonists spread a shadowy green roof up and down the valley. In San Ignacio you can explore the well-stocked store in the plaza and the massive stone church built by the Dominicans in 1786 and still in use today. In autumn you'll find racks of drying dates in the narrow streets up behind the plaza.

No airline touches down here, but light planes can land at the short, rough, rocky strip bulldozed out of the cactus-covered lava east of town—buzz town for a taxi.

Palm-studded *San Ignacio softens harsh desert landscape.*

Swimmers stroll *away from pool at plush Cape resort to view Cabo San Lucas bay beyond.*

Santa Rosalia—northern port for Cortez ferries

Curiosity is the best reason for visiting bustling Santa Rosalia, long famous but no longer functioning as a French-owned, French-operated, French-speaking copper mining town. The town is Mexican now, though some French names and customs persist. View the prefabricated metal church designed by Alexandre Gustave Eiffel (of tower fame) for a Paris exposition; it ended up here around the turn of the century.

A ferry accommodating up to 500 passengers and 120 cars operates between Santa Rosalia and Guaymas on the mainland. Private planes and a "commuter" plane service from the mainland use an airstrip just south of town.

Palms, papayas, and mangroves in Mulege

As far inland as you can see, the valley of the Santa Rosalia River is a forest of majestic date palms where you can hear the rustling of breeze-stirred fronds, the trickling of water, and the calls of tropical birds. Just upstream from the sheltered village, the river is dammed and partly diverted to irrigate citrus, mangoes, papayas, bananas, and palms. Downstream it's a brackish tidal estuary where big snook lurk—try for them if you can resist the lure of the Sea of Cortez beyond.

Mulege is a sleepy palm oasis located 672 km/420 miles south of the border along the river. The village is so small that, even at a stroller's pace, you can visit all the shops and

displays in a few hours. Highlights include the restored mission, built in 1766 on a high point upstream from the rest of town, and the imposing state prison, on a hillside north of the plaza. Prisoners who may have jobs and families on the outside are paroled during the day, but must return to the prison at sunset.

Everyone who visits Mulege should spend at least a day on an excursion (preferably by water, though you can get there by road) to Bahia Concepcion, deservedly famous for its fine white beaches, sheltered inlets, warm water, and good fishing. This is the place for the get-away-from-it-all beachcomber. Here you can dive for scallops and lobsters, scoop up clams and oysters by the bucketful, and, if you wish, sleep out overnight on a beach of your own discovery.

You'll find Posada Concepcion trailer park just 21 km/13 miles south of Mulege, and two and three-bedroom cottages fronting part of the beach at Coyote Bay. Primitive beach campsites reached by detours off the highway can be found at Playa Santispac, Coyote Bay, and El Requeson. Water is sometimes a problem; you might want to take your own.

A large fly-in resort and several smaller hotels in Mulege provide the visitor with a choice of adequate overnight accommodations.

Loreto—the original heart of Baja

Leaving Bahia Concepcion, the highway snakes up into spectacularly rugged mountains before dropping down to Loreto on the gulf. Loreto, Baja's first city (founded by

Salvatierra in 1697) and capital for 132 years, still enjoys its one-time prominence and is rapidly gaining a new reputation as a favorite haunt for fishing enthusiasts. Located here is the Mother of Missions—Baja's first—rebuilt again and again, and most recently restored in 1941. It was from Loreto that Junipero Serra began his northward march in 1769.

A canopy of date palms covers parts of town and extends right down to the beach; the trees lean out over the sand very much as coconut palms do in the South Seas. Resorts front this beach, and a seaside walkway makes a good spot for watching the spectacular sunrises and sunsets.

Loreto's International Airport is the landing strip for both commercial airliners and private planes. Waiting taxis take visitors to hotels around town or to Nopolo Bay south of town (see below).

Fishing is great. In proportions that vary with the seasons, all the valiant game species are ready to do battle — yellowtail, marlin, sailfish, roosterfish, tuna, bass, sierra mackerel, bonito, cabrilla, pompano, and others. For shellfishing and shore casting, you can go south of town a few miles to where the hills come right down to the water, forming headlands and sheltered coves.

You don't like to fish? Visit the mission museum to see the artifacts collected from all over Baja; stroll along the side streets until you discover the outdoor mud-and-brick oven of Loreto's bakery; visit the few shops for souvenirs; sit in the plaza and people-watch; or lie in a hammock and look out to sea. Most hotels have pools and tennis courts. The large island in the channel is Isla Carmen, noted for its spectacular grottos and good skin diving.

A visit to San Javier, a little community hidden back in a spiny mountain gorge, takes almost all day. Ask your hotel to pack a lunch; then hire a truck and driver and allow 2 hours for the 35 km/22 miles each way. The first half of the road has recently been improved and there's a fine picnic spot at the first wide stream crossing. The goal of this rough but beautiful trip is to see the finest example of mission architecture in Baja — the only original mission church remaining intact. It was finished in 1758, has never been restored, and still serves the ranchers and townspeople.

South of Loreto at Nopolo Bay, an ambitious new resort development similar to Cancun and Ixtapa is underway. A beachfront El Presidente Hotel, with swimming pools, restaurants, and tennis courts was completed first; a nine-hole golf course is under construction. In winter months, when currents and winds combine to pile up schools of small fish, you'll see scores of pelicans feeding at Nopolo.

Farther south along the 360 km/225 mile drive between Loreto and La Paz is Puerto Escondido, a natural harbor where you can rent a boat or fish off the dock. At Puerto Escondido the road swings inland; Villa Insurgentes and Ciudad Constitucion are the two principal inland towns. Near Ciudad Constitucion a paved road cuts across to Magdalena Bay on the Pacific. Fishing, clamming, and even swimming are great, but don't expect any facilities.

La Paz to the Cape

From La Paz to the tip of Baja you're in resort land, where campers are outnumbered. Almost everyone arrives here by air or by water, exactly as if this area were an island—an island about 160 km/100 miles long and 80 km/50 miles wide, with sea and land mixed in most agreeable proportions. It is also a desert island, though, and that is one of its special qualities. Cactus comes right down to the beach, even in the lower half of the peninsula (which lies south of the Tropic of Cancer). Many of the beaches are as empty as Robinson Crusoe's. Going inland usually means going up a little (peaks are over 6,000 feet), so you're always looking out toward sea.

Private pilots make Baja's tip a favorite target. Surprisingly luxurious resorts south of La Paz have their own airstrips—also used by the air taxi service from La Paz.

You can drive through this region in a loop trip from La Paz (rental cars available) down the gulf side of the peninsula to Cabo San Lucas, and then up the Pacific side by way of Todos Santos. The entire loop is now paved, including the stretch on the Pacific side. You'll see campgrounds and new hotels under construction; this is a major area of Baja's new development.

A friendly welcome in La Paz

La Paz, capital of Baja California Sur, lost part of its drowsy charm when it geared up for the tourists who arrive by ferry from Mexico's west coast resort cities and by jet from the U.S. No longer a backwater town, La Paz is nevertheless an intriguing city of 80,000 that most visitors remember fondly. The city's major attractions are within 2 or 3 blocks of the coconut palm-lined waterfront drive — a circumstance encouraging strolling, even though cabs hover about waiting to transport you to other areas.

The life of the city centers on the water. Even the bandstand—traditional center of the Mexican town plaza — adjoins the *malecon*, the beach walk alongside the sea wall, in La Paz. You'll see two piers: one serving sportfishing boats, the other serving commercial shipping. Farther west is the Topolobampo ferry terminal; the ferry to Mazatlan is 19 km/12 miles north of the city at Pichilingue.

La Paz seems quite different from cities of mainland Mexico, and many travelers find it more friendly. More than a few of the buildings are quaint and almost Victorian in appearance. The most conspicous landmark is the mission, a large rose pink church facing the plaza. On the opposite side, a theater and museum have replaced the old Government Palace. An impressive state capitol has been built in the south part of town.

(Continued on next page)

...Continued from page 19

Accommodations. Several hotels face the malecon (only La Posada is on the beach); others are located in the northwest corner of town or to the south (see page 149). You'll also find several recreational vehicle facilities.

Water sports. Superb angling brings most people to La Paz. You can rent fishing equipment, boats, and guides from the tourist pier near the center of town; reservations are advised from April through June. The *Baja Anglers' Guide* by Tom Miller (Baja Trail Publications) is a good directory to the fishy waters.

Snorkelers and scuba divers-for-sport will enjoy bay waters that are warm, wonderfully clear, and teeming with brilliantly colored fish not at all frightened by a human presence. Around the rocks near the beaches, you'll find legions of hermit crabs or enormous chitons, and starfish with 20 or more feathery rays.

You can rent a small boat to reach the sandspit across the estuary—a fine place for beachcombing. The swimming beaches of Coromuel and La Ramada, 3 km/2 miles from shore hotels, are best reached by round-trip taxi excursions.

Shopping. La Paz is a free port, so you'll find a few stores offering bargains. The best shopping is around Hotel La Perla, but remember that stores close in the afternoon for siesta. Some shops carry native crafts brought in from surrounding villages and from the mainland. The gulf waters' spiny, puffy blowfish are caught, cured, and sold by small boys; price depends on your bargaining ability.

Countryside villages and remote resorts

From La Paz the highway through El Triunfo and San Antonio—towns that whisper of a mining past—climbs gradually into foothills pocked with prospectors' holes and draped with yellow flowering *palo de arco* shrubs. A tall

Tips for the Baja driver

How's the highway? Usually pretty good. It can be an enjoyable experience to drive the length of the peninsula. What was formerly accomplished only by jeep or pickup is now easily managed by an ordinary passenger car. The key to a pleasant trip is to be well informed and well prepared.

• Arm yourself with a good road map and a mile-by-mile guidebook. *The Baja Book II,* by Tom Miller and Elmar Baxter (Baja Trail Publications, Huntington Beach, CA 92646) offer maps keyed to road logs, descriptions of major towns, and beachcombing and fishing opportunities. Other suggestions include the AAA and Automobile Club of Southern California publications on Baja, or Dan Sanborn's Mexico Travelog (available from his insurance office in San Ysidro). The Mexico West Travel Club (P. O. Box 6088, Huntington Beach, CA 92646) publishes a bimonthly newsletter with Baja fishing information and road conditions.

• The Transpeninsular Highway is slightly narrow; there are no shoulders; curves may be poorly banked; and *vados* (creek beds that cross the road) may hide not only water but cattle. The moral of the story: Don't drive at night!

• Fill up with gasoline wherever you find it—the next service station may be "just out." Carry Mexican pesos or only small U.S. bills. Brush up on your Spanish and carry a good translating dictionary, because Baja's rural folk know little English.

• Carry a complete set of tools and such replacement parts as a fan belt, spark plugs, points, condenser, and extra motor oil and radiator coolant in your car.

• Travelers staying in motels should carry a day's supply of food and at least a gallon of water per person.

• If you plan to travel anywhere off the main highway, you'll be on gravel or dirt roads. It's a good idea to carry a shovel and tire chains, and to put inner tubes in your tires—cactus spines can puncture a steel-belted radial tire, and you may have to drive a ways to find someone to repair it. Unless you have an all-terrain vehicle and know where you're headed, stay on the main road. Remember—no road holds any terror for the Mexicans who shake cars and trucks to pieces with utter nonchalance.

• Keep a lookout for green utility trucks with *Secretaria de Turismo* printed in orange on the side. These are the "green angels"—the traveler's friend. A fleet of seven of these trucks is supposed to cruise all sections of the highway at least twice a day to help motorists. Service is free; you pay for parts or gas. In a true emergency, they will relay messages by radio to your family at home.

smokestack, landmark of El Triunfo, towers black against the distant sky. Two yellow church towers rise between the smokestack and mine buildings on the hill where once $50,000 worth of gold and silver were produced monthly. San Antonio, now a cattle ranching center, possesses a church of rare simplicity—one of the most handsome in this region. From San Antonio come the baskets, hats, and ornaments sold in the shops of La Paz.

A short drive takes you to Los Barriles and the gulf. Here several fishing resorts (see page 149) provide comfortable accommodations for anglers, most of whom arrive by private plane. (Taxi service or rental cars are also available from La Paz.)

Inland, past the high peaks of the cape region's jagged blue ranges, you'll come to Miraflores, well known for its leather work. Craftsmen here make fine saddles, belts, shoes, and holsters; practically all the *cueras* (leather gun belts worn by cowboys throughout Baja) are made in Miraflores. Nearby Caduano also turns out leatherwork. Leather goods bought in these two towns cost slightly less than they do in La Paz. Whether or not you're shopping, take time to stop and watch these craftsmen at work.

Land's End: Cabo San Lucas

The end of the great Baja peninsula comes into sight at last. Gradually the desert shore curves westward toward the green splash of San Jose del Cabo, then on and on to the final tall rocks that stand apart and unapproachable—The Friars.

Here Baja California reaches a climax of sorts, not only in geography but also in the beguiling settings, extravagant spaciousness, and elaborate embellishments of its hotels. Prices don't really soar until you get past San Jose del Cabo, a neat, sunny little town that invites exploring.

Between San Jose del Cabo and the end of the Cape you'll pass many protected coves with small white beaches that, unfortunately, are often fenced off and inaccessible to the visitor. In bygone years, pirates lay in wait, planning to loot the richly laden Manila galleon, a trading ship on its annual voyage to Acapulco with stores of Oriental finery and spices and sometimes a fortune in gold. After the long voyage of 6 months or more, the ship headed in toward shore to stop at San Jose del Cabo for fresh water and supplies. Frequently, bold sea dogs—Thomas Cavendish among them—made off with the rich booty. (That wreck on the beach just east of the Cape is the Japanese longliner *Inari Maru No. 10* that ran aground in 1966, lured ashore by local fishermen using a transmitter placed in the hills above the rocks. Old traditions die hard.)

Miles and miles of spectacular shores are unbelievably deserted except for a few opulent resorts sprinkled along the white sands of the rocky headlands. The tiny town of San Jose del Cabo boasts a new El Presidente; other major development (including another hotel and nearby golf course) is underway.

Next along the line of deluxe accommodations at the Cape is the Moorish mirage at Punta Palmilla, followed by the sparkling concoctions at Chileno Bay — spreading grandly and improbably on a desert shore where a few years ago only an obscure ranch stood.

At the very tip of the peninsula is Cabo San Lucas, a small village. It has several modest hotels and a handful of luxury establishments (see page 149) set beside the skin-diving bay formed in the shelter of the southernmost headland. There are also trailer parks and a couple of good places to eat. Cabo San Lucas is the terminal point for major airlines and the Puerto Vallarta ferry, and a shore port for Mexico coastal cruises.

Avid deep-sea anglers put Cabo San Lucas on the map, and they return year after year to pit their skills against the big ones that managed to escape the last time. Families come along, trying out the latest in swimwear around improbably shaped pools, most of them complete with swim-up bars and underwater stools.

Though fishing is the name of the game, you'll find tennis courts, an upcoming golf course, a regional arts center, and the shop of Baja's top ready-to-wear clothing and jewelry designer.

Boats are available for a trip to El Arco, a natural arch in the sea where the Gulf of California and the Pacific Ocean meet. A multitude of beaches and clear waters provide endless scope for snorkelers.

A loop trip through Todos Santos

For the next 80 km/50 miles northward the road parallels the Pacific, sometimes within view of the water, sometimes well inland. This section of the road was scheduled for completion by 1983.

Once you reach El Pescadero, it's about 13 km/8 miles to Todos Santos, a village surrounded by a verdant valley close to the sea. Tall mango trees, light green and shiny-leafed, line the roadway. Sugar fields and towering palm trees mark fertile lands.

The primitive sugar cane mill attracts visitors. The cane, delivered by donkey cart, is crushed to produce a liquid. This liquid simmers and later thickens in a great wooden vat; then it hardens in hollowed-out forms. The blow of a mallet knocks the cone-shaped pieces of candylike *panocha* (raw sugar) from the forms, ready to be packed in shipping cases woven of palo de arco branches.

The mission (founded in 1732, rebuilt in 1840, and remodeled in 1941) retains evidences of age in its hand-carved doors and handhewn benches; a bell-ringing rope hangs down from the high tower within hand's reach.

Todos Santos is about 80 km/50 miles from La Paz (a 1½ to 2-hour drive over paved road). It's a pretty route in spring and after the summer rains. The desert glows with yellow clouds of *palo verde* flowers, pink blossoms come out on the cholla, and the wands of the *palo adan*, relative of the ocotillo, are tipped with red flowers.

A few miles from Todos Santos on the Pacific side of Baja is San Pedrito, a languorous beach with dangerous waves—swim here with caution.

West Coast

Resort Land

(For "Facts at Your Fingertips," see pages 150–151)

The Golden Coast and Mexico's Riviera—these are two of the names bestowed on the western side of the Mexican mainland. Mexico's west coast offers the nearest tropical destination for motorists from the western United States. It is also the closest by sea, and regularly visited by cruise ships from Los Angeles, San Francisco, and the East Coast (Miami and Tampa). The cost of air travel from the western U.S. to Mexico's west coast is comparable to (or even slightly less than) airfare to the nearest tropical destination—Hawaii. Ferry service to and from Baja makes it an increasingly popular leg on a triangle trip from California or Arizona.

The region's natural attractions include great mountain ranges, grand canyons, lush jungles, and sparse deserts. Its bay-notched coasts are ringed with superb swimming beaches, and the many rocky points lure anglers. Mixed emotions greet the increased accessibility of formerly remote spots now easily reached by the "sunshine route" (Highways 15 and 200), which stops only a few miles short of a coastal connection between the U.S. and Guatemala borders.

Luxurious hotels cover spaces where fishing huts used to stand. Today the bare feet on once-secret ribbons of sand belong not to native fishers but to tourists.

Weather is best during winter and early spring; the "in" season is from November into May. Hotel prices drop sharply during the rest of the year and many a canny traveler braves the warmer temperatures and summer rains to sun at half the price. One interesting exception is Guaymas. You pay more in the summer for rooms there because of the necessary additional air conditioning.

From the border to Guaymas

One of the most accessible portions of Mexico is the northwest corner of the state of Sonora, which includes the 405 km/253 mile stretch of Highway 15 from Nogales to Guaymas.

The desert in this area is spacious and unscarred. Flying over the desert or driving through it, you see how light civilization's touch has been—out toward the coast, vast areas have never been inhabited; in many regions, European culture and industry gained footholds three centuries or so ago, but the only traces of them now are ruins.

The people who still live in the desert have attempted to transform their environment, though they and their goats and cattle are scattered too thinly to change the look of the land very much. The brown adobe houses, barns, and corral walls blend easily into the desert setting.

Nogales—border town in a new style

Nogales, Arizona, and its Mexican counterpart, Nogales, Sonora, are primary entry gateways for Mexico's west coast beaches. From one year to the next, you'll never find Mexican Nogales as you left it. It is a border town of constant change — of rebuilding, tearing down, and restoring.

The customs offices at the border are open 24 hours a day; here you can acquire tourist permits, if you haven't

Colorful sail boards punctuate beaches at many resorts along Mexico's western side.

Fishing boats *form holding pattern to await next day's venture.*

already. The sheer joy of shopping brings weekend visitors to Nogales and attracts travelers on their way to other points within Mexico. Handicraft shops and markets, a shopping center called Casa Margot, and artisans' galleries are scattered throughout the town. For those interested in sightseeing, La Caverna restaurant (where Apache chief Geronimo was briefly imprisoned when the restaurant was a jail), Sacred Heart Church, and the old Customs House provide historical interest.

For trailer facilities, motels, and hotels, the U.S. side of the border offers more selection with higher standards.

The Gran Desierto: population zero—almost

Mexico's Highway 2 follows the border on the Mexican side from Tijuana through Mexicali and San Luis Rio Colorado to Sonoita, and then turns southeast to meet Highway 15 at Santa Ana.

The thin track of the old Camino del Diablo once wandered uncertainly for about 202 km/126 miles along the Arizona-Sonora line, among the rocks, cactus, and soft sand between San Luis Rio Colorado and Sonoita; it was no place for the casual traveler. Today there's still a long gap between gas stations, but the smooth pavement of Highway 2 invites—and gets—speeds of 96 to 112 km/60 to 70 miles per hour. The nearest thing to the old "Devil's High-

way" is the sandy trail on the U.S. side, used by the U.S. Border Patrol.

From San Luis Rio Colorado, Highway 2 heads east into the flat, silty, creosote-dotted desert. The road reaches out for the nearly featureless horizon ahead; on your left you can see the Gila Mountains of Arizona, and far off to the right the faint blue line of Baja California's 10,000-foot-high backbone.

It's always wise to take certain precautions when driving long distances on barren roads: avoid driving at night, sleeping in your car, and picking up hitchhikers. Take along plenty of water and extra gas. For a less hazardous and tedious trip, drive to Baja California and take a ferry across the Sea of Cortez.

El Golfo de Santa Clara, 112 km/70 miles south of San Luis Rio Colorado on a paved road, sounds more impressive than it is—a remote fishing village in an unspoiled, natural setting on the Sea of Cortez. Wide white beaches with soft, clean, inviting sand stretch for about 35 km/56 miles. Tides are among the highest in the world, rising as much as 25 feet. Fishing is the prime attraction, but you can also explore the beaches in a dune buggy, or swim and sun. Facilities include a gas station, a drug store, a grocery store, restaurants, and trailer parks (no hookups).

About halfway to Sonoita, the highway forsakes the straight-arrow course out of San Luis Rio Colorado to wind easily among some of the cinder cones and basalt mesas of Cerro Pinacate. It is hard to find a more massive volcano than this anywhere in the world. The volcano's broad, symmetrical, black lava mass, studded with hundreds of cinder cones and pocked with explosion pits and calderas, lies south of the highway, which cuts across some of the lava flows. U.S. astronauts practiced here before their first moon mission.

The final approach to Sonoita is through a natural conservatory of desert vegetation. If you drive this route in the spring, you may see the spectacular golden blooms of the palo verde. Other perennial plants that blossom in the spring are the cholla, giant saguaro, ocotillo, creosote, and organ pipe cactus. Watch, too, for such annuals as poppies, mallows, and mariposa lilies.

Sonoita, though on the border, is a typical Mexican country town except for its modern gas stations and an air-conditioned motel. The scenery becomes slightly more attractive south of Sonoita.

Puerto Penasco, or Rocky Harbor

The 99 km/62 mile paved highway to Puerto Penasco (also called "Rocky Harbor") starts at Sonoita. This Mexican shrimping port is fast becoming a tourist town, but the beach-camping settlements of Choya Bay and Sandy Beach nearby are more primitive than Sonoita. The sun, clamming, and tidepool exploring, as well as the long empty beaches and good shell-hunting, appeal to beachcombers. The Sea of Cortez is renowned for its abundance of fish. Hotels, motels, and restaurants are more plentiful in Puerto Penasco than in Choya Bay. You'll find boats for hire in both areas; launching is better at Choya. Launch permits are required for Mexican waters.

If you want to camp, check the trailer parks in Puerto Penasco, or head toward Sandy Beach and Choya Bay beach. There you can park recreational vehicles for a small fee, but you'll find no facilities, wood, or running water. (You can buy water and some food at the grocery store.)

(Continued on page 28)

Crumbling Cocospera, *original 18th century Kino mission, stands mutely in Sonora desert.*

On green *at Ixtapa, golfer pars hole with short putt. Course is only a stroll away from beachfront hotels.*

For a tropical tan *sans sand, take a tip from sun worshipers in Zihuatanejo Bay.*

Details at a glance

How to get there

Most travelers pick a resort and find the fastest way to get there, allowing themselves maximum time on sunny beaches.

By air. Several international airlines, including Aeromexico and Mexicana, reach resort areas directly from the U.S. and Mexico. Mexico's carriers also supply connecting service between major Mexican cities and resorts. Since flight schedules change constantly, check with a travel agent.

Private pilots may obtain a copy of *Airports of Mexico* from Arnold Senterfitt, J-V Fulfillment Center, P.O. Box 11950, Reno, NV 89150.

By car. Westerners often drive to northern resorts. Highway 2 from Tijuana and Mexicali joins Highway 15 from Nogales. Follow this route to reach Kino Bay, Guaymas, Mazatlan, and San Blas. At Tepic, take Highway 200 to Puerto Vallarta and Manzanillo.

By boat. Ferry service connects Baja California and the west coast between Santa Rosalia and Guaymas; between La Paz and Topolobampo/Los Mochis, Mazatlan, Guaymas, and Puerto Vallarta; and between Cabo San Lucas and Puerto Vallarta.

Cruise ships often stop at Mazatlan, Puerto Vallarta, Manzanillo, Ixtapa/Zihuatanejo, and Acapulco, allowing on-shore excursions.

Tours

You can save money with a package tour. Price usually includes transportation and accommodations; bonuses such as city tours or discounts for local events may be offered.

Accommodations

"Varied" best describes hotels, motels, and recreational vehicle parks along the coast. Finding suitable accommodations is limited only by season and your budget. (See the "Essentials" section on page 150.)

Climate and clothes

The farther south you travel, the warmer it becomes. The "in" season is winter and spring. Summer, a rainy time, brings a decrease in room price (Guaymas is an exception) to compensate for heat.

In northerly areas you may need a jacket during windy weather; otherwise, take cool, casual clothing for beach or street. Good buys in local attire make it wise to wait and add to your wardrobe in Mexico.

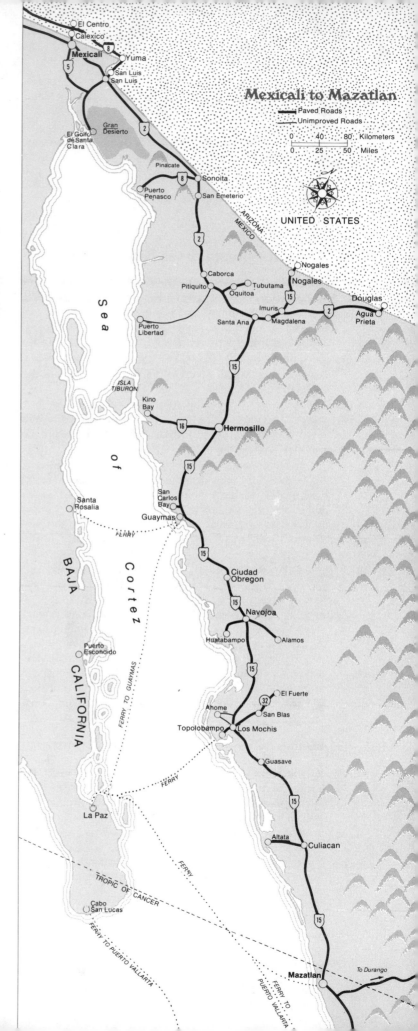

...Continued from page 25

What to do? The "night life" is usually on the beach. Special events include the Marine Carnival on June 1 and the Choya Bay Fishing Derby on Father's Day weekend in mid-June.

About the only sightseeing attractions in this area are the desalting plant and hothouse experimental station, the new seaside community of Las Conchas with its Moorish architecture, and the marina on the bay where ferries will dock when service is established across the Sea of Cortez to Baja.

A chain of missions in Kino country

An Italian Jesuit priest, the incredibly tough and daring Father Eusebio Kino, settled in the vast Sonoran desert and endured thirst, hunger, and hostile Indians while exploring (often alone) great stretches of northwestern Mexico, including parts of what are now Arizona and California. By the time he died in 1711, he had founded 25 missions.

The only traces of these original structures are the crumbling, weathered remains of the mission at Magdalena. In recent years the number of visitors to this town has been on the rise; this increase is attributable to the 1966 discovery of Father Kino's remains, now on display in the carefully tended town plaza.

In addition to establishing missions, Father Kino is remembered for converting seven Indian tribes to Christianity and teaching them how to farm as well as for discovering the Gila River and mapping much of the surrounding desert area. He is credited as being the first person to learn that Baja California was a peninsula, not an island.

Other than its significance as Father Kino's final resting place, Magdalena offers very little in the way of sightseeing except for the attractive plaza surrounded by arched, missionlike buildings housing restaurants and shops that sell religious articles. Magdalena is a mining and agricultural center and serves as a departure point for trips to Mission San Ignacio de Caborica, one of five original Kino missions in the area. The other mission locations are at Pitiquito, Oquitoa, Tubutama, and Caborca. Motels at Caborca and Magdalena offer overnight accommodations.

Hermosillo—clean capital of Sonora

Well worth a stopover, Hermosillo is a lovely, clean city with wide, tree-lined boulevards and tiled walks. The town offers a variety of places to stay and things to do. Much of the original ornate colonial architecture still lines the plaza, but old adobes are being replaced with brick, and many modern public buildings have sprouted up. Despite the smartness of Hermosillo's modern appearance, the "old" Mexico is still there — in the evening promenade in the plaza, and in the shops filled with a wide selection of Mexican crafts and imported goods from Portugal, Italy, England, and Scotland. Markets are clean, and the seafood from Guaymas is plentiful and inexpensive.

The University of Sonora is located on the highway in the north central part of the city. Other points of interest in Hermosillo include the cathedral, handsome museum, and attractively planted Parque Madero. Several motels offer golfing privileges; or you may enjoy the excellent hunting and fishing available in nearby areas.

Kino Bay: Land of the Seri Indians

Beautiful Kino Bay is one of the few accessible spots for the motorist on the long undeveloped coastline stretching from the northern end of the Sea of Cortez down to the resort center of Guaymas. Kino Bay and the little town of "Old" Kino are 106 km/66 miles from Hermosillo by good paved road. A long landing strip is a convenience for pilots of private planes.

The residents of the tiny village, with its simple chapel and single cantina, make their living chiefly by fishing from small boats or dugout canoes.

South of the village are some luxury condominiums, but most of the new development is north of the town in the newer, more urban shoreline community of "New" Kino, a modern development with paved streets, sidewalks, and sewers. A progressive seaside resort with attractive homes springing up along the beach, "New" Kino has several modern motels, recreational vehicle facilities, and a few restaurants (including the interesting Caverna del Seri). Shore fishing is good, boat rentals are available, and swimming is fun because the high salt content of the water makes floating effortless.

Large Tiburon Island, in Kino Bay, is the homeland of the Seri Indians and a focal point for these people. Basically nomadic at heart, the Indians never settled into an agricultural way of life and have spent much of their time pursuing the sea turtles that provide a small living for some of them. You'll see many of the Seri (their population is slowly dwindling) in and near towns selling trinkets, especially hardwood animal carvings and shell necklaces. Their gentle smiles make it difficult to imagine that they are believed to have once been cannibals and fierce warriors.

Guaymas—a watery utopia

Guaymas is really three communities: the city is divided from the two resort areas by a mountainous peninsula ending at jutting Cabo Haro. The original port and city face the Bay of Guaymas; 3 km/2 miles northwest is Miramar Beach on Bacochibampo Bay; and another 19 km/12 miles up the coast is New Guaymas on San Carlos Bay.

The city—a major seaport hub of the Mexican shrimp industry, and fishing capital of the world—is encircled by a range of steep cliffs and mountains. Visitors enjoy the variety of stores, an attractive church, and a landlocked harbor. Native families bring their children to Las Playitas, a small public beach facing shallow water.

Guaymas is also the terminus of a popular car ferry route from Santa Rosalia and La Paz in Baja California. It's a

Try Club Med for sun & fun

If an alternative to resorts and hotels sounds inviting, you might consider the "Club Med Experience." Three resorts dot Mexico's coastline, and five archeological villas are scattered among the Aztec, Maya, and Toltec ruins in central and southern Mexico.

Meals, accommodations, and activities are covered in one fee. Though sports are the main attraction, dance and art classes are offered at the three coastal locations; doing nothing is fine too. Romping or lazing, it's your choice.

Expect mealtime to be sociable. Where you sit and with whom is beyond your control—seating is arranged at tables of eight by order of arrival. The idea is to mingle; one of Club Med's many philosophies is that guests should get to know each other.

Complimentary wine and beer are offered at lunch and dinner. If something a little stronger appeals to you, expect to pay for it with the local currency—plastic pop beads worn as a necklace or bracelet. Liberation from the trappings of cold cash is another Club Med philosophy.

The staff sets the tone for the club. Trained as activities instructors, hosts, and entertainers, the *gentils organisateurs* (amiable organizers or G.O.s) mix with guests on all levels.

Ixtapa. This facility is located 224 km/140 miles north of Acapulco and 24 km/15 miles from the village of Zihuatanejo. Temperatures hover in the 80s. Most activities center on the sea, though you'll also find such land sports as archery and tennis. A nearby Robert Trent Jones-designed golf course is available for use by Club Med members.

Playa Blanca. Bougainvillea tumbles down the hillsides surrounding the club; greenery offers solace from the sometimes stifling Mexican heat. Situated on Chamela Bay, this village is tucked away in a relatively untouched portion of Mexico.

Cancun. Close to the heart of the Yucatan, this complex overlooks a horseshoe-shaped bay on the Mexican Caribbean. The protected reef, known for its outstanding scuba diving, has been designated an underwater park by the Mexican government. You can try your hand at water skiing, windsurfing, and sailing.

Archeological villas. For those intrigued with Mexico's past, Club Med has five small colonial inns 5 minutes from the archeological zones of Uxmal, Chichen Itza, Coba, Cholula, and Teotihuacan. Tennis and swimming are the only sports available. Well-stocked libraries at each villa offer books on the different Indian cultures.

The three coastal resorts offer 1 or 2-week packages; the archeological villas are available for one or more nights at a time. For more information write to Club Med, 40 West 57th Street, New York, NY 10019.

---

good idea to have reservations, but if you don't have them, you can arrange for your passage at the terminal building. For rail transportation, take the speedy Fiat Autovia, a daily train to Hermosillo or Nogales.

To reach Bacochibampo Bay, you'll drive through a long line of private beach homes. Where's the water? It is well hidden by the congested arrangement of hotels, trailer parks, and houses. But remember—all Mexican beaches are public and you'll soon find an access to the rocky shore. Two large resort hotels and one small beach concession offer rooms for rent.

San Carlos Bay, about 8 km/5 miles north of Guaymas and about 13 km/8 miles west of Highway 15, has become quite popular with American tourists. The multimillion-dollar complex is made up of a luxury hotel, several motels, a yacht club and marina, restaurants, tennis courts, a par three golf course, a large recreational vehicle village, a subdivision of seashore homes and cottages, and a small trailer park. There is also a convenient landing strip for private planes.

The waters are filled with an abundant and bewildering variety of game fish. Summer offers the most spectacular fishing, though after May the weather is sometimes oppressively hot. The big runs of marlin and sailfish come in July and August, but game fishing will satisfy the soul of the average angler during fall and winter months. The most exciting (and most crowded) time is in July, during the annual International Deep Sea Fishing Rodeo, which marks the peak of the sport-fishing season.

The best way to learn the techniques of game fishing is to charter a boat with a knowledgeable skipper who has been fishing the waters for years and knows where to find the type of fish you're after, as well as the best way to angle for them.

Cabin cruisers complete with light and heavy fishing tackle, bait, ice, ship-to-shore radio, and English-speaking crews may be chartered by the hour or by the day. Rental skiffs and outboard motors are also available; if you wish to take your own boat, it can be launched at Miramar Beach. For big game fishing, though, the larger inboard cruisers are best. Make reservations to charter a boat, especially during the tournament season.

(Continued on next page)

...Continued from page 29

Desert headlands and calm estuaries attract shore and rock fishers. The most common fish you can expect to catch are corvina, sierra mackerel, roosterfish, and a variety of rockfish. For surf fishing, bring tackle from home because not many supplies are available in the stores of Guaymas.

Conchologists enjoy the abundance and variety of shellfish. You can use a diving mask to look for them or follow their tracks in the mud at low tide.

The transparent, blue waters of Guaymas are made to order for those who enjoy skin diving and snorkeling — very few hazards exist, water temperature and underwater visibility are nearly ideal, and lobsters and turtles are plentiful. Lobsters can be caught most easily on nights when there is no moon or wind, because they hide in daylight but feed in shallow water at night.

Besides fishing, Guaymas offers a good spot for relaxing and soaking up the sun. If you want to combine exercise with your siestas, try the tennis courts. The swimming, good riding horses, and shopping should also help to keep you occupied.

If you're the self-sufficient soul who likes to do things independently, you'll find ample opportunity and an abundance of free advice in the Guaymas area. Plenty of elbow room along the coastline enables campers to enjoy freedom and solitude; you'll have to carry your own water, though.

An annual 4-day carnival begins at the end of the third week in February. You'll see parades, aerial acrobats, fireworks, and cock fights. The town is crowded then, so be sure you have reservations.

From Guaymas to Mazatlan

South from Guaymas, Highway 15 threads its way through expansive, scrublike desert with the foothills of the Sierra Madre Occidental always visible to the east, and the coastline of the Sea of Cortez barely discernible on the horizon to the west.

This is Mexico's great agricultural frontier. Here vast acreages of tomatoes, wheat, melons, and other crops interrupt the monotony of the wide Sonora and Sinaloa deserts. Cultivation is mechanized, and farming goes on all year on a large commercial scale. Tractor and farm equipment salesrooms, full of shiny new machines, are much more common in the cities here than in the United States.

Many of the cities you pass have come to life in the last 20 years, some of them mushrooming to surround old adobe settlements.

The highway is generally good, though the pavement has deteriorated in some sections and you'll encounter occasional detours around road-widening and improvement projects. Principal cities along this coastal route are Ciudad Obregon, Navojoa, Alamos (a short side trip from Highway 15), Los Mochis, Culiacan, and Mazatlan.

An agricultural boom town: Ciudad Obregon

Ciudad Obregon is edged by cotton gins, mills, and granaries. Planned before the boom began, Obregon reflects the disorder and incongruities typical of rapid city growth. Yet its streets are well lighted, and some are creatively landscaped. In the spirit of modern urban planning, Obregon's power lines are underground. An impressive church and a brewery highlight sightseeing in town. The Alvaro Obregon Dam, 56 km/35 miles north of town, represents the first step in a huge federal irrigation program for this area.

Hunters come to this region (especially from October through February) to shoot the wild ducks, doves, and quail that flock together at sunset over the rice fields near town. Deer, wild turkeys, bears, and wild pigs live in the mountains within 80 km/50 miles of Obregon. Arrangements for hunting trips may be made at motels.

Alvaro Obregon, the Sonoran farmer for whom the town was named, was a leader in the Revolution of 1910 and later president of Mexico.

Navojoa's old town

An old town dating back to 1614, Navojoa was devastated by a flood in 1914, and subsequently relocated on higher ground. It is a crossroad point for departures to nearby Alamos, to the Mayo Indian village of Yavaros, to isolated Huatabampito Beach, or to other west coast cities.

Alamos — Colonial architecture and jumping beans

The colonial ambience of Alamos, a fascinating town 54 km/34 miles east of Navojoa, pervades all aspects of the town's architecture and even influences the local inhabitants and their activities. Alamos has been declared a colonial monument by the state government, and a conscious effort has been made by its residents to maintain the image the town had when it was a silver mining center in the late 1700s. Though some of the buildings are little more than a century old, they blend to form a collage of colonial antiquity.

Founded in 1540 as a camp for one of Coronado's expeditions, Alamos later became the capital both of Sonora and of what is now the neighboring state of Sinaloa. In the 18th century, Alamos and its suburbs were the world's richest source of silver.

Moorish arches, delicately fashioned iron grille work, and *portales* (covered walks) are indispensable elements in the Spanish personality of Alamos. Don't miss the graceful fountains, splashy gardens, and elegant mansions that once belonged to silver barons. Art galleries, cantinas, courtyards, leather shops, and the Plaza Mayor are some of the unique highlights of this treasure out of Mexico's mining past.

(Continued on page 32)

A corking good *fishing port, Guaymas,*
west coast resort city, nestles along bay.

Arched arcades *fronting Alamos plaza*
offer cool retreat against noontime sun.

Train takes *high bridge, burros take low bridge in different-paced travel.*

...Continued from page 30

Alamos is also known as the major producer of jumping beans—not really beans at all, but little three-sectioned nuts with a tiny worm in each section. It is the movement of the worm that makes this so-called "bean" jump. There's a man in Alamos known as the "Jumping Bean King" because he buys all the beans from the natives who gather them, and then ships them in drums to the U.S. and all over the world. The beans are gathered in midsummer and must be sold before late September, when the worm burrows his way out of the shell, curls up, and dies, unable to exist in his new habitat.

To get to Alamos you can drive, fly by private plane, or take a bus. Some excellent inns, motels, and trailer parks are available.

Places to explore near Alamos

Once you've explored the town of Alamos, you may want to look at the surrounding country—the tropical forest on nearby Alamos Mountain, the foothill oasis of the great Sierra Madre to the east, old mines and silver smelters, scattered ruins, and the bays and beaches along the coast.

La Ubalama. This cluster of thatched huts is known as a pottery village. It is an easy, leisurely drive from Alamos. Here you'll see women making clay ollas and bowls.

Aduana. Here stood the great smelting works where Alamos silver was cast into ingots. Today, not more than a dozen families remain in the countryside village. The tall cactus growing from the wall of the church has a special significance. According to legend, the cactus was on the site before the church was built, and an image of the Virgin appeared on top of the plant and pointed out a rich silver lode. Every year on November 20 a religious festival commemorates the event, attracting thousands of Mayo Indians to Aduana.

Cuchujachi River. Deep pools in this river are hemmed in by bedrock banks, making it a good place for a swim. The river road is narrow, rocky, and rough, but passable for the ordinary passenger car. You might see flocks of parrots overhead, ducks in the water, and white-tailed deer in the brush. Great *sabino* trees grow along the watercourse.

Mocuzari Dam. This dam has backed up water and covered the tropical oasis of Aguas Calientes where hot springs once bubbled out of the rocks. Bass fishing is excellent, and you can park a recreational vehicle right on the shore of the reservoir. A visit to this area makes a worthwhile trip for people interested in Sonora's new agricultural boom.

Mocoyahui and San Alberto Tungsten Mine. For the rough, 48-km/30-mile drive to the ruins of Mocoyahui Mission, you'll need a guide from Alamos. Along the way through upland farm country you'll pass burro trains carrying firewood, sesame seed, and oranges to Alamos. You'll see kapok trees laden with masses of silky fibers hanging from open pods.

The bells of the old mission (built about 1728) are supposedly in the possession of Mayo Indians who bring them out for special occasions. The trip from Alamos to the ruins takes about 3 hours. Beyond Mocoyahui about 6 km/4 miles is the San Alberto Tungsten Mine, named after its discoverer, Alberto E. Maas, a native of Alamos.

Alamos ruins *lend Grecian touch to Mexican countryside.*

Take off from Los Mochis or Topolobampo

Intriguingly enough, Los Mochis was founded by an American—Benjamin Johnston—who came from Virginia to build a sugar refinery and stayed to lay out a townsite that had the wide streets and square blocks of most American cities. Johnston also built a magnificent mansion with an inside swimming pool, an elevator, a huge banquet kitchen, and elegant formal gardens.

After Mr. Johnston died in 1938, the family moved back to the United States; the estate house was abandoned and later torn down, but the gardens are worth a visit.

Sugar cane is one of the most important crops in this area, and the Los Mochis sugar mill is the largest on Mexico's west coast. To go through it, drop in at the mill office on the northwest edge of town.

From Los Mochis you can take a rail trip through some of the most spectacular mountain and canyon country in the world (see page 125).

Rugs create splashes *of riotous color along Mazatlan waterfront.*

Mazatlan cathedral *interior reveals vaulted dome, gilded altar, tile design.*

Topolobampo, a deep water port on the Sea of Cortez, makes an interesting side trip from Los Mochis. A boat is helpful for touring the numerous coves, estuaries, beaches, and islands. The shrimp packing plant welcomes visitors. Sportfishing is excellent if you can go out with one of the local commercial fishermen. Topolobampo is also the eastern terminus for a passenger and auto ferry from La Paz, across the gulf.

Culiacan—Sinaloa's state capital

Culiacan sits in the center of an immense, flat, unbroken, fertile plain that reaches toward the Sea of Cortez. Here the quiet colonial sections of Culiacan contrast with modern tractor showrooms and new downtown shops. The town is a blend of desert and tropical elements. Though the surrounding uncultivated land is semiarid, the river banks are green and lush.

The Golden Coast— Mazatlan to Manzanillo

When you reach Mazatlan you've crossed the Tropic of Cancer, and you expect glistening sands, leaning palms, and beach resorts. You won't be disappointed.

Resort towns are varied. Fishing is a fetish in Mazatlan; people-watching is the most popular sport in Puerto Vallarta, though shopping is definitely a close second.

Paved Highway 200 starts just north of Puerto Vallarta and continues south to the Mexico-Guatemala border. Have a current road map or highway information at hand, since some stretches of highway are still under construction.

Marlin and Mardi Gras in Mazatlan

Long ago Mazatlan outgrew the small peninsula on which it was originally founded and spread northward along a series of crescent-shaped beaches that extends for miles. The main shopping centers, some of the best restaurants, and the older hotels are located in the downtown area; new subdivisions and hotel developments are strung out along the beaches running north.

The boulevard along the sea wall connects old and new Mazatlan; it starts at Olas Altas Boulevard and runs for several miles—with several name changes. In other Mexican cities the evening promenade takes place in the park or plaza; in Mazatlan, it is along the malecon.

Life in Mazatlan is leisurely. Quaint, two-wheel, horse-drawn carts called *aranas* can be hired for sightseeing trips. A three-wheel, three-passenger *pulmonia* (because you can catch pneumonia riding in one) is an open-air taxi similar to a fast golf cart. Benches in the several quiet, shady plazas invite you to sit and surrender yourself to the Mexican sense of mañana. Palms, bananas, papayas, mangoes, and flowers give the town a tropical aura.

Shopping is centered around the southern beach, Olas Altas Boulevard, the public market, and the northern hotel area. At the city market (Mercado Municipal) visit seemingly endless rows of fruit and vegetable stalls with appetizing displays of pineapples, mangoes, bananas, and other tropical delights. Buy curios, try on huaraches, toss a lacy shawl over your shoulder, and bargain to your heart's content.

To watch artisans at work carving, braiding, weaving, or molding, visit the Mazatlan Arts & Crafts Center in northern Mazatlan. Here, you can see—and buy—items from all over Mexico. Los Sabalos, a shopping center with Mediterranean style architecture, has many beautiful shops.

Landmarks include the usual town plaza with old-fashioned bandstand, a yellow-towered cathedral, and some majestic hills. Atop one of the hills is the El Faro Lighthouse, a rewarding goal for rugged climbers; underneath, a blue grotto entices visitors in small boats. An ancient observatory on another hill welcomes guests. Farther north stands Icebox Hill; its tunnels were once repositories for blocks of ice brought by boat from San Francisco and delivered by mule cart to stores and homes.

For a few pesos, daredevil divers leap from the 40-foot El Mirador view tower on the malecon. To the north, gigantic figures of fishermen form a monument to the force of the sea.

To the south is the colorful harbor, where you can catch the daily ferry to La Paz. Also located here are the yacht and sport-fishing anchorages, and docks for fishing vessels, cruise ships, freighters, and tankers.

Big game fishing developed Mazatlan. Marlin and sailfish swarm in the waters, and the pursuit of these fish is expert and businesslike. Fleets of sleek cruisers cluster at neighboring piers along the docks. Normally as many as four persons fish from a boat fully manned and equipped with everything needed for "billfishing" except muscle. All you need to carry aboard is your camera and a box lunch from your hotel. Make fishing reservations well in advance for March and April.

Local fishermen who catch their fish from dugout canoes hold a market on the beach at the southern end of Plaza Norte.

At the beach a thatched-roof pavilion features picnic tables, a juke box, and a refreshment stand. On weekends, families from Mazatlan frequently take picnic lunches over to the island beach, spreading their meals across the tables in the pavilion. Often jovial, noisy affairs, these gatherings are characterized by much singing and dancing. Beyond the pavilion is the fine white sand of a gently curving beach, uncluttered except for an abundance of large sand dollars.

Tennis and golf are available all year; check with your hotel for locations and other details. Bullfights usually take place from January to April, but events are also scheduled during the rest of the year. The bullring is right downtown.

(Continued on next page)

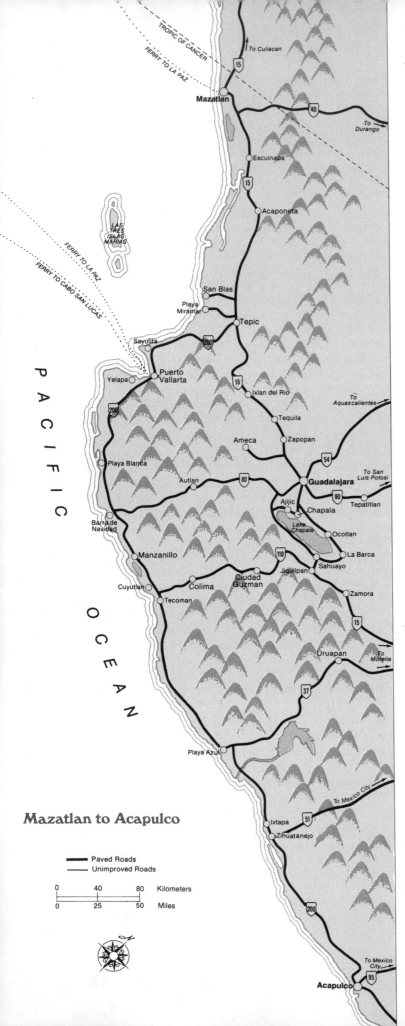

Mazatlan to Acapulco

Paved Roads
Unimproved Roads

| 0 | 40 | 80 | Kilometers |
| 0 | 25 | 50 | Miles |

...*Continued from page 35*

Check with your hotel or the excellent Department of Tourism for formal tours to outlying areas. You might want to arrange a private tour with an English-speaking guide. You'll get a look at green, forested back country valleys and mountains on a daylong excursion to Copala, a picturesque former silver mining village. Along the way you might stop at tidy little Concordia to see furniture makers and other craftsmen at work, and to view the richly sculptured small church.

Visit the aquarium just a block from the pier in downtown Mazatlan. You'll get a chance to see almost 200 different species of fish from the waters off Mexico and other countries around the world.

Festivals range from the weekly Friday Fandango (a street party on Olas Altas Boulevard sponsored by local merchants) to the Annual International Mardi Gras celebrated during the 5 days before Ash Wednesday. During Mardi Gras you'll see parades, official receptions, colorful floats, dances with exuberant mariachis, and fireworks. Forget sleeping and be prepared for a steep hike in prices.

Other outdoor activities center around the north end of the malecon and the district of on-the-beach hotels (some of them new), condominiums, and recreational vehicle facilities. This is where parachuting, water-skiing, swimming, and sunning take place. Here you can rent bilingual horses (they take commands in both Spanish and English) to ride on the beach or along a secluded trail.

You can take a boat cruise around the bay, travel through a jungle by inland waterways, or visit an island offshore. Isla de Piedra (Stone Island), only a 10-minute boat trip from downtown Mazatlan, offers one of the most beautiful beaches on the entire west coast of Mexico. You can find someone at Mazatlan's downtown dock area ready to take you across to the island at almost any time of day. (Reach a firm understanding about the cost of a round-trip voyage before you leave the dock, or you may find that the price of the return trip has suffered a sudden inflation.) You won't need a guide on the island; just follow the one and only road past the stick-and-mud houses of the islanders, through groves of tall coconut palms, and over to the beach. Even at a leisurely, sightsee-as-you-go tempo, the walk across the island takes less than half an hour.

South of Mazatlan

As the coastal route winds southward, the vegetation becomes more varied and lush, characterized by ebony, rosewood, lignum vitae, mahogany, and brazilwood. Palm trees resemble overdecorated Christmas trees because of the yellow, purple, and pink-flowered tropical vines climbing through them.

When the coastal lagoons come close to the highway south of Mazatlan, you'll see bright pink flamingos standing resolutely in the mud flats. Bananas, papayas, pineapples, mangoes, and citrus fruits grow in jungle clearings. Farms become smaller, and the big sophisticated tractors of the north are replaced by simpler farm equipment. Many farmers still till their fields with plows drawn by oxen.

About 27 km/17 miles south of Mazatlan, Highway 40 branches inland across the mountains to Durango, and Highway 15 swings away from the coast. Your only access to beaches from here south is on side roads that lead off to the west. One of the best of these roads leaves the highway about 35 km/22 miles north of Tepic and winds down through a luxuriant tropical forest to the old seaport of San Blas.

Sleepy San Blas is a peaceful, quiet, picturesque destination for travelers who shun the luxuries of more tourist-oriented towns.

Tropical jungles surround the village. The beautiful beaches near Mantanchen Bay are ideal for sunning and beachcombing; offshore islands abound with colorful tropical birds and offer rewarding finds for shell collectors. Near the fishing area in San Blas, you can charter a boat for fishing or sightseeing, or take an excursion boat to several remote beaches accessible only by water.

You can drive from Mazatlan to San Blas in about half an hour on a 35-km/22-mile paved road (off Highway 15) past thatched huts, small streams, and jungle denser than any other you'll see on the coastal route. The streams almost always flow near the roadside, and you'll probably see people bathing and doing their laundry along the banks. Marshy flats replace coquito palms, and dark estuaries wind through the low vegetation, their banks solidly lined with mangroves too thick to walk through. Exposed roots are encrusted with oysters.

Today, life in San Blas drifts slowly and languorously along. A few small dress, craft, and jewelry shops are scattered among the adobe-and-wattle huts clustered around the church and the rose-scented central plaza. Neat cobblestone streets lined with coconut palms lend a South Seas atmosphere to the area.

During colonial days San Blas was a bustling port; now the impressive customs house near the end of the main street remains as a decaying relic of a bygone era. On the crest of a small hill overlooking the newer section of town is old San Blas, built during the reign of the Spaniards. Hike or drive up here for a look at the crumbling remains of the fort, the church, and other small buildings overgrown with vegetation. (Mosquitoes are often numerous, so don't plan a long stay.) You may see some iguanas —scaly lizards sometimes growing to more than 2 feet long —inhabiting the ruins.

At the main beach, a wide sandy strip about a mile from the center of town, swimming is good all year. Along the beach you'll find bathhouses and hotels, and stands selling tantalizing sweets. Accommodations are adequate, but a bit below standards usually demanded by most U.S. tourists.

One popular excursion is a jungle boat trip up La Tobara tributary. The 2½-hour journey begins at the bridge over the San Cristobal River and passes through mangrove swamps and crystal clear jungle pools, giving visitors a chance to see orchids and other tropical vegetation and stopping at coffee and banana plantations. Colorful birds such as egrets, herons, and ibises abound, and you might see a coatimundi (a relative of the raccoon) or an iguana.

The best time to go to San Blas is between November and May. Strong winds usually blow across the beach in the afternoon. Summers are hot and humid, though it's sometimes cool enough for a blanket at night. One warning: Take some insect repellent. Though insect control is improving, small gnats called *jejenes* often swarm around the estuaries and beaches from late afternoon until 9 A.M.

Tepic, an old colonial city with a solid, prosperous look, is the capital of the small state of Nayarit. The main streets are wide; to widen other streets, the city planners are cutting away old buildings and adding modern facades that contrast sharply with the old walled cemetery and the arcaded buildings around the plaza. Soccer games in the stadium at the edge of town and promenades and concerts in the attractive city park provide entertainment for visiting spectators. Points of interest include the main plaza's cathedral, which was built in 1750 and has two perfect Gothic-type towers, and the Church de la Cruz, once part of the Franciscan Convent de la Cruz (founded in 1744). Pay a visit to the state museum, rich in treasures of the past.

The town, situated 3,186 feet above sea level at the base of an extinct volcano, is noticeably cooler than the nearby coast. The broad valley south of Tepic produces sugar cane, corn, and tobacco. A large cigarette factory in town employs many of Tepic's residents. Small banana and papaya groves surround some local native settlements.

Among Tepic's natural attractions are two waterfalls: Ingenio de Jala Falls, which flow with full force during the rainy season, and El Salto (west of the city). About 32 km/20 miles southeast of Tepic lies Laguna Santa Maria, a crater lake.

You'll find adequate accommodations in downtown Tepic and on the highway near Parque Loma.

Puerto Vallarta—still unspoiled

The cobblestone streets are as rough, uneven, and jolting as ever; the perilous descents from hillside casas, casitas, and condos are rugged and scary; and the number of shops, restaurants, and resorts keeps on growing. By some strange grace, though, Puerto Vallarta retains the charm and simplicity that have made it world famous.

Described in superlatives by most visitors, Puerto Vallarta's environs look more tropical and tidier than those of Mazatlan or Acapulco. Though you'll glimpse much of the native life, the presence of the American tourist is sometimes more obvious because the town is still small.

Donkey carts still rattle along the streets among the taxis, autos, and jeeps. Flaming bougainvillea and blue jacaranda hug stucco walls; sweet jasmine perfumes the night. Even if it's no longer an idyllic retreat, "PV" is certainly one of Mexico's fun spots and a highly picturesque town in a perfect away-from-it-all setting.

(Continued on next page)

...Continued from page 37

The town is crowded between the foot of the mountains and beautiful Banderas Bay. To get acquainted, locate the Cuale River, the *zocalo* (plaza), the malecon, and the Church of Guadalupe. The river (which runs in an east-west direction) serves as a natural dividing line within the city, separating the business sections from the south beach. The two bridges across the Cuale provide scenes of constant bedlam rivaling the confusion on any large city's freeway. One of the town's two major shopping districts starts north of the bridge; the other is south on Lazaro Cardenas and parallel streets. Farther up the river loom steep cliffs where luxurious homes cling precariously. One ravine is dubbed "Gringo Gulch" because of the number of Americans maintaining homes there.

In town you'll find a number of deluxe hotels (see page 150) and condominiums for rent. Excellent restaurants often feature both Mexican and American foods. Seafood, especially lobster, is a specialty.

Beaches—lovely, wide, and uncluttered—to the north and south of town are ideal for sunbathing, swimming, water-skiing, hiking, tennis, and horseback riding. Although a few beaches run beside the malecon, swimming here is not too good. Playa del Sol, south of the Cuale, has the action: vendors with goods and fish-on-a-stick, thatched-roof snack and cocktail bars, wandering mariachis, and boat and surfboard rentals. Taxis and buses run to and fro..

To the north, an excellent marina adjoins Playa del Oro. It has a number of slips for yachts and for fishing and excursion boats, a concrete dock for cruise passengers, and a terminal building for Cabo San Lucas and La Paz ferries.

Tours take you to Mismaloya Beach, a jungle hideaway discovered by Hollywood and converted into the setting for the 1964 film *Night of the Iguana*. Foliage has obscured most but not all traces of "el set." The view is worth your time, though the beach may be cluttered.

For a novel all-day excursion that includes swimming, sunning, hiking, lunching, and shopping, take a boat trip to the sequestered fishing village of Yelapa. If you want to linger, make reservations in advance; accommodations are modest and the choice is limited. Living is slow-paced and the people are friendly and hospitable. A handful of Europeans and Americans have made Yelapa their retreat from the bustling modern world.

After lunch you can climb into a hammock under a palm umbrella, hike to a nearby waterfall, wade in a warm lagoon, or shop at the small boutique displaying embroidered dresses, handloomed articles, and handprinted cloth.

Highway 200—sunshine route to Barra de Navidad

With the completion of the road between Puerto Vallarta and Barra de Navidad, auto visitors can "resort hop." The 140-mile stretch of coast (a 4-hour drive) is scenic enough to merit a side trip from Puerto Vallarta or Manzanillo, the area's two major destinations. You'll pass through mountain pine and oak forests, rugged high desert, thorn forests, and savannas. Jungles teem with colorful birdlife. Inviting detours can easily prolong your trip.

The highway crosses four major rivers flowing from the Sierra Madre Occidental to the Pacific; these rivers are life lines for farming villages and cattle ranches. Bays south of Rio San Nicolas are slated for development. The coast north toward Puerto Vallarta — important breeding grounds for sea turtles — will be kept in its natural wild state.

Except for the Club Mediterranee at Playa Blanca, resorts are so new that your travel agent may not know about them. But you should have little problem getting a room upon arrival. Accommodations range from inexpensive to moderate to expensive.

For more adventurous types, several villages offer primitive bungalows or *palapas* (palm-covered shelters) for just a few dollars a night.

Camping is permitted along most beaches; the only developed campgrounds are about 13 km/8 miles south of Rio San Nicolas.

Manzanillo—regal refuge for the rich

Squeezed onto a slender spine of land that separates two bays, Manzanillo is fast becoming the new resort haven for the world's jet setters. This long-ignored coastal town (now one of Mexico's most important ports for trade with the Orient) has turned into a holiday destination for graduates of Acapulco, the Costa del Sol, and the Greek islands.

The entrepreneur-millionaire Antenor Patino is responsible for the resort complex called Las Hadas, which includes — in addition to the luxury hotel — a marina, several tennis courts, a golf course, swimming pools, and boutiques and other shops. Cinemas, restaurants, a few small nightclubs and bistros, villas, and the usual shops make up the town. The central hotel complex consists of dazzling white buildings that project a Mediterranean air with Moorish overtones.

Manzanillo has everything going for it — vast open beaches, great swimming, excellent fishing (dolphinfish, marlin, sailfish), and a comfortable climate.

Manzanillo's evolution to this dreamed-of-resort-for-all is taking its toll on the sleepy, slow pace and low prices of bygone days. But if you're looking for an enjoyable atmosphere, Manzanillo won't disappoint you. The city's paved central streets are narrow, crowded, and often noisy. The waterfront, significantly, is clean and spacious — a place where families stroll at sunset when remnants of afternoon thunderclouds over the distant Sierra Madre cast their reflections on the blue bay. North and south of town, coconut and mango plantations edge the sea.

Chief attractions are beaches of yellow sand streaked with black on sheltered Santiago Bay and at Las Hadas Cove. Many Mexicans vacation at Manzanillo and at Santiago Beach (also becoming popular with Americans).

(Continued on page 41)

Filigree-crowned *church tower stands sentinel over passing boats at Puerto Vallarta's popular waterfront.*

Extemporaneous oven *roasts fish-on-a-stick to supply Puerto Vallarta beach vendors.*

Look familiar? *Ruins of Night of the Iguana set rise above bay at beguiling Mismaloya.*

...*Continued from page 38*

Nearby destinations north of Manzanillo include the beach resort of Melaque and the quaint fishing village of Barra de Navidad, both about 61 km/38 miles out of Manzanillo. Hardly more than 5 km/3 miles separate these neighboring towns, but the beaches are quite different. Barra de Navidad, with one of the cleanest beaches along the coast, has deep waters and vigorous waves that attract surfers and water-skiers. Melaque fronts on the calm tranquil water of the more protected bay. Buy shrimp and fish from seaside stands.

At Cuyutlan, south of Manzanillo, watch for the famous "green roller" — a miniature tidal wave. At certain times during April or May, the ocean gathers itself into a huge, hurtling force and rushes toward the beach with a thunderous roar. An awesome sight, the "green roller" reaches heights of up to 30 feet. Cuyutlan is suggested for daytime sojourns, not for overnight.

Colima, capital of one of Mexico's smallest states, is easily reached by following Highway 110 inland from Manzanillo. A balmy metropolis dating back to 1523, Colima lies a short distance from the foot of Mexico's second highest active volcano (it last erupted in 1941).

Colima is an attractive town. Colonial buildings with luxuriant gardens line quiet streets. Life is leisurely. The city's principal attraction is the Museum of the Cultures of the West. Antique car buffs will enjoy the Museum of Old Cars, located 6 blocks south of the city's plaza. On display are more than 100 vehicles dating back to 1912.

Other notable buildings around town are the government palace, cathedral, and a few churches.

About 15 km/9 miles south of town is Agua Caliente, one of the health resorts springing up in this area. Comala, a little town 10 km/6 miles north of Colima, is your best bet for handicrafts — handpainted furniture and wrought iron items.

Moorish style *marks Las Hadas, gleaming hotel complex on bay near Manzanillo.*

Shutterbugs and boaters *focus on diver leaping from La Quebrada cliffs to ocean below.*

Built to resemble *an Aztec pyramid, Acapulco Princess boasts five pools, one with waterfall and swim-up cave bar. Luxury hotels ring bay, climb hills above coastal resort.*

Parachute, *pulled by power boat, is readied for beach liftoff. Parasailing is popular beach sport.*

Southern Coast contrasts: Acapulco, Zihuatanejo, and Ixtapa

You have several options for getting to the Southern Coast beaches, depending on your point of departure and your method of transportation. If you are driving, newly completed Highway 200 links all of the western and southern beaches of Mexico. To get to Acapulco by road from Toluca or Mexico City, take Highway 95 to the coast. Jetting to Acapulco is easy from the U.S.; from Mexico City there's a shuttle service with a dozen flights daily. You can also get air service to or from Guadalajara, Puerto Vallarta, and other southern cities.

Getting to Ixtapa/Zihuatanejo is just as easy and convenient. Daily flights from the U.S. and Mexico City land at the airport serving both communities. Bus service is also available from Acapulco; the 4½-hour drive takes you through verdant countryside where you'll pass by small pueblos and wayside cemeteries and see women washing clothes and children in the rivers.

But go soon. The area is growing quickly; it's been designated for super-resort status and is well on its way to becoming just that: a super resort area.

Acapulco—still exotic, still the most popular

Acapulco is the big city of coastal resorts, with the most visitors and the most hotels (over 400) of any Mexican coastal city. Its visitor attractions are divided between those for foreigners and those for the many Mexicans who swell the winter population. In spite of the heavy tourist traffic and the wealth of diversions that have been introduced for tourists, the area has retained its exotic natural beauty, and steps have been taken to guarantee its preservation.

Winter is probably the best season to visit, but the resort is popular all year (most hotels lower their rates during the off season from May through November). The weather never gets very cold, and the water temperature is always perfect. Vegetation is lush, fragrant, and tropical. Shoppers beware, though — prices are generally higher here than in any other Mexican city (especially from Christmas to Easter).

The town is set at the base of the mountains that all but encircle a blue bay. When approaching town along the highway, you descend to beach level and drive along hotel row, a long line that reaches in toward the center of town. You'll discover newer resorts (and more expensive ones) on Revocaldero Beach and near lovely Puerto Marques Bay south of the city. The great high-rise structures are the second generation of hotels, air-conditioned and equipped with swimming pools. Completed this year is the rebuilding of the Costera Miguel Aleman. Palm trees line this boulevard, where Acapulco's best shops, restaurants, and nightclubs are clustered.

This tropical parkway parallels the beach for a while. At the last center of commerce before the street turns south, a broad, divided boulevard heads inland; the vast public market complex is located near here.

The market is fun, whether you're shopping for picnic ingredients or just looking at what may be the most fascinating place in town. Here you'll find unfamiliar groceries, fresh breads, bulk seasonings, and produce both familiar and strange. Flower vendors brighten the courts between pavilions, and truckloads of bananas and other products crowd the streets.

Where the boulevard turns west again, you'll see Acapulco's one real antiquity—Fort San Diego, built by the Spanish in 1616 to protect the port from Dutch and English pirates. The fort is now a regional anthropology and history museum. This area is the center of town, where the zocalo, cathedral, and malecon are located.

A city of parks. Acapulco is becoming a city of parks. Newly dedicated Papagayo Park, considered one of Mexico's prettiest, stretches along the beach for 20 blocks. The grounds contain a botanical garden, an aviary, a regional museum, and amusement rides. Coming in the future are an aquarium, an art cinema, and some restaurants.

Cici Park, on the Costera near the Acapulco Center, concentrates on aquatic activities: performing dolphins and seals, water slides, and a pool with artificial waves.

El Veladero Park is Acapulco's national park of the future. The mountainsides surrounding Acapulco are being reforested to prevent erosion, and recreational areas are being created. The 12,500 families who once lived on the mountainsides have been relocated in Ciudad Renacimiento (Renaissance City), 10 minutes beyond Acapulco's hills.

The Acapulco Center, a multilevel convention facility on 35 acres of parklike grounds, serves as the city's new entertainment complex. Fountains and meticulously landscaped gardens greet visitors. A small entrance fee gives you entrée to a wide range of dining, shopping, and entertainment possibilities. Folkloric shows (such as that featuring the famous Flying Indians of Papantla) and a variety of musical performances are presented in the auditorium, theater, open-air amphitheater, and plazas. Music also pours forth from the center's bars and restaurants. The center is especially lovely at night.

The city's miles of beaches are justly famous. Though most beaches around the bay are crowded, the best for sun-worshippers are from Condessa east to Icacos. For solitary ocean front, head south to sandy stretches around the Princess and Pierre Marques hotels (under Mexican law all beaches are public), or take a boat across the bay to a quiet spot.

People-watching is one favorite activity: parasailers taking off and landing, water-skiers sliding through the water, or vendors offering everything from cold drinks to bead jewelry. Open-air restaurants front onto main beaches.

Beyond the malecon, the waterfront boulevard is less picturesque. You approach the hilly peninsula that shelters the harbor; the first big hotels and costly houses were built on its slopes. Across the peninsula is La Quebrada, an observation point over the rocky cliffs of the town's seaward side. Acapulco's famous high divers leap from these cliffs to the water 137 feet below; you can get a good view of them from La Perla lounge in the El Mirador Hotel.

Caletilla and Caleta (original morning beaches), on the low side of the peninsula, are the center of water-oriented activity, with a small harbor for sport-fishing boats, glass-bottom boats, and launches taking visitors to La Roqueta Island to enjoy the beach, have lunch, or indulge the beer-drinking burros. Parachute rides are popular: the parachute, pulled by boat, lifts you from the beach and takes you for a brief, breathtaking tour of the beach—with a bird's-eye view.

Several boat excursions—sightseeing trips by day or partying trips by night—explore the harbor or go out to sea and around the peninsula to the dramatic coast of La Quebrada.

To the north and south of the mountains lie lagoons; both have boats for fishing and exploring, and both are destinations for hunting and sightseeing excursions.

Sporting activities center along the beaches. All beaches and beach hotels offer complete water sports facilities, including power boats and sailboats, pedal boats, surfboards and paddle boards, and water skis. Angling, especially for sailfish, is exceptionally good; you can rent tackle and power boats. Less athletic visitors may enjoy watching greyhound and horse racing at a track near Las Brisas.

Two championship 18-hole golf courses (at the Princess and Pierre Marques hotels) and over 80 tennis courts —some indoors and air-conditioned—help keep you fit.

Shopping is good—but expensive. You'll find everything you need (or didn't know you needed) in downtown stores, hotel boutiques, or convention center shops. For handicrafts, take a look at the government Fonapas store near the Acapulco Center. The best of crafts from all over the state are displayed and sold here; there's also a small museum on the grounds.

Street and beach vendors will expect you to bargain for baskets, sarapes, beach hats, and jewelry; store prices are usually set.

Night life in Acapulco begins late (around 11 P.M.) and goes on until dawn. Hotels, nightclubs, and beachfront restaurants vibrate with music and laughter. Discotheques are popular, and entertainers are exotic; at top spots, you can expect a cover charge. The Acapulco Center features a variety of continuous entertainment nightly.

Some hotels offer 3½-hour nightclub tours, which include stops and sips at three shows; prices include drinks, cover charges, and tips. English-speaking guides are your escorts. You may not visit the current hot spots, but it's a good way to glimpse the city's entertainment variety.

Zihuatanejo—a simple village grows up

A different experience awaits the visitor arriving in Zihuatanejo from Acapulco. Only 200 km/125 miles up the coast, it's far removed from Acapulco's crowded beaches and cosmopolitan air; but change is definitely on the way. Nestling at the base of Mexico's Sierra Madre del Sur, the town's protected 3-km/2-mile-wide bay is surrounded by low, brush-covered hillsides and coconut plantations. A trim white lighthouse on a jungle-clad crag far out in the surging sea guards the bay. A few boats bob in the water, and outrigger dugout canoes are drawn up on the sand. You'll see no high-rise hotels, though there are a few good hotels scattered around town.

Along the highway, though, new construction has changed the entrance to this once-sleepy town. Streets have been paved, downtown shops have new fronts, and a pedestrian-only shopping mall leads to the beach. The government project underway at nearby Ixtapa is turning an isolated region into a topflight resort area. Sample Zihuatanejo as soon as you can, while it still holds its provincial simplicity and charm.

Around the bay. At Playa Principal (the main beach) and Las Gatas beach you can rent equipment for water-skiing, scuba diving, and surfing; arrange rentals in advance through your hotel. You can hail a water taxi anywhere along the shore for a bay tour, or rent a deep-sea boat with a guide and go fishing for tuna, roosterfish, and an occasional marlin. At tidepool-studded Isla Grande, a few miles north, cooks will prepare your catch; or you can cook it yourself, native-style, on a mainland beach.

The clarity of the water, the abundant variety of underwater life, and the intricate beauty of its coral reefs make Zihuatanejo Bay popular among skin divers. Even if you've never tried the sport before, take along a snorkel and face mask and begin your underwater adventure by floating quietly over the coral reefs. If the appeal of the underwater world becomes irresistible, diving instruction is available.

From the beach, a few primitive roads invite you to take a short hike into the surrounding jungle with its flowering tropical trees and shrubs, great birdlife, and occasional palm-thatched hut.

Around town. Shopping for handicrafts, native clothing, and gifts in the town's small stores can be intriguing. It's a place to bargain. You'll also discover a few good restaurants in the small downtown area. Zihuatanejo's hotels (see page 150) are mostly cliffside, above the bay; seclusion and a good view are their prime offerings.

Cruising Mexican waters

The warning gong sounds, the band strikes up, the streamers fly—and you're off on a cruise to Mexico. Will it be as glamorous as the popular "Love Boat" television show? Probably not. But for those who enjoy an abundance of food, 24-hour entertainment, and colorful ports of call, Mexican cruises are a tempting form of transportation.

Your schedule and your budget will determine your choice of cruise line; depending upon the length of the trip, ports of call are the same. Bahama, Costa, Carnival, Norwegian Caribbean, Princess, Royal Caribbean, Royal Viking, and Sitmar lines offer 1 to 2-week trips. If a shorter vacation better suits your schedule, pick Western Cruise Lines or Royal Viking for 3 to 5-day excursions.

Ports of call for longer cruises include several of the resort cities of Acapulco, Cabo San Lucas, Ixtapa/Zihuantanejo, Manzanillo, and Mazatlan on the west coast; Cancun, Cozumel, and Playa del Carmen on the east coast. The shorter cruises concentrate on Ensenada or Mazatlan and Puerto Vallarta. U.S. ports of departure are Los Angeles, San Francisco, Miami, and Tampa.

Some cruise lines offer trips the year around. The only exceptions are Bahama, Costa, and Special Expeditions Inc., who have only winter and spring departures. Though prices are lower in the warmer months and shipboard temperatures will be pleasant, the cities you visit may be quite hot and humid.

Special Expeditions Inc. offers 15-day in-depth looks at Baja California from January through April. Sailings coincide with the migration of whales to Scammon's Lagoon (see page 17).

Cruise costs vary, depending on the line, the length of the cruise, and the type of cabin. The price includes all meals (up to eight a day), lodging, shipboard activities, and entertainment. It does not include land tours, tips, and alcoholic beverages. Airfare may or may not be included in the total price—if it's not, you may be able to save by booking your air travel in connection with the cruise.

Few, if any, unpleasant surprises usually associated with vacation travel arise when you take a cruise. Once you're aboard, there's no possibility of mysteriously missing reservations or lost luggage. Your only decisions during the day will be whether to court the sun, engage in a lively game of deck tennis, swim, play bridge, see a movie, shop, sightsee, eat, or sleep. At night you can gamble, dance, watch the entertainment, or curl up with a good book.

Contact your travel agent for more details on the delights of visiting Mexico by ship.

Zihuatanejo's handful of restaurants also attract Ixtapa's visitors. Ask for recommendations at your hotel. Restaurants may be simple, but the seafood (and its preparation) is impressive.

The best way to get to Ixtapa, 15 minutes away from Zihuatanejo, is to take a cab. Confirm the price before you get in.

North of Ixtapa lie the Club Med facility and Playa Linda, an inexpensive coastal resort that attracts Mexican vacationers. You'll find trailer hookups, outdoor cooking areas, a pool, a small store, and boat rentals.

Ixtapa—a new super resort

Ixtapa lies 24 km/15 miles north of Zihuatanejo. Here, Mexico's second computer-planned wonder resort is partially completed — among 5,263 acres of coconut palms, mangroves, colorful flowers, and foliage, along miles of beach that, up to now, were known only by tropical birds. Surprisingly, not even the dozen or so hotels spoil the region's beauty.

This is beach and pool life at its casual best. Except during the summer and early autumn rainy season, you'll almost always find good weather and balmy offshore breezes. When you tire of sitting around a beach or pool, you can play a round at the nearby 18-hole Palma Real Golf Club (take your clubs along or rent them there). A number of lighted tennis courts encourage evening play. Sailboats, water-ski boats, and fishing boats can be rented, and parachute rides arranged, in front of the hotels or from the marina.

A small shopping center across the street from the row of hotels contains a few good shops, gift stores, and restaurants. Hotel dining rooms and bars, plus one disco, supply nighttime action.

Taxis or buses take you to Zihuatanejo for shopping or dining; your hotel will offer several specialty tours of the surrounding area.

Guadalajara

The Colonial Circle

(For "Facts at Your Fingertips," see pages 152–153)

For many visitors, Guadalajara makes an attractive base from which to explore Mexico's colonial past. To the east is the heartland of the 1810 Revolution of Independence—Guanajuato, San Miguel de Allende, and Queretaro. To the south are Morelia, a living museum of Mexican history, and the enchanting towns of Uruapan and Patzcuaro. In between lies a profusion of colonial villages packed with historical monuments, buildings, and legends. Several of these towns have diligently tried to maintain the colonial ambience and historical authenticity that so often dissipate after years of renovation and new developments.

Guadalajara

Capital of the state of Jalisco, Guadalajara is Mexico's second largest city—and a favorite of many American tourists who find a contrast to the rest of Mexico in the unique blend of modern and traditional architecture, as well as in the tree-shaded residential streets, temperate climate, and cosmopolitan atmosphere.

If you have the time and want to explore a place where the best of Mexico is expressed, plan a long stay in Guadalajara. You're not likely to get bored with a place where horse-drawn cabs and caravans of laden burros share the right-of-way with the latest model limousines and sports cars; where street widening (needed to transform a country town into a brisk metropolis) was done only on one side of the street, so only half the ancient buildings had to be removed; where people who hardly gave a passing glance to the erection of an architecturally superior department store pay tireless tribute to the architecturally grotesque cathedral; and where the siesta is a jealously cherished ritual that shuts down businesses for 2 hours every working day, causing four daily commuter-traffic rushes.

Guadalajara's partial conversion to a sleek metropolis has been attained at some sacrifice of Mexican mellowness, and there may be moments on Avenida 16 de Septiembre or Juarez when you'll have to remind yourself that you're a thousand miles below the border. But Guadalajara still has much that is "old" Mexico, and a very evident enthusiasm for new things has not displaced affection for the old.

Getting around

A slight handicap in learning your way around Guadalajara (and many other Mexican cities) is that the city is divided into different sectors — so most street names change as the streets pass from one sector to another.

Guadalajara has four sectors; the boundaries are Avenida Morelos, Calzada Independencia, and Avenida Gigantes. Thus Avenida 16 de Septiembre suddenly becomes Avenida Alcalde when it crosses Avenida Morelos near the cathedral; Avenida Juarez changes its name twice, becoming Avenida Javier Mina before it gets to the Mercado Libertad, and (going the other way) Avenida Vallarta where it passes the university.

Even if you're self-reliant and arrive in your own car, it's a good idea to take a preview tour of the city—or to hire a guide, either through a travel agency or from the government tourist office located in an old convent on Avenida Juarez. If you go out for half a day or longer in the city or to

Guadalajara's expansive Plaza de la Liberacion is only one of city's handsome plazas.

visit nearby points of interest, you may want to choose a package itinerary with guide, car, meals, and hotels from the choices offered by a Guadalajara travel agency.

Taxicabs are plentiful. Rates are fixed by a government ordinance; determine the fare before entering the cab.

You won't get much Guadalajaran lore out of the preoccupied driver of a *calandria* as you clip-clop around town, but you might enjoy the experience. These horse-drawn antiques, complete with black-liveried drivers, once were the private conveyances of well-to-do families. When some vehicles went into public service, their drivers put on yellow armbands to indicate the calandrias were for hire. The armbands must have reminded someone of a yellow-shouldered lark, because the carriages have long been known as calandrias (larks or buntings).

For more extensive sightseeing you may wish to join one of the bus tours available in Guadalajara. Morning and afternoon tours last about 4 hours each (including time for shopping) and take in the famous pottery suburb of Tlaquepaque in the southern part of the city, as well as the state Arts and Crafts Center (Instituto de las Artisanias Jalisciense).

Brooding beauty *of Orozco murals covers stone walls and ceilings of Centro Cultural de las Americas (formerly Hospicio Cabañas). Benches provide "lie-down" viewing.*

Fountain jets, *colorful plantings enliven front entrance to gracious Degollado Theater.*

A look at the new and the old

Downtown Guadalajara is undergoing a facelift. New pedestrian malls (some with limited traffic) offer grand opportunities for strolling and shopping. The mall between the Centro Cultural de las Americas (formerly the Hospicio Cabañas) is a good place to start your downtown walk. Stroll along the block-wide, newly renovated Plaza Metropolitana; you'll pass fountains, waterways, and colorful tilework on your way from the Centro Cultural de las Americas to the back of the Degollado Theater. Colonial monuments are just steps away from the plaza.

The cathedral: Be sure to explore the interior, especially beautiful when the huge chandeliers are lighted. Begun in 1571, completed in 1618, partially destroyed in 1818, and modernized in 1944, the cathedral reflects a potpourri of architectural styles and is recognized as the universal symbol of the city.

The churches: The Church of Santa Monica, intricately carved in the Churrigueresque style, was completed in about 1720. The churches of San Francisco and Aranzazu both face the shady Jardin de San Francisco. San Francisco has the most impressive exterior by far, but the Churrigueresque altar in Aranzazu is perhaps the masterpiece of its kind.

The Centro Cultural de las Americas, once an orphanage, is now a cultural center devoted to art, concerts, and theater presentations. This impressive building also houses the best work of the muralist Orozco; to get the best view of the painting on the ceiling, lie on one of the benches provided. Wander through numerous flower-filled patios, preserved and enhanced by recent remodeling.

The museums: The State Museum & Library is located on Avenida Corona near the central plaza; the original building was constructed in the 17th century as a Jesuit seminary. Here you'll find historical, zoological, and archeological exhibits, as well as art galleries. The collection of contemporary art includes Murillo paintings and a great three-dimensional mural by Gabriel Flores (the mural is on the ceiling of the auditorium dome).

Instituto de las Artesanas, on the northwest corner of Parque Agua Azul, displays crafts from Jalisco. The Museo Regional de Guadalajara, covering a square block along one side of the cathedral, features western Mexico's cultural development. Orozco's Museum Workshop displays over 90 works by this well-known artist; open daily except Monday, it's close to the arch on Avenida Vallarta.

The government buildings: At the Government Palace (Palacio de Gobierno) you're welcome to go in and look around the 17th century building and peruse several powerful murals by Orozco (located near the stairway) depicting episodes in the building's history. From the second floor, a narrow stairway leads to the rooftop view.

The Municipal Palace (Palacio Municipal) is built in the colonial style to harmonize with neighboring buildings.

(Continued on next page)

Sunlight sparkles *on blown glass, product of a principal craft in Jalisco state.*

...Continued from page 49

This is the place you go to buy back your front license plate —if you park illegally, a policeman will remove it from your car. The transaction will cost you an hour; but while you wait, you'll have the chance to see a truly distinguished mural by contemporary painter Gabriel Flores.

The Degollado Theater: The theater's classical facade can be seen from the central plaza. To assure yourself of an opportunity to enjoy the elaborate interior, buy tickets to whatever is being performed. Home of the famous Guadalajara Symphony, the theater also hosts a wide variety of other performers.

To discover what's going on when, buy the *Colony Reporter* (published every Saturday). It gives the current information on the English-speaking community, plus lots of news for the retired.

A city of parks and plazas

The Plaza de la Liberacion is a major result of the modernization of Guadalajara. Two blocks of old buildings were removed to create this long rectangular "square," now rich with fountains and bright flowering *tabachin* trees.

You'll hear the word *tapatio* mentioned frequently around town—it refers to any quality of Guadalajara. Very tapatio is the Plaza de los Mariachis, where mariachi bands gather in the narrow mall to serenade you as you sip sangria or tequila at a parasol-shaded outdoor table. Since they require a small fee for their musical services, check the price per song in advance.

Hand-burnished duck *bears finely detailed decoration typical of Tonala.*

The Parque Agua Azul — only two blocks from the Sheraton — is a great place to people-watch each Sunday afternoon, when a free performance is presented in the outdoor theater. Children will appreciate the zoo and the rides, and everyone will enjoy watching the park's many colorful macaws. Though these birds have complete freedom, they usually stay on the canopied perches suspended over the walks.

Another tree-shaded and fountain-cooled escape from the bustle of the city is Parque Revolucion on West Juarez. Here the Latin dating game, the *paseo*, takes place on Sunday evenings.

Sports and sporting events

Cockfights are legal and occur in their own arena. At the Santa Rita polo grounds, games are played several times weekly; the best matches are at noon Sunday. Perhaps the most colorful and typically Mexican events are the char-readas, Mexican rodeos performed with great skill by dressed-up charros. Rodeos are usually held before noon on Sunday; you'll have to check the location. The inevitable bullfights are held at the Plaza de Toros opposite the Mercado Libertad, though Guadalajara's younger generation must be credited with an overwhelming preference for *futbol* (soccer) and good old *beisbol* (baseball).

Visiting golfers can get a guest card at the Guadalajara Country Club on the northwest side of town, at the Santa Anita Country Club on the southwest side, or at the Altas Golf Club on the road to Chapala.

Places to shop

To put your thoughts in order, go first to the large Instituto de las Artesianas Jalisciense. Located at the entrance to Parque Agua Azul, it's an intriguing museum-salesroom where you can examine exquisite products typical of various regions of the state. These include furniture, pottery, tinware, glass, ceramic sculpture, and fabrics. Everything's for sale. The prices are generally higher (in some cases, much higher) than elsewhere in Guadalajara and in nearby Tlaquepaque and Tonala—but you'll be sure of top quality, and many items are still only half the price of similar articles sold in the United States. You can have your larger purchases shipped directly home.

Many of the city's fine shops and good restaurants are concentrated in the Pink Zone (Avenida Chapultepec) and on the west side (Avenida Union to Avenida de las Americas). You'll find everything from fashionable boutiques to handloomed fabrics.

Mercado Libertad. You can haggle over prices at only a few places in Guadalajara, and the *Mercado*, claimed to be the world's largest market under one roof, is one of them. Nearly destroyed by fire quite a few years ago, it was only recently rebuilt in a more modern style. As you work your way through the overwhelming confusion of merchandise,

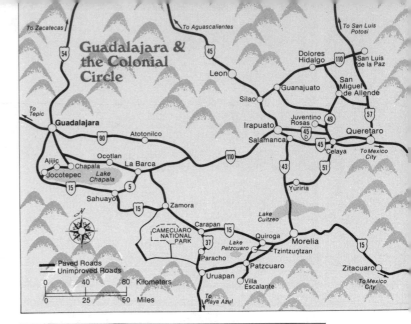

Details at a glance

How to get there

Guadalajara, a major tourist destination in its own right, is also a jumping-off spot for visits to Mexico's colonial towns. Most travelers fly to Guadalajara (or Mexico City), then rent a car, take a bus, or join an organized tour for a look at the colonial loop.

By air. Guadalajara is easily reached by direct flights from the U.S. and Canada. Domestic carriers offer frequent service from Mexico City and other large towns.

By car. Highway 15 is the most direct route from Mexico City to Guadalajara (via Morelia). Using Guadalajara as a base, you can drive the colonial loop in 4 or 5 leisurely days. Park your car in the city; then take cabs (agree on fare beforehand), hire a car and driver, or join bus tours.

Accommodations

Guadalajara offers hotels ranging from inexpensive to deluxe; most convenient downtown hotels have recently had a facelift. Recreational vehicle parks are available in Guadalajara and most smaller towns. For more information, see the "Essentials" section, pages 152 and 153.

Climate and clothes

Guadalajara, at 5,200 feet above sea level, has clear, bracing weather; temperatures may be higher in other cities along the route.

For women, pants are acceptable both in the city and in small towns, though you may find a loose shift more comfortable if you're visiting in summer. Outside of Guadalajara, men need not bother with a tie.

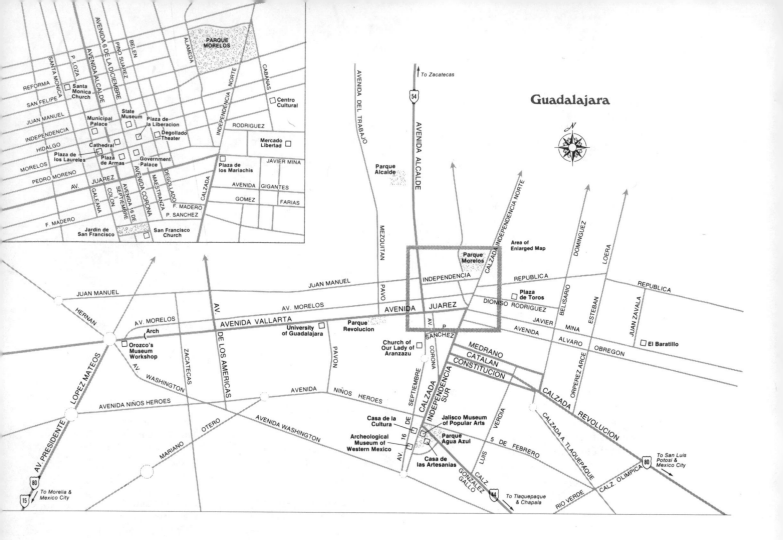

you'll come upon everything you can think of (and a few things you can't), from renowned Paracho guitars to dried iguanas for witches' brew.

El Baratillo. "The bargain counter" is open for business every Sunday morning. Though most customers are Guadalajarans, more and more tourists who enjoy garage sales, flea markets, haggling, and browsing are discovering this market. Of special interest are the dealers in antiques, picture frames, odd pieces of porcelain, and wrought iron. A staggering display of items awaits you — many new, most used—including fake and genuine artifacts, bottles, medicinal herbs, ancient typewriters, and even washing machines. Located on Juan Zavala, a 5-minute drive east of the Mercado Libertad on Javier Mina, this flea market displays 12 long blocks of merchandise. You can always hope that a priceless item has been overlooked and has found its way to the Baratillo.

Plaza del Sol. This plaza is one of Latin America's largest shopping centers. Opened in 1969, it covers over 12,000 square yards and provides an astounding range of goods and services. It's located in an area of new hotels and motels in the southwestern section of the city between Mariano Otero and Avenida Lopez Mateos.

Tlaquepaque. Guadalajara has sprawled east to merge with San Pedro Tlaquepaque. Though this town is best known for its pottery, other arts are practiced here as well; silver jewelry, leather goods, glassware, rugs, and much more can be found in this folk art center, which is usually included in a tour of Guadalajara.

Red brick malls lead the way to the shops (many have patios sprinkled with potted plants and flowers). Weary shoppers will appreciate the bars and cafes along El Parian. If you're interested in a bit of history, visit the Regional Museum of Ceramics and the Gallery of Culture and Art.

Tonala, an Indian village just 20 minutes east of Guadalajara, is one of the best areas to shop for ceramics. You'll usually find better quality merchandise in established shops, but visit on market days (Thursday and Sunday) to see more color and variety.

Tonala is also popular for copies of "pre-Columbian" figures. Their "weathered" look comes from being buried for a few months.

Craft towns around Guadalajara

Mexico produces a tremendous amount of exuberant folk art—primarily handicrafts designed for household use. Notably rich in handicrafts is the region around Guadalajara. Artists in each of these craft towns produce pottery, baskets, sarapes, and toys for sale in local markets; you'll often be able to buy a craft item from the person who made it. After you've visited several towns, you'll begin to appreciate their distinct artistic styles.

Guadalajara is a recognized craft center, partly because so many artisans are at work in surrounding communities. If you're visiting Guadalajara, reserve a little time for Instituto de las Artesanias Jalisciense. Located at the north end of Parque Agua Azul in a state-operated building, this center both displays and sells regional handicrafts. Here you'll find examples of the crafts made in each village; you'll also see some unique articles and begin learning to identify high quality and top workmanship.

A few miles southeast of the center of Guadalajara, between Highway 80 and Highway 35, is the well-known craft center with the fun-to-pronounce name of Tlaquepaque (tlockay-pockay). The town was once known only for pottery—not all of it good—but local craftspeople have now branched out into furniture, textiles, glass, and other crafts. The Regional Museum of Ceramics, located in an elegant colonial house on Avenida Independencia, has a collection of pottery from the Valley of Atemajac, including *barro de olor* (odoriferous earthenware) and the unique *petatillo* pottery. Typical of this region, petatillo is characterized by its distinctive, almost Oriental designs of stylized animals against a background of tile red slip with white crosshatching. Don't miss the glass factories on Avenida Independencia, where you can buy glass objects and watch glass blowers at work. Gift shops line the main street.

Drive east from Guadalajara for about 20 minutes to reach Tonala, which produces some of Mexico's most unusual pottery and stoneware. In addition to more practical pieces, its artisans produce many beautifully decorated, handburnished birds and animals, and sculptured objects. Small boys often linger around the town plaza and flag down tourists, hoping to earn a few pesos by conducting a tour through one of the several ceramic factories.

If you follow Highway 15 south of Guadalajara for 56 km/35 miles, you approach Lake Chapala at Jocotepec. This lakeside town is noted for handwoven sarapes—in traditional styles with geometric designs and small flowers in pastel colors on an off-white background, and in contemporary designs featuring birds and flowers in cheerful patterns typical of the state of Jalisco. For information on individual shops, inquire at the Hotel La Quinta, located about a mile off Highway 15 toward Ajijic. Ajijic, a community even smaller than Jocotepec and 19 km/12 miles farther northeast on the same road, is also known for weaving. Numerous artists and writers, many of them American, have settled in this quaint, picturesque fishing village on the edge of Lake Chapala. Several boutiques and gift shops in town display high-quality handwoven cloth and embroidered clothing. Two studios specialize in refined weaving done on hand looms: Helen Kirtland's Studio and Neill James' Studio, both located near Posada Ajijic.

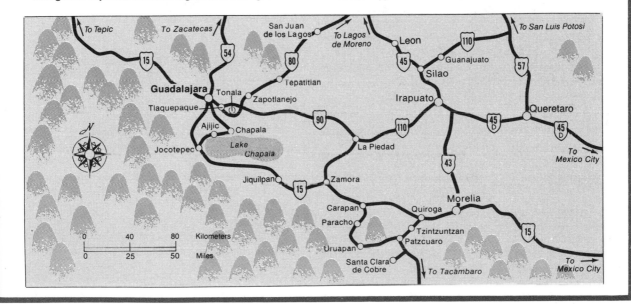

Suburban attractions

Just outside Guadalajara's city limits, you'll discover a fruit producing region, one of Mexico's largest waterfalls, and a revered relic.

Barranca de Oblatos (Monk's Canyon). Thermal rivulets plunge down the red walls of this 2,000-foot-deep gorge; the tropical valley below produces much of the fruit marketed in Guadalajara. From the city, follow Calzada Independencia 11 km/7 miles to the canyon rim.

Juanacatlan Falls. This waterfall — one of the largest in Mexico—is at its best from June through September. In the nearby village you can view several iron and textile mills. From Guadalajara take Highway 44 southeast about 23 km/14 miles; then turn onto a paved road and continue driving for another 12 km/7 miles.

Zapopan. From her 17th century basilica at Avenida 20 de Noviembre and Pino Suarez in this little suburb of Guadalajara, the revered Virgin of Zapopan ventures forth each summer to tour all of the city's churches, returning to her own in October. Through a travel agency, you can reserve seats for the unusual and emotional return procession on October 12.

Lake Chapala area

Lake Chapala lies 56 km/35 miles southeast of Guadalajara; surrounded by mountains, it's accessible by several good roads. Stretching alongside Highway 15, this hyacinth-dotted lake is the largest lake in Mexico, measuring 104 km/65 miles long and 32 km/20 miles wide. It's fed by the Lerma River and empties into the Grande de Santiago River. A 29-km/18-mile paved road connects the villages circling the lake. The road from Highway 15 skirts the southern shore, taking you to the village of Chapala on the northern shore. On the way, you'll pass through picturesque villages of Jocotepec, with its narrow cobblestone streets and a profusion of tropical flora, and Ajijic, where you can buy beautiful handloomed textiles. The road also passes several residential subdivisions, where many of the homes are occupied by retired North Americans.

The climate is temperate and mild all year in the lake region. Fishing for sunfish and Chapala whitefish is popular, as are boating, bird watching, and swimming.

Chapala

Traditionally the destination for Sunday outings by Guadalajarans, Chapala has a large community of retired and foreign residents and was a favorite with the international set long before any of the other lakeshore resort villages became popular. Two private clubs extend their privileges to visitors: one features a golf course, the other is a yacht club. A 500-seat Civic Cultural Center is a center for regional performances. Chapala has several restaurants, most serving the one dish that everyone who comes to town should sample—Lake Chapala whitefish. These fish had been unavailable for consumption in recent years; because the lake was polluted, eating fish caught in it was not recommended. The situation has improved, though, and residents and visitors are once again enjoying this regional specialty.

If you continue eastward along the north shore of the lake, you go through the lakeside towns of Ocotlan and La Barca. At La Barca you cross the Lerma River just before it flows into the lake; then you can follow the highway down to Sahuayo where it joins Highway 15, or continue ahead and join Highway 15 at Zamora, a strawberry town.

Ajijic—lakeside artist's community

Since about 1945 Ajijic has been the home of many foreigners, from lively young liberals to quiet, well-known artists. An international atmosphere, along with neat whitewashed buildings and cobblestone streets, make Ajijic a delightful village to visit for an escape from bustling Guadalajara. Shopping is a rewarding adventure; you'll come upon art galleries, weaving studios, and craft shops of all kinds. The retired community represents a large part of the village population.

The fishing village of Jocotepec

Founded in 1528, Jocotepec radiates a quiet contentment with its long history. Evidence of the village's age is apparent in a few crumbling walls, and in the old colonial architecture and rough streets; the air of antiquity gives Jocotepec a quality that makes it unique among the lake resort villages. Heavy, handmade white sarapes with a colorful central design motif are a specialty here. Fishing is the chief livelihood here; you'll see fishers' huts, and yards of fish nets strung out to dry.

The Colonial Circle

Between Guadalajara and Mexico City, Highway 15 is a paved road. It's two lanes wide from Guadalajara to Toluca; from there into Mexico City, it increases to four lanes. You'll find slow going, though, in the mountainous sections east of Morelia and in the shallow, barren canyons and ravines east of Zitacuaro.

The sights east of Guadalajara will make you more aware of Mexico's history: a wealth of arched aqueducts dating from colonial days; small farm plots which Indians still till with ox-drawn plows; huge old crumbling haciendas; burros on their way to market; small towns dominated by the reassuring presence of the parish church's ornate tower; and the Tarascan Indian villages, located around Lake Patzcuaro.

Lakes Chapala, Camecuaro, and Patzcuaro, the falls

On net-draped shore *of Lake Chapala (Mexico's largest), fishermen chop boat channel through water hyacinths.*

near Uruapan, and the heavily forested mountains make the region between Guadalajara and Morelia one of Mexico's most scenic stretches.

East of Zitacuaro, you leave the cool pine forests for high, semiarid plains. The wind sweeps freely across the rolling countryside, hills are covered with sparse grass, and erosion has seriously furrowed the thin, drifting soil. Much of the wide, flat valley of Toluca is divided into small farms, each with its small house of raw adobe and its adjoining stack of fodder elevated on poles. In the windy late winter and early spring, gossamer clouds of dust hover over the landscape, obscuring the countryside.

Just before reaching the Valley of Mexico, the road climbs to its highest point in the Sierra Madre Occidental—10,000 feet—and you go through another stretch of pine and fir forests. Miniscule farms sit in clearings on the steep mountainsides; as you start the descent into the valley, clusters of attractive, expensive homes come into sight.

You can avoid the mountains (though you'll miss some of Mexico's most beautiful scenery) by taking the northern route to Mexico City along a combination of Highways 110, 45, and 57.

South of Leon and the Comanjilla road junction is a small city named Silao. Atop a mountain just east of the city is a huge stone statue of Christ called "Cristo Rey" (Christ the King); it can be seen from Highway 45 for several miles in both directions. The mountain on which the statue stands is said to be the exact geographical center of Mexico — if it's possible to determine the exact geographical center of a cornucopia-shaped country. A road leads up to the statue from near the Guanajuato highway junction just east of Silao, but it's unpaved and quite difficult to negotiate. A better, slightly longer road leaves Highway 110 a few miles east of Guanajuato.

South of the Silao and Guanajuato junction, Highway 45 winds into a huge valley which the Mexicans call El Bajio (The Depression). It's the largest of the seven valleys making up the vast Central Plateau and is also one of Mexico's most fertile agricultural areas, providing metropolitan Mexico City with food and dairy products. Down Highway 45 you'll see the Mexican food processing plants of several North American companies (largely owned and run by Mexicans) — Del Monte, Campbell, Kellogg, Carnation, Ralston-Purina, and others.

Like an ivory egg, *Guanajuato nestles among velvet hills, once rich in silver.*

Leon—Mexico's sole town

Accorded with generous acclaim as "The Shoe Capital of Mexico," Leon is a bustling, industrious city in the state of Guanajuato. Shoes aren't everything here; Leon is also well known for all types of leather goods.

The general atmosphere reflects the city's highly industrial economy. Leon is a large city with many big city problems: you'll probably discover traffic is terrible, and you may find difficulty getting comfortable accommodations.

Nevertheless, the city retains many charming colonial buildings, and has a central square surrounded by old archways and flower-filled plazas. The Palacio Municipal (City Hall), on the main plaza, has an exquisitely carved exterior. A spacious, wide boulevard runs the length of the city; trees bordering the plaza are trim and lush.

A few miles south of Leon and 9 km/6 miles east on a blacktop road is the popular health resort of Comanjilla. Here, thermal spring waters are piped into large swimming pools and also into the bathtubs and miniature pools of the guest rooms.

Guanajuato—18th century silver capital

Founded by the Spaniards more than 400 years ago, Guanajuato grew into a city of wealth and extravagance during the heyday of its legendary silver mines. It saw some of the fiercest fighting of the War of Independence, then went into a long, slow decline. Today, it has emerged as a small, stately city with a strangely provocative and medieval European air.

A unique feature of Guanajuato is its subterranean street — a stone-arched tunnel that meanders under the city. The tunnel was built on the dry bed of the Guanajuato River and follows its original course for almost 3 km/2 miles (the river now flows in a different channel). One of North America's greatest floods occurred in Guanajuato in 1905, when the dams at the south end of the city broke during a storm. The flood waters rampaged through the narrow, ravinelike channel of the normally unassuming Guanajuato River, drowning thousands of residents.

Guanajuato is a city made for walking. Built where three ravines meet, the city offers the delight of random

Gently climbing *a hill to its cathedral, San Miguel de Allende is an undisputed gem in Mexico's colonial crown.*

Colorful yarn *hangs in hot Uruapan sun to hasten drying after dying.*

Handcrafted *iron scrollwork, wooden doors, plastered walls convey colonial character.*

strolls along the narrow, cobbled byways that wind up the hillsides, turning into flights of stairs when the going gets too steep. You'll find yourself drawn on by the unusual facades of houses (no two alike), beckoned by the filigree of street lamps and overhanging balconies, and diverted by narrow passageways into unexpected squares. And for all your wandering, you're never really lost — the center of town is always waiting for you down the hill.

Sightseeing. Jardin de la Union — a good place to begin a day's exploration — is a delicate and graceful plaza. Here you can sit on ornate wrought iron benches and listen to band concerts each week.

Facing the plaza is Teatro Juarez, a theater in the classic style of the late 19th century. One of Guanajuato's few examples of postcolonial architecture, it once rivaled Mexico City's opera house in prestige and splendor. Don't miss seeing its opulent, Moorish interior. (The eight bronze figures that top this building are by an Ohio sculptor.)

Next to the theater is the Franciscan Church of San Diego (built in 1784). Its facade is magnificent, though the interior isn't especially impressive. A block away you'll come to Plaza de la Paz, dominated by La Parroquia Church; its baptistry and sacristy date back to 1696.

Up a narrow alley from this plaza is a comparatively recent building of the University of Guanajuato, designed to blend with the colonial town.

La Compania (built in 1747), a beautiful church inside and out, is also part of the university. Its colonnaded dome will serve as a landmark as you stroll about the town.

Three other destinations require longer walks: the marketplace (Mercado Hidalgo), with local craft products for sale (Sunday is market day); the pleasant parks by the two dams that hold back the Guanajuato River; and the granary, better known as the Alhondiga. The Alhondiga, scene of a bloody battle in revolutionary days, now houses a regional museum reputed to be one of the most informative and well-organized museums in Mexico.

58   Colonial Circle

A roundabout drive (or a steep climb) takes you up the hill behind Teatro Juarez to the Statue of Pipila. At the start of the War of Independence of 1810–1821, the miner Pipila, with a flat stone strapped on his back as a shield, braved enemy bullets and molten lead to set fire to the door of a loyalist stronghold at the granary. Guanajuato became the first major city to fall to the forces of independence.

An attraction you may prefer to miss is the collection of well-preserved mummies at the Catacombs, doomed to exposure because their descendants fell behind on crypt rental fees.

Three miles from the midtown plaza, a church and mine bear witness to the glories of the past. La Valenciana is considered one of the most perfect and elegant churches in Mexico. Its architecture, the craftsmanship displayed in its intricate facade and carved altars, and the impressive view all merit a visit.

Across the highway you'll find the crumbling ruins of La Valenciana Mine, which for half a century poured millions of pesos annually into the treasury of the Spanish vice-royalty and financed the construction of the elegant homes and churches of Guanajuato and its suburbs.

City tours leave from the Juarez Theater in the morning and afternoon. If you prefer to sightsee on your own, it's best to hire a guide and car — you'll save hours of getting lost.

Shopping. Guanajuato offers many fine shops within walking distance of the central plaza. Quality is generally good; prices are reasonable. Look for silver, brass, crystal, mirrors, and jewelry. Brown is the newest color for local pottery; the best place to look is at the marketplace.

Culture. Guanajuato is known as one of Mexico's most culturally oriented states—and every spring, the city lives up to its reputation with an International Cervantes Festival. During the last week in April and the first two weeks in May, the city hosts an impressive (and international) array of performing artists. Many events take place in churches and other historical buildings.

Dolores Hidalgo—the spark of independence

In this little village, on a Sunday morning in mid-September of 1810, Father Miguel Hidalgo y Costilla spoke to his followers from the front steps of his parish church. Burning with the fire of his conviction that the Mexican people should be freed from their Spanish conquerors, he exhorted his congregation to take arms against their oppressors. This incident was the beginning of Mexico's fight for self-rule; today, all Mexicans revere Hidalgo as the "Father of Mexico's Independence."

Several large commemorative monuments have been erected in Dolores Hidalgo, but it is the quiet reverence for the parish church and the historical significance of its well-worn front steps that make an indelible impression on those who visit the town. Hidalgo's house, a block south of the plaza, is now a museum. Also of interest are two ceramic tile factories.

The old church of Atotonilco

Off the highway, between Dolores Hidalgo and San Miguel de Allende, is the village of Atotonilco. While on his way to

Days of the Dead: cause for celebration?

Around Halloween time, the streets and markets of Mexico may surprise you with their great array of confections and simple toys or figures with skull, skeleton, or coffin motifs.

These items are for the Days of the Dead, celebrated November 1 and 2. This Mexican holiday is a curious blending of the Christian All Saints' Day and a pre-Hispanic feast day. The figures reflect the unique Mexican attitude toward death: serious, but also mocking and humorous.

Downtown shops display paper flowers and unusual Halloween-style trappings. Bakeries feature a special bread (pan de muerto). Markets sell children's dolls and masks, toy coffins, and miniature skeletons.

Many Mexican families gather to eat an elaborate meal. Often an altar is set up with burning candles and zempasuchitl (the flower of the dead). Pan de muerto, tamales, turkey mole, pulque, and confections are offered in the belief that the souls of the departed will return to enjoy the meal.

If you visit any of Mexico's cemeteries on this day, you'll see families and friends gathered to chat while cleaning and decorating the graves.

Days of the Dead celebrations are of special interest in Lake Patzcuaro's island village of Janitzio. Residents bring food to the cemeteries and keep an all-night vigil. Hundreds of candles burn on the graves—a spectacular sight.

battle the Spanish royalists, Father Hidalgo stopped at the parish church here with his disheveled independence "army." He took from the church an embroidered tapestry showing the image of Mexico's patron saint, the Virgin of Guadalupe, and made it the banner of his cause.

The plain facade of the sanctuary of Atotonilco belies the fact that it's a treasure house of religious paintings, sculptures, and examples of early Christian-Indian art. Literally hundreds of art works fill the church, including stone carvings, miniature murals, statuary, and manuscripts.

Atotonilco means "place of hot water." The church was built in 1784 over hot springs; mineral baths are available to the public. Pilgrims come here by the thousands to do penance.

Just south of Atotonilco is the well-known Mexican thermal springs resort of Taboada.

Irapuato's strawberry harvest

First of several booming cities in the valley of El Bajio is Irapuato, probably most famous as Mexico's strawberry-growing area. It produces huge quantities of these juicy, red berries, and has several ultramodern quick-freezing and preserve-making plants.

In recent years, Irapuato's former drab downtown business section has been transformed into an attractive mall where no automobiles or other vehicles are allowed. The colonial-style development has been built around the town's ancient cathedral and market plaza. The city now has a nine-story hotel, a modern block-square market building, and innumerable shops—all in keeping with the mall's colonial decor.

If you drive into Irapuato, you might want to continue about 48 km/30 miles west on Highway 110 to Rancho Corralejo, birthplace of Father Hidalgo. The ruins of the old hacienda where the "Father of Mexico's Independence" was born, and the adjoining humble ranch chapel, are 6 km/4 miles north off Highway 110 on a good, slightly narrow, blacktop road. The turnoff is just beyond a branch of the Lerma River, some 9 km/6 miles west of the town of Abasolo—site of another of Mexico's larger thermal spas.

San Miguel de Allende—
a national monument

Strolling the picturesque streets will be your main pastime in San Miguel de Allende, for this is an exceptionally fine example of a Spanish colonial town—so much so that the Mexican government has made it a national monument in order to preserve its charm. All new buildings must be in harmony with the Spanish-style architecture.

Then. Juan de San Miguel, a Franciscan friar, founded the town in 1542. The "Allende" was later added to the name to honor Ignacio Allende, a hero of the struggle for independence.

San Miguel's narrow cobblestone streets climb the slopes in gradual stages. During a walk around town, you'll see fine old colonial houses, many of them with plaques telling what famous figure was born there, or lived there, or what important event took place inside the thick walls.

Of the dozen churches in San Miguel de Allende, the most unusual is the parish church of San Miguel on the central plaza, which reflects a crazy potpourri of architectural styles. Originally this was a rather plain Franciscan building. In the 19th century, it acquired a Gothic appearance—the work of an Indian mason who studied postcard pictures of French Gothic cathedrals, then created his own unique version with ornate towers and a stone facade.

West of the church is the house where Ignacio Allende was born in 1779. The Latin inscription over the doorway reads, "Here was born he who is widely known."

Buildings worth exploring include the 18th century Church of San Francisco, which has a 17th century monastery attached to it, and the other group of religious structures on Insurgentes—a photogenic collection of domes, steeples, niches, and scalloped roofs. Inside, examine the "miracle paintings," votive paintings made by pilgrims grateful for miraculous cures.

Now. The beauty and quiet of San Miguel de Allende have attracted a sizable colony of foreign artists and writers. Instituto Allende, an accredited school of fine arts, attracts students from all over the Americas. The Institute has a beautiful hillside setting on the edge of town. From time to time, exhibits of student arts and crafts are displayed. Academia Hispano Americana offers intensive Spanish and related courses. A branch of the National Institute of Fine Arts (Instituto de Bellas Artes) is housed in a former monastery—a handsome, two-story building with gracefully arched corridors enclosing a tree-shaded patio.

The city contains many fine shops, offering a wide variety of local merchandise as well as goods from all over Mexico. Interesting art studios abound.

You'll find an appealing resort-type hotel, another with colonial charm, nice motels, and other inexpensive accommodations. For further information, see the "Essentials" section (page 153).

Several excellent inns and restaurants are available in town. One of the most unique is the attractive colonial Posada de Ermita, built on the hillside site of the Ermita family's home and owned by relatives of Cantinflas, the famed Mexican comedian.

Queretaro—a haven for historians

To reach Queretaro from San Miguel de Allende, you first ascend a steep hill at the eastern edge of town; then take a blacktop road at the junction with Highway 57 a few miles north of Queretaro. Or you can travel south on Highway 49 from San Miguel de Allende to Celaya on Highway 45 and then continue to Queretaro on this route (a toll road).

Easter in San Miguel

San Miguel de Allende celebrates Easter with pageantry and fervor. Colorful religious observances take place during the entire week preceding Easter, but two of the most spectacular processions occur on Good Friday.

Early that morning the faithful from nearby mountainside villages fill the streets of the old city for church services, awaiting preparations for the "people's procession."

About 10 A.M., men dressed as Roman soldiers appear, marching in front of a wooden cross and led by a piper playing a haunting Indian melody. Following them are boys painted to resemble lepers, girls carrying their dolls, and other children costumed as shepherds, leading their pets. Life-sized images of various saints are collected from churches, dressed in satin and velvet robes for the occasion, and carried through the streets. (You may even see a replica of an apple tree with a serpent coiled around its trunk.)

Because the procession departs from San Juan de Dios Church and stays mainly on the side streets, it attracts little attention from the downtown population, and business proceeds as usual.

It's a different story for the well-organized late afternoon burial procession. All stores are closed, and houses along the parade route are draped with purple ribbons; people line the main streets hours ahead of time to ensure themselves of a good view.

Three young priests bearing candles and a cross lead the pilgrimage. Little girls dressed to resemble angels pass by with eyes downcast and hands folded in prayer. In striking contrast to the white-gowned girls are long lines of solemn, black-clad señoras carrying flickering lanterns. Climaxing the street procession is a special honor guard, bearing a large glass coffin with flowers at its base. By now, it's almost dark, and the onlookers head for home.

Easter Sunday begins with morning Mass; the rest of the day is spent in festive celebration. Bands play in the plaza and the citizens wear their finest and most colorful costumes.

Tourists usually outnumber San Miguel's hotel rooms during this period, so be sure to make reservations well in advance. For more information on accommodations, see the *Essentials* section on page 153.

At the northern edge of Queretaro, Highway 57 passes the Mexican plants of four American firms — Singer, Carnation, Ralston-Purina, and Kellogg.

At Queretaro, the route merges with Highway 45 near the town's impressive, modern bullring, and together the two routes proceed to Mexico City — 221 km/138 miles on a high-speed expressway.

Much of Queretaro's charm lies in its history. The townsite was occupied by the Otomi Indians long before the discovery of the New World. It became a part of the Aztec empire in the 15th century and was overcome by Spanish forces in 1531. (The "conquest" by the Spaniards consisted of a one-day, weaponless confrontation.)

Secret plans for national independence were formulated in this city, and it was here that the Treaty of Guadalupe-Hidalgo was ratified, ceding California, New Mexico, and a portion of Texas to the United States.

Emperor Maximilian and his two faithful generals were executed in 1867 on the "Hill of the Bells" at the western edge of town; the spot is marked by a chapel, a gift of the Austrian government. The constitution under which Mexico is now governed was drafted in Queretaro in 1917.

Today, Queretaro is a fascinating colonial city with intriguing and colorful parks and plazas. At the heart of town is Plaza Obregon, dominated by the Church of San Francisco, with its dome of colored tiles brought from Spain in 1540.

One downtown building of significance is the post office, formerly the government palace. An engraving of this lovely example of colonial architecture appears on the back side of Mexico's old 20-peso bill. Another attractive nearby building, housing La Marquesa Restaurant, was the gift of a Marquis to his bride. The Marquis supervised the construction of the largest of Queretaro's arched aqueducts; 400 years ago, these carried water from the mountains to the city. Several aqueducts still stand — monuments to the engineering brilliance of their builders.

Queretaro is reputed to be Mexico's center for the gem industry, and around the well-manicured main plaza you'll find several reputable shops selling opals mined in the nearby mountains. Not all of the stones sold in Queretaro are mined in the area; Queretaro is also a center for gem cutting. Many of the stones sold locally are from the United States, Brazil, and other countries, but have been cut in Queretaro. You should try to make your purchases only in a well-established shop — the "gems" sold by itinerant peddlers frequently can turn out to be pure "pop bottle."

Celaya — masterpiece of Mexico's Michelangelo

Celaya is probably most famous as the home town of Francisco Eduardo Tresguerras—architect, artist, and poet, often called the "Michelangelo of Mexico." El Carmen

Church of Celaya is considered to be his greatest architectural work. Tresguerras is buried in a little chapel of his own design in Celaya's ancient San Francisco Church, the newer altars of which he also designed.

Celaya is also famous as the source of a favorite sweet, *cajeta*, made of goat's milk boiled down with sugar to a thick, gooey syrup. You'll note many cajeta shops along Lopez Mateos Boulevard, one of the streets cutting through town.

Juventino Rosas—a town for waltzes

The unassuming town of Juventino Rosas lies 24 km/15 miles north and west of Celaya. Formerly called Santa Cruz, the town was renamed in honor of one of Mexico's most famous composers (born here in 1868). Rosas wrote the beautiful waltz "Sobre las Olas" (Over the Waves), which we know in English as "The Loveliest Night of the Year." He received only a few pesos for his composition, and though he wrote many other pieces, none achieved the fame of "The Loveliest Night." He died in poverty at the age of 26 in a Cuban fishing village.

The black gold of Salamanca

If you're in a hurry after leaving Irapuato, you may wish to by-pass Salamanca and Celaya, and take the modern, limited-access Highway 45-D toll road. The entrance is 5 km/3 miles beyond Irapuato. If you continue on Highway 45, the next place of any consequence after Irapuato is Salamanca, best known for the huge Pemex oil refinery located just east of town near the Lerma River. Oil for the refinery comes from Poza Rica in the State of Veracruz. After being processed in Salamanca, oil is distributed to cities throughout the highlands.

The highway runs south through gently rolling hills from Salamanca to Morelia, at the junction of Highway 15. Two features of this pleasant 104-km/65-mile trip are the renovated church and monastery at the lakeside town of Yuriria and, 20 miles farther, the 3-km/2-mile causeway across Lake Cuitzeo. Fishers' dugout canoes dot the glassy, mirrorlike surface of the lake, enhancing its natural beauty.

Morelia—for Old World atmosphere

Morelia lies about halfway between Guadalajara and Mexico City, and makes a good stopover midway in the 16-hour drive. Highway 15 turns into the main street of town.

So many of Morelia's elegant old buildings have been preserved that the city is practically a museum of Spanish and Mexican history. Ordinances require that all new construction conforms to the style of the early architecture.

For strollers. Downtown Morelia is an inexhaustible outlet for the energy of those who love using their feet to explore a new town. The most intriguing old buildings are clustered around two central plazas—Plaza de los Martires and Plaza de la Paz. Many visitors think the Plaza de los Martires is one of Mexico's most beautiful. Lacy detail and ornamental ironwork soften the tall, mosquelike arches of its nostalgic old band pavilion; the delicate foliage of stately jacaranda and other flowering trees casts latticed shade across the broad paseo (walkway). Especially on Sundays, Morelia's plaza is full of activity and the atmosphere of Mexico.

Just a few steps away from the Plaza de los Martires is Morelia's lovely old cathedral. The construction of this graceful, twin-spired building took over a century (from 1640 to 1744).

From the cathedral, it's an easy stroll to the Museo del Estado. This museum is small—you won't get "museum legs"—yet interesting enough to make a visit well worthwhile. Of particular interest is the collection of whimsical pre-Colombian sculpture.

Morelia's central market is at the end of Valladolid Street, about five blocks east of the Plaza de los Martires. On market days (usually Sunday and Thursday), the market overflows the big central pavilion and extends along Valladolid Street for several blocks. Among the many handicraft articles displayed, huaraches and hammocks are the best bargains.

Near the market is the Casa de Morelos. Besides having historical and architectural importance, the old home contains memorabilia of the famous patriot Jose Maria Morelos.

At the eastern edge of the city you'll see an imposing stone aqueduct (its arches are 30 feet high) extending down the middle of Highway 15. Nearby is the beautiful Sanctuary of the Virgin of Guadalupe. On the outskirts of town is a neoclassic church, La Iglesia del Nino de la Salud.

Where to stay. Overnight visitors are attracted by Morelia's languid Old World tempo and charm—features that, combined with sunny days and moderate climate, explain why so many come here for extended vacations.

A charming colonial hostelry facing the plaza, and also several inexpensive hotels, are ideal for short stays. Patrons planning longer visits usually head for one of the informal resort-type complexes on the hill overlooking the town. A public golf course adds much to Morelia's recreational pleasures.

Patzcuaro—near an island-dotted lake

Patzcuaro sits on a hilly landscape about 3 km/2 miles from vast Lake Patzcuaro. The shallow 21-km/13-mile-long lake is dotted with a profusion of inhabited islands; there are also several villages along the shore (communication among them is chiefly by boat). The village dwellers spend most of their time either fishing on the lake or producing a variety of handicrafts at home.

Around town. The 16th century city of Patzcuaro still uses many churches and mansions built in colonial days (1521-1810). Once the political seat of the Tarascan Kingdom and

Butterfly-net fisherman *heads out for early morning whitefish catch on Lake Patzcuaro.*

later an important Spanish settlement, Patzcuaro now blends the best of two heritages. At the basilica on the hill, the Colegiata, you can see the Virgin of Health — a compromise entity used to bridge the gap between the pagan beliefs of the Indians and the dogma of the Church. The Virgin, made of cornstalk pith and orchid mucilage, is revered throughout Mexico and thought to have great healing powers. The Virgin's feast day on December 8 brings visitors from miles around.

Remarkably, life in the city today is much as it was in colonial days. The Tarascan Indians practice a variety of crafts and hold frequent fiestas. *Los Viejitos* — a dance in which men or boys hobble around on canes and wear grotesque masks to make them look like old men — is a traditional dance performed frequently.

Touring. After you've seen the city and visited the Friday market and the excellent museum, you may want to take one of the excursions the region offers—boat trips to some of the islands, or a 15-minute ride to the top of El Estribo for a view of the city and lake. Janitzio Island is a classic for photographers; the butterfly-net fishermen provide ideal early-morning subjects. Boat or automobile trips are available to some of the villages (Chupicuaro, Erongaricuaro)

Woodchoppers *and laden burros plod purposefully along country road near highway to Morelia.*

Final touches *give high sheen to lacquer tray in Uruapan.*

around the shore. Consider taking a 19-km/12-mile trip south of Patzcuaro on paved Highway 120 to Santa Clara del Cobre (Villa Escalante), where several small copper foundries produce graceful urns, pitchers, and pots.

Shopping. Best buys in this region include lacquerware, silver jewelry, pottery with fish designs, ceramic animals, red-checked wool fabrics, woodenware, and copper. An excellent place to find everything at bargain prices is in Tzintzuntzan, a small village about halfway between Patzcuaro and Quiroga; the market is on both sides of the highway.

Specialties. At restaurants, ask for the delicate and delicious pescado blanco, a small, almost transparent whitefish caught in the lake. The fish are a nationally known delicacy of the Patzcuaro region.

For a taste of colonial life, you can stay at a renovated hacienda or a colonial-style motel.

Handpainted lacquerware in Uruapan

Uruapan, 77 km/48 miles from the Highway 15 turnoff at Carapan, exudes an air of drowsy remoteness. The town is set in a verdant, floral landscape—a burgeoning mixture of pine, cedar, oak, and ash, with banana, avocado, mango, and other tropical trees and plants. Uruapan is another of Mexico's extremely lush areas; it has been awarded the title of "the flower garden of Mexico."

Lacquerware — especially trays and masks — is produced in several small shops in Uruapan and the surrounding area. The best work has engraved designs cut through layers of lacquer. Guitars are made in Paracho, on the highway 24 km/15 miles south of the junction town of Carapan. Be on the lookout, too, for beautiful wooden articles, especially those made of cedar.

Uruapan's pride is its unique park, Parque Nacional Licenciado Eduardo Ruiz. Tree-shaped paths lead along a meandering, cool river and up to its headwaters—a series of bubbling springs. Local residents often bathe in Baño Azul, one of the river's pools. Orange groves, coffee plantations, and banana plantations surround the area and provide ideal settings for picnics, picture taking, and siestas.

For another purely relaxing excursion, ride out about 9 km/6 miles to Tzararacu Falls. The waters of the Cupatitizio River gush from many points around a natural stone amphitheater and drop about 90 feet into a pool surrounded by tropical trees, plants, and flowers. Rustic, circular rest houses on a trail to the pool make cool picnic spots.

Also located near Uruapan is the volcano Paricutin. In 1943, the volcano pushed its way 1,700 feet up from the cornfields in the valley floor—since then, it's been quiet. You can drive out to view the weird, blackened landscape; if you're possessed with greater curiosity, you can explore the lava fields on horseback. It's a 38-km/24-mile round trip from Uruapan on a cinder-surfaced road.

An icy swim in Lake Camecuaro

Off the highway, half a mile from the humble village of Camecuaro (14 km/8½ miles beyond the town of Zamora), is Lake Camecuaro, a little-known but refreshing and idyllic spot where you can stop for a picnic lunch, take a restful boat ride, or walk around and stretch your legs. On Highway 15 watch for a small sign pointing out the spur road leading south to the lake. The half-mile road is paved, but the road at the lake itself is rough (you can park at the entrance to the lake park and walk through the grounds).

Lake Camecuaro is narrow and only about half a mile long. Giant cypress trees protrude from the clear azure water; white ducks glide among the gnarled roots, and usually there are a few bronzed boys swimming in the shaded water. If you join them, you'll find that they're a hardy bunch—the water is incredibly cold.

Painter captures *cool vista at Lake Camecuaro Park.*

Golden Angel atop Monument to Independence seems to direct traffic on Paseo de la Reforma.

Mexico City

Country's Capital

(For "Facts at Your Fingertips," see pages 154–155)

A tour of Mexico City, the country's capital, can be telescoped to fit into almost any tight vacation schedule. Or, if your time is unlimited, you can slowly savor and meticulously explore the city. Mexico City lies in a mountain-rimmed valley 7,400 feet above sea level. On a rare clear day, you can see the snow-capped volcanic peaks of 17,591-foot Iztaccihuatl (ees-tak-*see*-watl) and majestic 17,893-foot Popocatepetl (po-po-kah-*teh*-petl) about 56 km/35 miles to the southeast.

With all of its big-city problems — the metropolitan population is over 14 million — Mexico City can hold its own along with any exotic foreign city. It's a place of hustle and bustle; its charm lies in its profusion of color and sound.

Mexico City marks the beginning and end of all major highways in Mexico. Kilometers to anywhere in the country are measured from this city.

Using the capital city as a base, first-time visitors can explore the surrounding countryside on 1 or 2-day trips. Within 80 to 112 km/50 to 70 miles, you can find a complete cross section of the country — pyramids, colonial towns, restored haciendas now operating as resorts, quaint villages with colorful markets, and dramatic scenery.

Getting around

For greater enjoyment of Mexico City's myriad delights, read about it before you go. If you're the independent type, you may prefer to wander through the city armed with a guidebook, a map, an English-Spanish dictionary, and your own self-inspired itinerary. Or, at your hotel or any travel agency, you can engage the services of an official, government-authorized guide (ask to see credentials) who will take you in his own car, or drive yours, wherever you wish to go.

To get advice, assistance, and helpful literature, or to register complaints on prices or services, consult the information office of the Department of Tourism at Avenida Juarez 92, a block off the Reforma. English-speaking police officers, with an embroidered insignia of the flags of Canada, England, and the U.S. on the sleeves of their dark blue uniform, also offer help to tourists. You'll find them along the Reforma, and in the Zona Rosa, Plaza Garibaldi, and other areas frequented by tourists.

Public transportation—buses and the Metro system— is inexpensive, and satisfactory once you learn your way around. Taxis vary in type and rates, and will give you more flexibility than public transport.

The automobile—patience and courage

Mexico City traffic is apt to dampen your enthusiasm for driving. Streets in the older sections of town are narrow, one-way, and congested. On the wider streets cars move fast, and the traffic circles (*glorietas*) at intersections along many main thoroughfares may give you the sensation of being caught in a revolving door. Taxi drivers, darting in and out of traffic with split-second judgment, are particularly skillful at sizing up the intentions of others. Bicycle and motorcycle riders who weave between cars are a constant menace in traffic. As in many European cities, motorists sometimes use only their parking lights when driving at night.

(Continued on page 69)

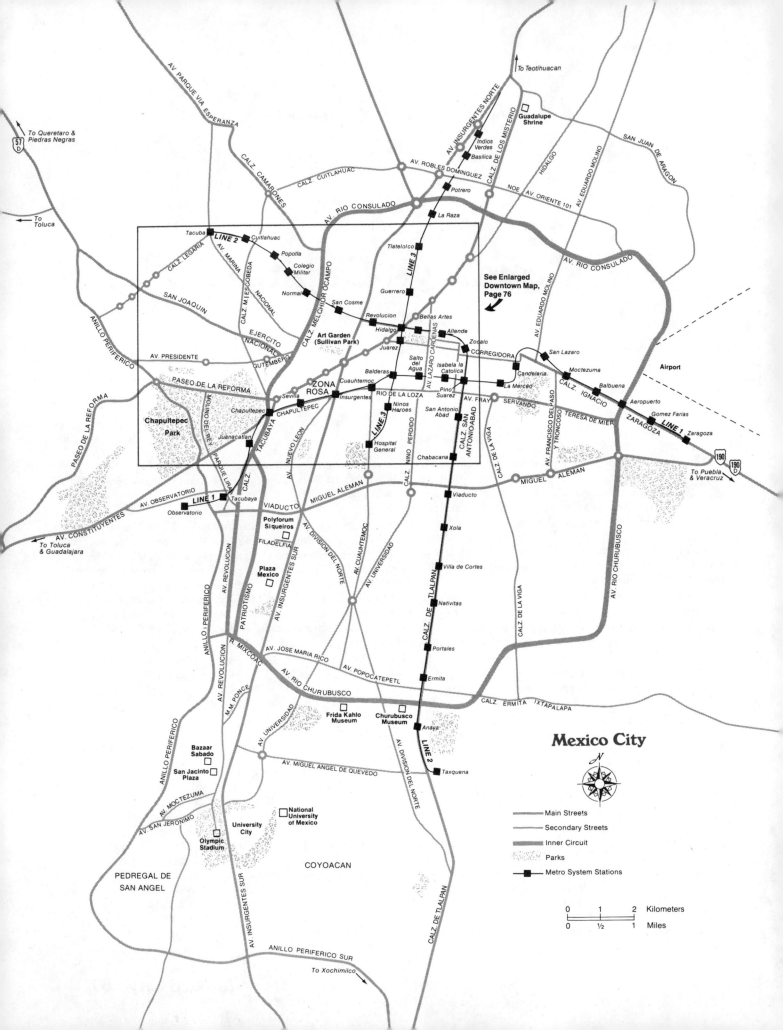

...Continued from page 67

Details at a glance

How to get there

Most visitors fly directly to Mexico's capital city. It's the country's most accessible location, and often a first stop for further exploration.

By air. Mexico City is reached easily by air from most large U.S. cities. Connections to other cities go through the capital. In addition to Aeromexico, Mexicana, and U.S. carriers, several foreign lines offer service.

By car. All main roads lead to Mexico City. Mileage is measured from the city to all other parts of Mexico. Drivers enjoy good highways, scenic variety, and sufficient gasoline (be sure to plan your stops ahead).

By bus and train. Trains offer low-cost transportation over thousands of miles of scenic routes, connecting Mexico City with almost all major attractions—and some offbeat destinations. National Railways of Mexico (the country's largest carriers) and Pacific Railroad depart from border towns. Pullmans and reserved seats are usually available. Rail routes from Mexico City include trains to the Yucatan, the west coast, Oaxaca, and Guadalajara. Rail tours from the U.S. are popular; check with a travel agent for details.

No American bus companies serve Mexico. Border gateway cities for Mexico City service include Tijuana, Mexicali, Ciudad Juarez, and Matamoros. From Mexico City's central bus terminal, local transportation is available to any point in the city. One popular bus route is from Acapulco to Mexico City via Taxco and Cuernavaca.

Accommodations

Hotels come in a wide assortment: budget to deluxe, colonial to resort with pool. Most are centered around three locations: downtown, along the Reforma, and in the Zona Rosa. Make (and confirm) reservations in advance. For additional information, see the "Essentials" section on page 154.

Climate and clothes

Mexico City's weather is springlike the year around. The rainy season—often limited to afternoon showers—extends from May to October.

Dress is sophisticated in this cosmopolitan city. During the day women wear pants suits and dresses, men are attired in suits or in sports jackets and slacks. Leave shorts for resorts. Evenings are dressy and often cool—you'll want to bring a jacket.

Street signs are black-on-white. Streets often change names every few blocks. Watch for the small blue and white *transito* (direction) and green and white *preferencia* (right-of-way) signs on the walls of buildings at corners. Traffic is regulated by lights at most intersections; at others a policeman may be stationed in the center. When he faces you or has his back to you, you must stop; when he turns his side to you, you may proceed.

As you enter the city on a major highway, you may be accosted by individuals who offer to guide you to your destination. Mexican travel authorities strongly recommend that you do not employ these or any other unauthorized guides.

It is important to park your car in a safe place, because Mexican car insurance doesn't cover the loss of component parts. When you park on the street or in a parking lot—even when an attendant is in charge and you lock up the car—don't ever leave clothing, cameras, or other valuables exposed inside the car; lock them in the trunk or, even better, take them with you.

At downtown parking lots (often very crowded), you must leave your keys in the ignition or deliver them to the attendant so the car can be moved if necessary. On the street, try to park near a khaki-uniformed car watcher and tip him a few pesos when you leave. Meters that register up to 4 hours have now been installed on many streets. Don't leave your car parked on the street overnight. You can always arrange to park in your hotel's own parking area or in a nearby public parking garage.

Taxis—tips on all types

You'll probably find taxis the most convenient way to get around in Mexico City. Taxi drivers have been supplied with cards showing the prices for service. Most taxis have meters, and drivers are supposed to use them. If the driver fails to put the flag *(bandera)* down when you enter the cab, politely remind him to do so. The law stipulates that you pay the meter reading if you hail the cab on the street; the fare is higher if you call a taxi from a stand. Tips are not expected. Though plentiful, taxis are sometimes difficult to find. If this is the case, call one from a cab stand listed under *sitios* in the yellow phone directory. The fare will be higher, according to the distance the taxi has come in response to the dispatcher's call. You can also arrange for hourly or daily taxi rates.

Up and down the 5-km/3-mile main route from Chapultepec Park to the Zocalo (down Paseo de la Reforma, Juarez, and Madero, and return via Cinco de Mayo, Juarez, and Reforma), you can take a *pesero* or peso cab (jitney). This is a euphemistic term, for the one-peso fare is a thing of the past; but jitney fares are less expensive because these cabs are shared. When the driver has room for more passengers, he holds his left hand aloft. You simply alight at the stop nearest your destination. There are many pesero routes in the city, but the Chapultepec-Zocalo route is the one of greatest benefit to the tourist because it passes most of the downtown attractions.

The Metro: fast and convenient

Since 1970 Mexico City has had a new transportation system—the Metro or subway. Construction was initiated in 1967, and excavations unearthed parts of the ancient city of Tenochtitlan. For a glimpse of some of the archeological finds, get off at the Pino Suarez station, where a small, round Aztec pyramid was left in place in the terminal lobby. Unlike some dark, dreary underground tubes, the Metro is well lighted and gaily decorated.

At present, 5 lines are open; lines 1, 2, and 3 are most useful to the tourist (see map on page 68). Other lines are in the planning stage. The Metro operates between 6 A.M. and 12:30 A.M. Because of the crowds, it's wise to be on the alert for pickpockets.

Buses—bargain travel to almost anywhere

Buses are still one of the most convenient ways to travel in the city — provided you know your way around. They serve almost every section of the capital, but will take at least twice as long as a taxi. Ask about direct (directo) bus routes at your hotel. Bus stops are indicated by a small, elevated sign with the word parada on it. Odd-numbered buses run north and south; even-numbered lines go east and west. Fares are very low and service is usually available until midnight.

The city's diversions

Mexico City offers an astonishing number of attractions for vacationers. You'd need to stay a week just to sample the city, and an additional week to visit some of the surrounding areas. There's something for everyone—from sightseeing in the Zocalo and shopping in the Zona Rosa, to mariachis in Garibaldi Plaza and museums in Chapultepec Park.

During the day

Because the city is so large, first-time visitors may wish to take a city tour to get oriented. Though basically the same, city tours vary according to the tour operator, length of tour, and type of transportation. Most half-day excursions include the Zocalo, Chapultepec Park, and University City. A separate half-day tour visits University City, Coyoacan, San Angel, and Pedregal. The full-day excursion adds such attractions as the National Pawn Shop, La Merced Market, and craft centers.

Many colorful daytime events take place on weekends: Toluca Indian market on Friday (see page 94); Bazaar Sabado in San Angel on Saturday (see page 90); Ballet Folklorico, Xochimilco excursions, Painters' Market, Thieves' Market, bullfights, and charrerias on Sunday. (For details on Sunday events, see page 83.)

Sundays and holidays are also the times when Chapultepec Park (see page 84) is filled to overflowing with family groups; vendors of balloons, soft drinks, candies, and tacos reap the richest harvest then. But many things go on every day in the park.

Ballet Folklorico. A highlight of Mexico City's nighttime entertainment is the beautifully executed and magnificently costumed performance at the Palace of Fine Arts. Known as Ballet Folklorico de Mexico, it's one of the liveliest and most satisfying combinations of Mexican music, dancing, costumes, and staging that you'll see anywhere. Try to get tickets at least a day ahead of time, preferably from a travel agent; they may sell out early during heavy tourist seasons.

Lottery. Every Monday, Wednesday, and Friday night there is a drawing at the National Lottery Building (at the corner of Juarez and Rosales) to determine the day's lottery winners. You'll have more interest in the proceedings if you've bought a ticket or two from a street vendor. Prizes range from hundreds of pesos to millions. (U.S. customs regulations prohibit bringing lottery tickets into the United States.) Often some entertainment enlivens the lengthy proceedings, in which the most active participants are small, uniformed page boys who call out the winning numbers they draw from revolving cages. The complete list of lottery winners is published the following day.

Movies are very popular and well attended in Mexico. Current films, including some not yet released in the United States, are available. Sound tracks on all foreign films, including American, are in the original language, with Spanish subtitles. You'll find the programs of the best movie houses listed in the entertainment section of *The News*, Mexico City's English-language daily.

Jai-alai. Jai-alai is played every night of the week except Monday and Friday at Fronton Mexico, facing the Monument to the Revolution. Usually, the games begin at 6 P.M. The greatest spectator interest centers on the betting, which is confusing to the novice. On every play the odds change, and "bookies" pace back and forth in front of the stands exchanging money with the bettors by means of a cut-open tennis ball attached to a long pole. Those who prefer a less strenuous betting system can use the windows in the lobby, where bets may be placed on the final outcome of the game or on quinellas.

...and at night

The city is as busy at night as it is during the day. Offices close late, cocktail time begins around 7 P.M., and nobody thinks about dinner until 9 or 10. Night spots attract crowds until early the next morning.

Many of the most elegant nightclubs, shows, and restaurants are concentrated in the Pink Zone. Larger hotels elsewhere in the city have one or more nightclubs or bars offering afternoon and evening entertainment.

Diego Rivera's mural *in the National Palace depicts turbulent history of Mexico.*

Indian ceremonial *dancers perform on the zocalo fronting Mexico City cathedral.*

Love for color *shows in cathedral illumi-nation on special holidays.*

Downtown Mexico City *street vendor sells lunch snacks.*

Rebozos *carry tiny passengers and groceries, leaving shoppers' arms free.*

More about sports

Golf courses and tennis courts are not easy to find in Mexico City. No public facilities are available, but you can play at private country clubs if you are a member of an associated club. Check with your club.

Bullfights are a big spectacle during the winter; in spring, novices develop their skills. For information on bullrings, see page 83.

Horse racing. Hipodromo de las Americas is the capital's beautiful racetrack on the northern outskirts of the city. Races are held on Tuesday, Thursday, Saturday, and Sunday afternoons all year around — except from mid-September to October 12. Tuesday racing is discontinued during the summer.

Futbol. Soccer or *futbol* (a faster, more agile game than U.S. football) is the most popular sport in the world and is played with verve to capacity crowds.

Mexico has soccer comic books, sand-lot soccer, and little league soccer—all indicative of the national preoccupation with the sport. In Mexico City, big-league games are played in the Estadio Azteca (seats 108,000) out on Calzada Tlalpan, on Thursday evenings and Sunday mornings. Occasionally, additional games are scheduled. Tickets may be purchased at the stadium.

Shopping—a Mexican mecca

In Mexico City, you can shop for a wide range of Mexican handicrafts — from exclusive fashion in fine Zona Rosa shops to bright paper products and handloomed sarapes in colorful public markets. In most stores, prices are clearly marked and usually not subject to bargaining. But you can haggle in markets and at sidewalk bazaars and street stands. The usual shopping hours are from 10 A.M. to 6 P.M. (until 8 P.M. on Wednesday and Saturday).

Palacios de Artesanias. At the government-sponsored store on colonial Plaza de Santa Veracruz at Hidalgo (north side of Alameda), two floors and a patio are crammed with handicrafts: jewelry, dolls, dresses, blankets, pottery, and so forth. While you watch, craftspeople ply such trades as glass blowing, painting, and weaving. It's a good place to look at a wide range of crafts.

Artesania Mexicana. This artists' cooperative offers a great collection of crafts; you'll find everything from furniture to gold and silver jewelry. The store has two locations: 117 Londres, and Versalles at Atenas behind the Fiesta Palace Hotel.

Polyforum Siqueiros. Inside the unique Polyforum building (see page 86), you'll find a fine array of reasonably

Colorful costumes, *intricate dances, native music highlight world-renowned Ballet Folklorico performances in beautiful Palace of Fine Arts.*

Blue and white *tile-faced facade distinguishes House of Tiles—once a palace, now a restaurant.*

priced handicrafts. Some of the very best designs and craftsmanship in all of Mexico are displayed here.

Markets. The multitude of public markets — particularly colorful on Sunday — offers plenty of opportunities for bargaining and photography. Among the most notable markets are Abelardo Rodriguez (pottery, flowers), north of the National Palace on Carmen at Calle Venezuela; Centro Artesanal (piñatas, basketry, weaving, leather products, flowers) downtown at Ayuntamiento and Miranda; Insurgentes Mercado, 154 Londres; La Merced (fascinating food market) on Iztapalapa off the Mexico-Pueblo Freeway; Lagunilla Market (clothing, housewares) on Ecuador between Allende and Chile; and Mercado Tepito — the Thieves' Market (see page 83).

San Angel. Site of the big Saturday market (Bazaar Sabado), charming suburban San Angel has a number of shops to browse through on other days of the week. For a particularly pleasant trip, combine shopping with lunch at the San Angel Inn.

Eating well

Like all metropolises, Mexico City has an abundance of excellent restaurants specializing in many different cuisines. But since it's here that you can savor Mexican food as it is prepared on its home ground, sample Mexican cuisine first. Check with your hotel for suggestions about restaurants noted for outstanding native dishes.

Leisurely mealtimes are the rule. The usual lunch hour is from 2 P.M. on; dinner is served starting at 9.

Mexican cuisine. Forget the familiar taco and enchilada and try some new exciting item on the menu instead. Don't overlook the seafood; *pescado blanco de Patzcuaro*, a small whitefish, is superb. *Huachinango a la Veracruzana*, red snapper in a sauce of tomatoes, onions, and olives, is another popular choice. Most restaurants have menus in both Spanish and English.

One of the world's few great, distinctive cuisines, Mexican cooking has been refined over a period of several thousand years. The cuisine was originally a simple one, based on corn, beans, and squash—but by the time of the Conquest, preparation was so complex and ingredients so varied that the Spaniards were amazed.

The discovery of New Spain meant that Europe's table was enriched by such Mexican foods and flavors as corn, tomatoes, avocados, chiles, chocolate, and vanilla; it also gave new direction to Mexican cuisine. The Spaniards brought with them oil and animal fats, and taught the Mexicans a new cooking process—frying. They also introduced cattle, hogs, and sheep (thus also milk, butter, and cheese), as well as sugar and rice. These new ingredients were rapidly incorporated into Mexican fare, and the wonderful result is your gain.

You'll also find Mexico City a delight for continental dining—from Arabian to vegetarian. No matter what the restaurant's specialty, you'll probably find delicious tropical fruits on the menu. Hot sauces are always available upon request.

For your sipping pleasure, try Mexican chocolate or "cafe de olla," spiced with cinnamon and sweetened with molasses. Tequila is the base for most cocktails; Kahlua is the best liqueur. Mexican beer is extremely good, and these Mexican brands of wine are highly recommended: Santo Tomas, Hidalgo, Terrasola, and Domecq.

Price. Meals cost about the same as you would pay at home for equivalent food and service. Ask for *la cuenta* (the check) just before you finish your meal, or you may have to wait for hours. A 10 percent Value Added Tax (IVA) is applied to all meals; expect to tip the waiter an additional 10 to 15 percent. (A cover charge may be added when there's dancing or entertainment at the restaurant.)

Restaurant choices. A restaurant's atmosphere adds to a good meal. Several excellent choices are Hacienda de los Morales (elegant dining in an 18th century manor house), Prendes (operating since 1892 in a building of the old San Francisco monastery), or the expensive Del Lago Mayor (on a lake in Chapultepec Park). Reservations are essential.

Other fine restaurants are scattered around the city; the largest collection is in the Zona Rosa. You'll also find surprisingly good restaurants in the city's leading hotels.

Around the Zocalo

Since 1325, when the Aztecs established their capital of Tenochtitlan on an island in Lake Texcoco, the area of the *Zocalo*, Mexico City's huge downtown plaza, has been the seat of government and religion for the entire country. Upon the Spaniards' arrival in 1519, the island (with an area of only 165 square blocks) was linked to the mainland by broad causeways and an aqueduct that brought fresh water from the western shore of the lake. Tenochtitlan had an estimated 80,000 inhabitants.

The conquerors were amazed at the beauty of the palaces, the luxury of their furnishings, and the impressive grandeur of the great ceremonial center immediately north of today's Zocalo. But during their 80-day siege of the capital in 1521, they systematically razed the Aztec structures and, upon the rubble, built a Spanish town.

Your visit to Mexico City, therefore, might well begin where the post-Conquest history of Mexico began.

Historic Center

On April 11, 1980, 668 square blocks of the downtown area were declared a Historic Center; the city planners' goal is to preserve, maintain, and restore the area's Aztec heritage as well as its colonial period and struggle for independence.

Great Temple. On a 2-square-block area at the northeast corner of the plaza (Calles Argentina and Guatemala), the

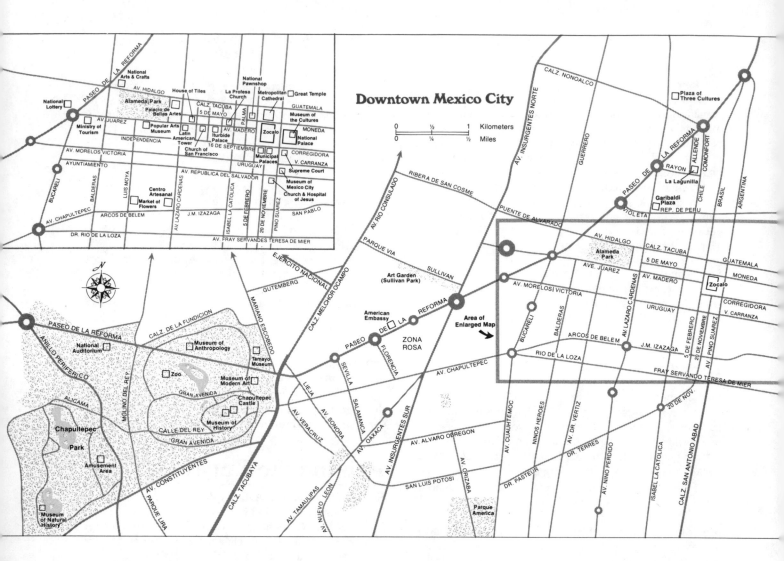

National Institute of Anthropology is slowly uncovering an archeological treasure. In 1978, a chance discovery of a huge monolith dating from the late 1400s led to further excavations that revealed the complete foundations of the Great Temple of the Aztec city of Tenochtitlan. Finds also included a small, still-intact temple and a number of stone chambers containing offerings to the gods. Plans call for restoration of a nearby 19th century building to house the Aztec relics.

The Temple Mayor is now open to the public Tuesday through Thursday with guided tours in English and Spanish. At the Museum of Mexico City (see page 77) an imposing mock-up of the present city and the Aztec city is on display. The museum is closed Monday.

Zocalo. Measuring 790 feet on each side and bordered by four broad streets, the Zocalo itself has had a colorful career. After the Conquest it became the very center of colonial life. Market stalls selling wares of every description filled it until 1789. A gallows stood in front of the National Palace; at one time fountains marked the four corners of the plaza. The Zocalo has been the site of a bullring and a park; until about 35 years ago, it was also the terminal for bus and streetcar lines. Now, because large crowds frequently assemble there, it is a grand expanse of concrete blocks broken only by a flagpole, mobile planters, and a subway entrance.

Coming into the plaza from Avenida Madero, you'll see the Hotel Majestic on the righthand corner. Its roof garden restaurant is a good place to eat or drink while you enjoy the panoramic view of the Zocalo and the historic buildings that face it. For the night of September 15 — the eve of Independence Day — the hotel is booked far in advance by those wanting a box seat for the spectacle staged in the plaza: as many as 300,000 people gather to hear the President repeat the Grito (call to arms) given by Miguel Hidalgo in 1810. Spectacular fireworks and the pealing of the cathedral bells follow the ceremony.

Turning right on the west side of the square, you pass through the *Portales*, a broad arcade in which merchants maintained permanent stalls from 1524 until some time after Mexico won its independence from Spain in 1821. Small shops and cafes now operate there, opening onto the arcade.

The two Municipal Palaces stand on the south side. The Old Palace, built in 1532, was almost destroyed by rioters in 1692. In addition to the city offices and archives, this building also housed the Royal Mint (established in 1536, it was the first in the Americas). The New Palace, between 20 de Noviembre and Pino Suarez, was inaugurated in 1948. Both buildings are now devoted to overall administrative functions.

The Supreme Court building at the southeast corner of the square was completed in 1940. Be sure to go inside for a look at Jose Clemente Orozco's powerful mural, a satirical critique of the judiciary.

The National Palace, a squat, three-story building, occupies the entire east side of the Zocalo, where the Palace of Moctezuma once stood. Cortes erected his official headquarters here; in 1562, the Spanish king purchased the building as a residence for the viceroys. Later on, Emperor Maximilian made improvements, and the building was enlarged when Porfirio Diaz became president. It wasn't until 1927 that the third story was added. The central balcony and the niche above it together form the focal point of the facade. In the niche hangs Mexico's Liberty Bell, rung by the president at 11 P.M. on September 15. Below the balcony, the main entrance gives access to the great stairway where, in 1929, Diego Rivera painted one of his finest murals — "Mexico: Yesterday, Today and Tomorrow." Behind the Palace, at Moneda 13, is the Museum of the Cultures, where you can see exhibits depicting the history of art throughout the world.

The magnificent Metropolitan Cathedral, on the north side of the plaza, has detractors who claim that it suffers from an overabundance of architectural styles—a result of its 200-year construction period. Be that as it may, it continues to be the most important Catholic church in the New World, housing a multitude of religious art treasures. Recently it has been totally renovated, from foundations to bell towers, in keeping with its status.

Cortes began erection of the first cathedral here in 1524, 3 years after the Conquest. Foundations for the present cathedral were laid in 1573, and work continued as funds permitted; the awe-inspiring Altar of the Kings was not completed until 1737.

First-time visitors should take special notice of the cathedral crypts (entrance on the west); the Altar of Forgiveness and the Choir, almost destroyed by fire in 1967, and now restored with painstaking care; the four huge oval paintings by Miguel Cabrera above the two side entrances; and the 85-foot-high Altar of the Kings, a glory in gold leaf, at the end of the central nave. Chapels of great artistic merit line the two lateral naves.

The Monte de Piedad or National Pawnshop stands at the northwest corner of the Zocalo, on the site of the palace where Hernando Cortes and his men were housed upon their arrival in 1519. The present mansion was constructed in the early 18th century and, in 1836, became this hemisphere's oldest credit institution. Anything except perishable goods may be pawned; if not redeemed within a specified time, articles are offered for sale here or at one of the numerous branches throughout the country. The huge complex, though interesting, offers little shopping value for tourists; it's run largely as a discount outlet for new merchandise.

Museum of the City of Mexico. On the northeast corner of Pino Suarez and Republica del Salvador, midway between the Zocalo and the Pino Suarez subway station, stands the magnificent town house of the Counts of Santiago de Calimaya. Its foundations were laid in the 1530s; but the mansion's recorded history begins in 1775, when it was totally restored by the count of that epoch.

The building is impressive because of its elegant simplicity and the excellence of its stone carving. Notice the massive stone serpent's head embedded in an exterior wall of the building; it once adorned the Aztec ceremonial center.

In 1960 the mansion was declared a national monument and, after restoration and adaptation, it became the Museum of the City of Mexico. Ground-floor salons depict the pre-Hispanic history of the Valley of Mexico, from man's appearance there until the defeat and destruction of Tenochtitlan in 1521. Second-floor exhibits transport the visitor through the colonial and independence periods to present-day Mexico City. From the last corridor you can look down upon an ingeniously illuminated scale model of today's metropolis and yesterday's Aztec capital. The mansion is open daily except Monday, from 9 A.M. to 7 P.M.

Church and Hospital of Jesus. Diagonally across the street, on the southwest corner of the intersection, stands the oldest hospital in the Americas; Cortes founded it in 1524, on the spot where Emperor Moctezuma greeted him upon his arrival 5 years earlier. In continuous operation since its founding, the hospital now occupies a square block; newer facilities surround the colonial core, which is still in use.

Under the terms of his will, which provided financial support for the institution, Cortes stipulated that the hospital be directed by his descendants. This stipulation was respected until the 1930s, when the government took over the hospital's administration from an unworthy scion of the family. An inexpensive health care plan for those not covered by social security and unable to pay for private insurance is now in effect.

Cortes' remains lie in the Church of Jesus Nazareno. The conqueror died in Spain in 1547, leaving instructions that his body was to be returned to Mexico 10 years later. After being moved from place to place, the remains were finally interred in the church in 1794; but hatred of the Spaniards reached such a pitch during the War for Independence that they were removed and hidden in another part of the church. Persevering historical investigators rediscovered the remains in 1946, and they are now entombed in the north wall of the sacristy. The church is open to visitors.

Along Avenida Madero

When a number of Franciscan friars arrived from Spain in 1524, Cortes granted them 4 square blocks of land on the western shore of the island capital. Then he ordered a narrow street to be cut through from the Zocalo so that the friars might have easy access to church and government offices. The street was first called San Francisco, and members of the aristocracy built their mansions along its 6-block length.

Eventually, as in all large cities, commerce began to move out to the less congested suburbs, leaving the downtown area to decay. Since 1970, however, all streets leading into the Zocalo from the west have been rejuvenated; the city government has eliminated unsightly signs and cables; sandblasted, painted, and repaired building facades; paved the streets with octagonal red tile and the sidewalks with pink stone blocks; planted trees and shrubbery; and installed colonial-type street lighting.

A stroll down Avenida Madero — renamed to honor the leader of the Revolution of 1910—is a delightful journey into the past.

The Church of La Profesa, corner of Isabel la Catolica, was built by the Jesuits in the 16th century. Here, in 1820, members of the clergy and other Spaniards plotted to defeat Mexico's bid for independence by bringing in a European prince to rule the country. Among the plotters was Agustin de Iturbide, who proclaimed himself emperor in 1822.

The Palace of Iturbide, just 2 blocks east at Madero 17, is an elegant building. Completely restored in 1972, it now houses the offices of a financial institution. Its construction as a private dwelling was begun in 1779 by the Count of San Mateo. When Iturbide entered the city in triumph on September 27, 1821, the building's owner invited him to make the palace his home. After having himself crowned emperor in July, 1822, Iturbide continued to live there, but only for 10 months — until he was forced to abdicate and fled into exile. The following year, when he attempted to reenter Mexico, Iturbide was captured and executed.

The Church and Monastery of San Francisco, nestling behind the Latin American Tower, played a dominant role in the spiritual and social life of the people from 1524 until the 1850s. Today's streets of Madero, Lazaro Cardenas, Venustiano Carranza, and Bolivar form the approximate boundaries of the 4 square blocks Cortes ceded to the Franciscans. The city's first church was built there in 1525; the present church, the third to stand on the site, dates from 1716. Recent excavations permit a complete view of the lovely facade and reveal that the heavy structure has sunk 12 feet into the spongy subsoil.

The House of Tiles, directly across the street at Madero 4, is one of the city's downtown show places. Another palatial residence, the building was erected prior to 1708 as the town house of the Counts of Orizaba. The facing of Puebla tiles it wears was added in 1737. For many years the exclusive Jockey Club occupied the building; then, in 1919, the first Sanborn's restaurant was installed in the spacious patio, where it continues to operate today.

The Numismatic Museum is just west of Sanborn's across narrow Condesa Steet, on the second floor of the Guardiola Building. The 20,000-piece collection includes duck quills filled with gold dust; cacao beans and jade beads used as media of exchange before the Conquest; coins brought in by the Spaniards and those they minted in Mexico during the colonial period; and money coined by insurgents during the War for Independence and, a century later, the Revolution of 1910.

The 44-story Latin American Tower, on the opposite corner of Madero and Lazaro Cardenas. Despite its enormous height and weight, the tower has suffered no damage from sinking or earthquakes since it was erected in 1956. This extraordinary stability is a result of the building's extrasturdy construction: it's built on a concrete slab resting on pilings anchored in solid rock 100 feet below ground. Water injected around the pilings helps to maintain the level of the tower. The 42nd floor is a *mirador* (scenic lookout) commanding a superb view of the entire valley; the Muralto restaurant and cocktail lounge occupy the floor below.

Avenida Juarez

Continuing westward, Madero becomes Avenida Juarez. After you cross Lazaro Cardenas, the first building on the right is the Palacio de Bellas Artes, home of the world-famous Ballet Folklorico, the National Symphony orchestra, and classical and modern ballet companies. It is also the opera house. Information on all events appears in *The News*, Mexico City's English-language daily, and in give-away tourist publications. Some of the best murals ever painted by Orozco, Rivera, Siqueiros, and Tamayo adorn the stairwell and walls; special art exhibits are held in the various salons. Your eyes will be caught by the 22-ton glass mosaic curtain by Tiffany, installed in 1910.

Begun in 1904 and built on land reclaimed from Lake Texcoco, the massive marble structure has sunk 6 feet below street level. The sinking has caused spectators' seats to tilt forward; at performances you may feel that you have to hold on to keep from falling out of your chair.

Alameda Park immediately west of the palace, is 2 blocks wide and 4 blocks long, and the largest green area in downtown Mexico City. Establishment of a park on the one-time lake bed was decreed in 1572. In 1973 the park was completely refurbished — its broad walkways paved with pink stone blocks, its several fountains cleaned and repaired, and its numerous classical bronze and marble statues burnished. Comfortable benches and attractive lighting fixtures were placed along the paths and on the periphery of the park.

(Continued on page 80)

Sweeping staircase *dramatizes Museum of Modern Art entrance.*

Curtain of water *cascades from umbrella roof in central patio of Museum of Anthropology in Chapultepec Park.*

Glistening bunches *of flowers, washed by afternoon shower, sell for only pennies.*

...Continued from page 78

Early in the colonial era, the stake at which victims of the Holy Inquisition were burned was set up on the west side of today's Alameda. Throughout the 19th century the park was enclosed by a wall and reserved for the upper classes, who promenaded there on Sunday in carriages or on horseback. Sunday in the Alameda is also the subject of Diego Rivera's mural (completed in 1947) in the lobby of the Hotel del Prado, across the street at Juarez 70. You'll enjoy the mural's (and the park's) colorful Sunday sprawl.

Midway along the Juarez side of the park stands the imposing Juarez Hemicycle, dedicated in 1910 to Benito Juarez, president of Mexico during the War of Reform and the Empire of Maximilian.

The Museum of Colonial Paintings, facing the west side of the Alameda at Mora 7, is housed in the 16th century Church of San Diego. Hidalgo Street borders the park on the north, and at No. 85 is the Hotel de Cortes, dating from 1780. It was built by the Augustinians as an inn for pilgrims

beside one of the causeways that linked the capital to the mainland.

One block east, two 18th century churches, San Juan de Dios and Santa Veracruz, face each other across a small sunken plaza.

Popular arts are well represented at two locations in the last block of Juarez before its intersection with Paseo de la Reforma. On the ground floor of the building at Juarez 92, sales exhibitions lasting from 4 to 6 weeks are offered. Each is devoted either to one type of craft object from different areas of the Republic—textiles, ceramics, basketry, woodworking, and so on—or to the varied products of a single state.

Across the street at Juarez 89 is the Museum of Popular Arts, a combination salesroom which opened in 1974. This charmingly restored colonial building started life as a convent; today, its two spacious floors are filled with a vast array of popular arts chosen for their authenticity and superb workmanship. The National Handicrafts Fund operates the museum and also arranges the six to eight exhibits staged each year in the museum.

Garibaldi Plaza. If you're addicted to mariachi music, and the louder the better, Garibaldi Plaza is the place to find it: 6 blocks north of Madero, 1 block east of Santa Maria La Redonda (northward extension of Lazaro Cardenas), between Honduras and Peru streets. The plaza and the numerous restaurants and night spots on its perimeter were completely refurbished in 1973. Groups of musicians begin to gather there about 10 P.M.; the later it gets the more music there will be, as mariachi bands that have been performing elsewhere join in the fun. Remember — you pay if they play.

Paseo de la Reforma

Stately Paseo de la Reforma was laid out by Maximilian, who reigned as emperor of Mexico from 1864 to 1867. Having established his royal residence in Chapultepec Castle, Maximilian desired a direct route to the National Palace and traveled it in an ornate carriage drawn by six buff-colored mules. At that time the roadway was known as Carlotta's Promenade.

From its intersection with Juarez westward to the park, the Paseo is punctuated by several impressive monuments. The oldest of them all — El Caballito (Little Horse)—used to stand where the two streets cross. Cast in Mexico in 1802, this magnificent bronze equestrian statue of Charles IV of Spain reigned on the Zocalo until 1979, when it was moved to the Plaza Manuel Tolsa, 2 blocks east of Alameda Park. As the statue's affectionate name implies, it's the horse that has captured the public's imagination—not the rider, who remains anonymous to most.

On the traffic circle in front of the Fiesta Palace Hotel is a splendid monument to Christopher Columbus, placed there in 1877.

Cuauhtemoc, last emperor of the Aztecs, keeps his vigil at the Reforma-Insurgentes intersection from a rather complex pyramidal monument of three bodies, completed in 1887. Surmounting the whole is the heroic figure of 22-year-old Cuauhtemoc in full battle dress, his spear at the ready.

Most beloved by Mexicans of all the Reforma monuments is the Independence shaft on the traffic circle where the Hotel Maria Isabel Sheraton and the United States Embassy stand. Begun in 1902 but torn down in 1906 because of a faulty foundation, the monument was completed in 1909 on pilings driven 70 feet through the spongy subsoil to solid rock. Aside from the weight of the 150-foot column, the foundation supports the 8-ton gilded angel poised on the shaft's tip. After the severe earthquake of 1957 hurled the angel to the marble flooring at the base of the shaft, and during the many months required for repairs, the benches around the traffic circle were occupied continuously by the monument's devoted admirers.

At the next glorieta, a new series of fountains form a graceful canopy of water. For a good look at the Paseo's latest adornment, visit the intersection at night, when the fountains are illuminated.

Once the lovely fountain of Diana the Huntress graced a traffic circle at the entrance to Chapultepec Park, but fountain and circle were forced to give way to the march of progress and construction of the vital inner-city expressway. Now that the section passing the park on the east is finished, Diana again presides over her fountain in a small park nearby, on the north side of Paseo de la Reforma.

To get your best view of the entire Paseo de la Reforma, visit the terrace of the Chapultepec Castle. From this vantage point even the flow of traffic around the glorietas appears to have a sense of direction.

(Continued on page 84)

Massive Tlaloc, *outdoor exhibit at Anthropology Museum, is the Aztec god of rain.*

Watery parking lot *holds boats at Xochimilco's floating gardens. Sunday playground is riot of people, food and flower vendors, mariachi music.*

Fancy ropework *and riding mark charreada. Losing sombrero during show loses points for charro.*

Always on Sunday...something to do

Any visit to Mexico City should be planned to include at least one Sunday, for certain activities of special interest can be indulged in only on that day. The questions are: where does one begin, and how does one fit all these activities into one trip? The only answer is to schedule more weekends into your visit to the capital city.

The three major attractions are the Ballet Folklorico, the bullfights, and the floating gardens of Xochimilco.

Ballet Folklorico performances take place at the Palacio de Bellas Artes on Sundays at 9:30 A.M. and 9 P.M., and at 9 P.M. on Tuesdays. This beautifully executed and wonderfully costumed spectacle, representing all of Mexico's regions in a 2-hour series of folk songs and dances, should be high on anyone's list of "must sees."

Travel agencies run group tours; the price includes transportation to and from your hotel.

Bullfights are, for many, one of the chief reasons for coming to Mexico. In the capital they take place in the world's largest bullring, Plaza Mexico on Insurgentes Sur, which seats 50,000 fans. The formal season begins around December 1 and lasts for 3 or 4 months. That's when prestige matadors fight brave bulls weighing in the neighborhood of 1,000 pounds. During the rest of the year, younger, less experienced *novilleros* fight smaller bulls.

When you buy your tickets—which you should do in advance through a travel agency, but can do at the bullring—specify whether you want to sit on the *sombra* (shady side) or the sunny side. Sombra seats are more expensive. Shun the ticket scalpers! The exciting spectacle begins promptly at 4:30 P.M.

Xochimilco, perhaps the second most popular Sunday destination, is about 24 km/15 miles southeast of the downtown area. Several hundred years before the Conquest, the Xochimilcas established a land base and floating gardens aboard rafts of varying sizes, long since anchored by plant and tree roots. They developed a thriving trade in green goods with the island capital of the Aztecs. When the lake was drained, the constantly enlarged raft-islands and the canals dividing them remained to become a colorful Sunday recreation area.

Nothing floats there now but canoes and gondolas. Until recent years each gondola proudly wore its name emblazoned in fresh flowers across the front of the canopy; unfortunately, plastic flowers are now used.

You can visit Xochimilco at any hour of the day, but it's best to go early. (Mexican family groups go in the afternoon and the traffic is terrible.) Along the banks are a number of restaurants where the pilot of your boat can put in; but we recommend taking a lunch. Authorized hourly rates for boat rides are posted at the docks. Agree on the charges before you set off.

You'll save time and money by visiting Xochimilco on an organized tour; check with the travel desk at your hotel.

Art buffs will enjoy a stroll through the Art Garden in Sullivan Park, one block west of Insurgentes and two short blocks north of Reforma. Between the hours of 11 A.M. and 5 P.M. every Sunday, some 250 artists struggling for recognition display works including paintings in all media, etchings, drawings, and sculpture.

Broad, winding, beige and pink pathways serve as exhibition halls. There are splashing fountains, large bird cages with a variety of colorful and musical birds, landscaped gardens and shade trees, and many benches where you can sit and watch the passers-by. An underground parking garage occupies the section of the park fronting on Insurgentes.

Charreria and the charreada are the progenitors of the Western-style cowboy and the rodeo. Neither cattle nor horses were known in Mexico until after the Conquest in 1521. At that time, those who had won the land for Spain were rewarded with immense haciendas, which they stocked with imported livestock. The tasks of everyday ranch life, as well as all the maneuvers required to herd cattle—rounding up, cutting out, and so on— gave rise to new and complicated skills, gradually refined into what became known as *charreria,* the art and showmanship of the talented man on horseback.

Charreadas are usually held Sunday mornings on Rancho del Charro or Rancho La Tapatia. Check with a travel agent for ticket information and times.

Mercado Tepito, long known as the Thieves' Market, is an open-air mecca for antique hunters, and particularly colorful on Sundays. Located on Calle de Aztecas, between Allende and Brazil streets, the colorful market is a confusion of people and junk. Take a cab or guide with a car. If there's a crowd, beware of pickpockets.

You'll find good buys, but it takes sharp eyes, patience, and knowledge of Mexican artifacts to separate copies from originals.

Pink Zone

The Pink Zone — Zona Rosa — is to Mexico City what the central plaza is to a provincial town. Bounded by Paseo de la Reforma, Insurgentes Sur, Avenida Chapultepec, and Florencia, the Zone covers an area of roughly 24 square blocks. Within its confines are numerous restaurants of all types, nightclubs, hotels, travel agencies, art galleries, and shops and boutiques in infinite variety, selling everything from colorful paper flowers to designer clothes and handsome wearing apparel in kid or suede.

Recent refurbishing of the swank setting included resurfacing walkways and streets with pink stones, painting and remodeling shops, and installing colonial-style street lamps. Niza is the main street of Mexico's "Greenwich Village." Copenhague and Genova streets, now closed to traffic, invite strollers; sidewalk cafes allow open-air dining.

This area is the ideal place to window shop, to run into friends or new acquaintances, to see and be seen. High fashion prevails on these streets; even the trees, trimmed to perfection, have carefully painted trunks.

Chapultepec Park

If you entertain the notion of "doing" Chapultepec Park in a day, forget it! This vast cultural and recreational center covers more than 2,000 acres. It is bounded by Avenida Constituyentes on the south-southwest, extends westward in an irregular form beyond Molino del Rey Street and the peripheral highway, and in some places overflows Paseo de la Reforma on the north. On the east, the park relinquished a portion of its land for construction of the Melchor Ocampo section of the inner-city expressway.

Located within the park's boundaries are five of the country's finest museums, two lakes with boating facilities, a zoo, a Coney Island type amusement park with all the usual rides plus one of the largest roller coasters to be found anywhere, and several miniature railways. There are also restaurants, botanical gardens, a number of handsome fountains and sculptures, bridle paths, and miles of quiet walkways shaded by centuries-old cypress trees (*ahuehuetes*). Los Piños, the president's official residence, is located on the southwest side of the park.

At the park's eastern entrance is the imposing Monument of the Boy Heroes, dedicated to a small group of military students who defended Chapultepec Castle against the American troops in 1847.

For those who shudder at the prospect of traversing so much ground on foot, first-class buses operate out of a terminal at the rear of the Museum of Modern Art. After winding through the old section of the park, the buses emerge onto Constituyentes, enter the new section by its main entrance, work their way north to the Reforma, and then return to the terminal. There are scheduled stops all along the route.

The zoo houses some 2,000 birds and animals of several hundred species. The newest inhabitants are giant pandas — a gift of the People's Republic of China. The zoo is closed on Mondays.

The Museum of Modern Art, a two-building complex set among the sculpture-filled gardens, was built in 1964: it's on your left as you enter the park on Paseo de la Reforma. Permanently displayed in Salon I are the works of Jose Maria Velasco, Mexico's talented prolific landscape painter. In Salon II, artists of a later period (1900–1960) are represented; exhibits include canvasses by Orozco, Rivera, Tamayo, Siqueiros, Dr. Atl, and others. The works of contemporary artists, active since 1950, are on view in Salon III. Special exhibits by artists of all nationalities are mounted from time to time. The museum is open daily except Monday, from 11 A.M. to 7 P.M.; there's an admission fee.

The National Museum of Anthropology, a miracle of architecture and museum planning, is easily identified by the 168-ton figure of Tlaloc, the Aztec rain god, standing at the entrance to a tunnel leading to the parking area. Pedro Ramirez Vasquez was the architect of this splendid structure, perhaps the most modern and functional museum in the world — and certainly the most spectacular.

Off to the right of the spacious lobby is the temporary exhibit hall with its ingenious mechanisms for lighting and display. At the rear of the lobby, opposite the ticket counters, is the Orientation Salon. Here, a 23-minute light-and-sound spectacle presents the chronological sequence of Mexico's ancient cultures in capsule form. The recorded lecture is in Spanish, but the display of pictures, bas-reliefs, figurines, and scale models of pyramids and temples is easily understood without the commentary, and serves as a valuable introduction to the exhibits inside.

As you enter the door into the mammoth patio, remember that the museum's treasures occupy 100,000 square feet of floor space on two floors; a complete view of the interior entails a 5-km/3-mile hike. For your convenience, each salon on the ground floor opens onto the patio, where you can rest on stone benches. A stairway on the lefthand side of the patio leads down to a restaurant. There are several restrooms.

On the ground floor are 11 exhibit halls containing relics from the various Mexican cultures (including the famed 22-ton Aztec Calendar). Upstairs are equally fascinating dioramas of contemporary Indian life.

The patio's outstanding feature is a 5,300-square-yard "umbrella" on a sculptured bronze column. From it falls a refreshing cascade of water that is also a cooling device for the water that flows through the museum's mechanical systems.

The museum is closed Monday; it's open Tuesday through Saturday, from 9 A.M. to 7 P.M. (Friday until 8); and Sunday and holidays, from 10 A.M. to 6 P.M. There's an admission fee, with an additional charge for a guided tour. You may find it rewarding to devote more than a day to your exploration of this museum.

Mexico's mariachi melody for sale

The music of the Mexican mariachis was born in Jalisco during the days of the grand ranchos; songs boasted of horsemanship or wailed about lost loves. Just as jazz originated in New Orleans and later traveled to Chicago, mariachi music was brought from Jalisco to Mexico City at the time of the revolution. From there it spread, becoming recognized as the country's national sound.

In the beginning, the orchestra consisted of *vihuelas* (small five-string guitars) and harps. But other variations of this musical tradition existed and are still heard today: Veracruz style features a harp accompanied by small regional guitars; *huasteca* style is characterized by wild violins and falsetto singing; and Norteño is a combination of button accordion, *bajo sexto* (large 12-string guitar), and, often, a saxophone.

Mariachi sound has undergone some transformation during the past 100 years. The first instrument to be added to the original orchestra was a six-string Spanish guitar. As mariachi groups became more mobile, the cumbersome harp became a liability. Because its principal function had been to provide balance in the lower register—a plucked bass effect—someone designed a giant vihuela. This became the *guitarron* (giant guitar), without which today's mariachi group would be incomplete. Last to be added were the dominant voices of the trumpets. Experts believe the trumpet traveled to Mexico from Europe, arriving in the 1920s.

Though you'll hear other types of Mexican music, this is the ensemble that blares forth in most of the country's cafes and nightclubs. Guadalajara is often called the "home of the mariachis"; some of the finest sounds are heard in the Mariachi Plaza. A visit to Mexico City's Garibaldi Plaza (see page 81) is like visiting a mariachi supermarket. Hundreds of musicians wait to be hired, for one song or for the evening.

A roadway through the park begins directly opposite the Anthropology Museum and leads to the Hill of Chapultepec and the castle that crowns it. There the National Museum of History was installed in 1934.

Chapultepec Castle, begun in 1783, was originally intended to be a weekend resort for the Spanish viceroys. But the War for Independence intervened, and the castle was not completed until 1841, when it was designated as a military academy. It was the last bastion to fall to the invaders during the U.S.-Mexican War of 1847. Then came Maximilian and Carlotta, who made the castle their private residence, adding many of the beautiful features it possesses today. Subsequent presidents of Mexico—with the exception of Benito Juarez — resided there, until Lazar Cardenas decreed that the history museum should be installed in the castle.

The eastern portion of the building displays the rich furniture and furnishings left behind by Emperor Maximilian. Notice Carlotta's exquisite bathtub. In the museum proper, the history of Mexico is depicted in various salons. Aside from their fascinating exhibits, several salons are adorned with murals by O'Gorman, Reyes Meza, Gonzalez Camarena, and Siqueiros.

The castle is open daily except Tuesday from 9 A.M. to 5:30 P.M. (10 to 2 on Sunday); there's a small admission fee.

The new Museum of History lies at the bottom of the hill below the castle. This multi-level structure contains colorful dioramas and recorded lectures about Mexico's colonial life. Through the large windows, you'll see striking views. The museum is open daily, from 10 A.M. to 6 P.M.

The Museum of Natural History, far out Constituyentes just before reaching Dolores Cemetery, is on the roadway on your right. Spectacularly modernistic in architecture, its exhibits are universal, not exclusively Mexican. Note especially the Rotunda of Illustrious Men (and women). The museum is open daily except Monday, from 9 A.M. to 5 P.M.; there's a small admission fee.

The National Auditorium, west on Reforma (lefthand side) shortly before its intersection with the peripheral highway, is the scene of classical ballet peformances, jazz concerts, and other cultural programs presented chiefly by troupes and bands from abroad. International sports events are also staged there. Check *The News* (English-language daily) for details.

(Continued on next page)

Tamayo Museum. The park's newest museum sits to the north of Reforma Boulevard, and is accessible from the street by a mall (which also leads to the Museum of Modern Art), or from the end of Ghandi Street. At the convergence of the two malls west of the Museum of Anthropology, an open-air sculpture court leads to the museum entrance.

Tamayo's personal collection of contemporary art is displayed inside the museum (two groups of exhibit halls connected by a central covered courtyard). The museum is open daily except Monday; there's a small admission fee.

Avenida Insurgentes

Mexico's longest street runs for over 24 km/15 miles, connecting central Mexico City with the University City area (and on to Cuernavaca) to the south, and with the Shrine of Guadalupe and Teotihuacan pyramids to the north. It also provides access to the suburbs of Coyoacan and San Angel, and to the Pedregal residential section.

Heading south, Avenida Insurgentes passes the Polyforum Siqueiros, Hotel Mexico (unfinished except for a resaurant and cocktail lounge at the top), and one of the country's largest shopping malls.

Polyforum Siqueiros

On the western side of Insurgentes Sur, on the grounds of the towering Hotel Mexico, stands the Polyforum Siqueiros, a four-story, 12-sided exposition hall covered with the dramatic acrylic murals of David Alfaro Siqueiros. Each of the 12 panels illustrates one phase of the artist's theme, "Humanity's Progress on Earth and in the Universe."

The underground level offers a select display of traditional and modern handicrafts for sale, including furniture, ceramics, crystal, and textiles. Also on this floor is a theater in the round and a snack bar. A glass elevator and a winding stairway lead to the ground floor and cupola. At ground level, changing exhibits of Mexican and foreign art catch the eye. The cupola is adorned with a continuous relief painting by Siqueiros that can be viewed from a revolving platform accommodating up to 1,000 persons. The Polyforum is open daily, from 10 A.M. to 9 P.M. For a small fee, you can see a light-and-sound show; it's presented in English at 5 P.M., Monday through Friday.

Along Insurgentes stretches an 80-foot wall on which Siqueiros paid tribute to the most important figures in Mexican art: Rivera, Orozco, Posada, Mendez, Murillo (Dr. Atl), and himself.

A visit to the southern suburbs

On the southern outskirts of the metropolis, three suburbs and University City form a section of particular interest to visitors. Two of these areas, Coyoacan and San Angel, are very old; the other two, the campus of the National University and the Pedregal residential section, are ultramodern. all four can be covered in a day by car; drivers or guided tours are available at all major hotels. More time is needed for a leisurely exploration of the many places that will attract your attention.

Coyoacan. Once an Indian kingdom, Coyoacan means "place of the coyotes." After the Spanish conquerors had razed the Aztec capital, they withdrew to Coyoacan until the island city could again be made habitable. Almost overnight Coyoacan became a Spanish town, and many buildings of the 16th and 17th centuries not only remain standing but continue to be used today, a typical trend in older sections of the city.

Plaza Hidalgo and the Centenario Garden together form the main plaza of Coyoacan. Facing this shady, flower-filled area is a house which supposedly belonged to Cortes—a doubtful claim, since the building dates from the 17th century.

On the walls of a chapel in an adjoining patio are modern murals depicting the Conquest.

Across the plaza from the so-called Cortes house stands *La Parroquia* (Parish Church), constructed in the 16th century. To the right of its facade, an arch gives access to the monastery of which it was a part.

Two other Moorish-style 17th century homes bear the names of Pedro de Alvarado and Diego de Oraz, two of Cortes' top lieutenants. But if either Alvarado or Oraz ever lived in the houses originally erected on the sites, it was only briefly; they were both fully occupied elsewhere in consummating the Conquest.

At some distance from the central plaza are two museums well worth a visit. One is the Frida Kahlo Museum on the northeast corner of Allende and Londres, established in the home the artist shared for 25 years with her husband, Diego Rivera, until her death in 1954. Open daily except Monday, from 10 A.M. to 6 P.M., it displays both artists' works, plus some pieces from their collection of ancient art. This is only one of two Rivera museums that you will enjoy visiting (see below).

You should also plan to stop in at the Churubusco Museum, installed in the Churubusco Monastery at the corner of General Anaya and 20 de Agosto. This, the first building raised by the Franciscans in 1524, was rebuilt and enlarged in the 17th century and again in the 19th century. During the U.S.-Mexican War of 1847, the monastery became a fortress, falling to the invaders on August 20, 1847. Now a museum devoted chiefly to relics of that war, it is open Monday through Saturday, 10 A.M. to 8 P.M.; Sunday, 9 to 2 and 3 to 5.

Don't miss a visit to Diego Rivera's Anahuacalli Museum in suburban San Pablo Tepetlapa (Calle del Museo off Calzado Tlalpan). The stunning lava rock structure, built in the style of a Maya pyramid, contains Rivera's collection of over 50,000 archeological treasures, in addition to examples of his work and a replica of his studio. The museum is open Tuesday through Saturday, from 10 A.M. to 1 P.M. and 3 to 6 P.M.; and Sunday from 10 to 2.

(Continued on page 88)

Monumental mosaic *designs like Juan O'Gorman's give unique look to Mexico's National University.*

Energetic climbers *atop Teotihuacan's Pyramid of Sun appear as mere dots. View is across Avenue of the Dead.*

University City. Inaugurated in 1953, the modernistic campus of Mexico's National University extends east and west of the highway over an immense lava flow — the result of the volcano Ixtle's eruption in about 200 B.C. The campus is an outdoor gallery of mural art expressed in every medium by leading Mexican muralists.

Clearly visible even before you enter the campus is the 10-story, wraparound, polychrome stone mosaic mural on the Central Library, for which Juan O'Gorman was both architect and artist. On the west side of the highway, you'll see a daring stone mosaic decoration carved and painted on the stadium; it was designed by Diego Rivera. Facing the stadium is the rectory, adorned on three sides by Siqueiros; the central mural is unique for its three-dimensional massiveness. The roster of other muralists includes Messeguer, Eppens Helguera, and Chavez Morado.

Of special attraction to those interested in Mexican flora are the university's Botanical Gardens, where exotic plants from all regions of the country are on view in two greenhouses and three acres of exterior plantings. The orchid and cacti collection is south of the stadium, over a clearly marked roadway. Cacti are arranged in a natural lava rock setting; the orchids grow in a ground-hugging conservatory. Tropical rain forest plants thrive under simulated natural conditions in a conservatory east and south of the Olympic swimming pool. In all, more than 2,000 species are displayed, each tagged with its botanical name and the area from which it comes.

The National University was founded in 1551 by royal decree in a building on the Zocalo just north of the National Palace. As the number of students increased, each professional school moved to quarters of its own. When the present campus was inaugurated, it drew together students from schools by then scattered all over the city. In 1975 — only 22 years later — enrollment stood at 245,000. Now dispersal is again in process, with the establishment of branch universities in other areas of the capital.

Jardines del Pedregal. West of the university stadium are the *Jardines del Pedregal,* "Gardens of the Lava Flow" — an extension of the same flow upon which the campus is built. To reach this incredible residential area, return north on Insurgentes Sur to San Jeronimo, taking off to the left just beyond Avenida Universidad.

The Pedregal must be seen to be believed. Its modernistic architecture incorporates black lava stone into homes and landscaping with dramatic results. The weird, beautiful trees and flowers that flourish on their rocky beds complete the otherworldly atmosphere.

There are no pre-Hispanic or colonial monuments here; you'll see only the uncommon beauty that sprang from the fertile imagination of a group of architects in the late 1940s.

San Angel. Exploring San Angel on foot through the winding cobblestone streets is a thoroughly enjoyable experience, if you are comfortably shod. The area was "discovered" in the 18th century by viceroys, members of the nobility, and high churchmen. Since it is higher and somewhat cooler than downtown Mexico City, San Angel became a fashionable spot for rest and recreation, especially in the summer. Many of the homes built by aristocrats still stand, mostly behind high walls, of course. Home and garden tours are arranged by the Ladies' Club of San Angel; ask your travel agent, or inquire at the American Book Store, Madero 25.

Your eyes will be drawn first to the enormous pile of El Carmen Church and Convent, built by the Carmelites from 1615 to 1617. Services continue to be held in this church resplendent with gold leaf, Puebla tile, and oil paintings. In the thick-walled convent, the National Institute of Anthropology and History maintains a museum of colonial art, as well as workshops where authentic copies of pre-Hispanic ceramic figures and jewelry are manufactured and offered for sale.

San Jacinto Plaza, a long block west of Revolucion, is surrounded by some of San Angel's oldest buildings. The

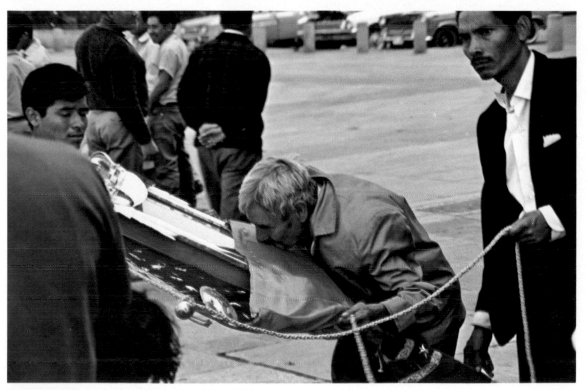

Reverent pilgrim *to Guadalupe shrine bends to kiss portrait of Virgin.*

Shopper can be sure *that turkey she buys at outdoor market near Mexico City is fresh.*

18th century Casa del Risco on the east side, for example, was a private residence until recent years. Now it is a museum displaying all the furnishings of a bygone era — furniture, paintings, chandeliers, and chinaware. Set in one wall of the patio is the huge fountain that gives the house its name — it forms a fantastic *risco,* or cliff, of multicolored tiles and fine porcelain pieces.

On the front of a building on the west side of the plaza is a bronze plaque unveiled in 1959, which reads: "In memory of the Irish soldiers of the heroic St. Patrick's Brigade, martyrs who gave their lives for the Mexican cause during the unjust North American invasion of 1847." The names of 68 officers and enlisted men follow.

Archives of the Library of Congress reveal, though, that these "martyred heroes" were actually deserters from the U.S. army who, in July, 1847, signed agreements to serve in the Mexican army in exchange for land grants. Many of them came from San Patricio, Texas — hence the name "St. Patrick's Brigade." After their capture and

court-martial by U.S. forces, 23 were hanged; 24 were lashed, branded, and dishonorably discharged. The fate of the rest is not known.

Also on the west side of San Jacinto Plaza is the Bazaar Sabado, or Saturday Bazaar. It occupies a 17th century mansion, from which the sleeping Santa Ana barely escaped with his life on the day U.S. troops took San Angel. On Saturdays only, from 10 A.M. to 8 P.M., some 100 craftsmen, Mexican and foreign, display their creations — many of contemporary rather than traditional design — running the gamut from exquisite silverware and jewelry to clothing and textiles to furniture. There's a restaurant on the patio.

If you haven't yet had lunch (or if it's time for dinner) try the charmingly different ambience of the San Angel Inn, Palmas 50. The early 18th century manor house of a 90,000-acre hacienda, it became a restaurant in 1963 and offers international cuisine. Dining is indoors or on the broad terraces that surround a lovely flower-filled patio.

Nearby attractions

You can make these excursions on your own, via bus tour, or with a car and driver-guide. Though none is very far from the city, you should figure at least a half day for short trips, a full day for others. Guided tours to Teotihuacan may include visits to the Plaza of Three Cultures, Guadalupe Basilica, and Acolman.

Plaza of Three Cultures

About 16 blocks beyond the intersection of Juarez and Paseo de la Reforma lies the Plaza of the Three Cultures. You can't miss it; from the time you start the drive north on Reforma, the high-rise buildings of the Tlatelolco housing project will dominate the horizon. Turn left around the traffic circle, and then west onto Calzada Nonoalco, the southern boundary of the project. Turn right at the first corner and the plaza is on your right.

The plaza gets its name from the interesting juxtaposition of buildings from three different periods. Below street level are the excavated remains of pyramids and platforms—a small portion of pre-Columbian Tlatelolco's ceremonial center. Behind the plaza is the attractive 16th century Church of Santigo Tlatelolco; adjoining it is the College of the Holy Cross, completed in 1536 for the sons of Indian nobles. It was in this college that Fray Bernardino de Sahagun, aided by survivors of the Conquest, completed a monumental work by recording in Nahuatl the history and customs of the Aztecs.

Guadalupe Shrine

A short distance inside the northern city limits is the Basilica of Our Lady of Guadalupe, Mexico's patron saint. As you approach the enormous plaza in front of the Basilica, you'll note the new Basilica on the left. The old Basilica, dating from 1709, is to become a religious museum.

It is said that on December 9, 1531, a young Indian convert named Juan Diego was on his way to Mass in Tlatelolco when a vision appeared in his path—the Virgin Mary, dark skinned and clad in the robes of an Indian princess. It was her desire that Juan should go to the Bishop, relate his experience, and express her wish that a chapel be erected there, on Tepeyac Hill, where she might minister to her Indians.

The Bishop was understandably skeptical. On the following day the Virgin again appeared to Juan and repeated her instructions. Still unconvinced, the Bishop requested that Juan bring him proof of the Virgin's identity. Reluctant to embarrass both the Virgin and himself, Juan remained at home on December 11. On the 12th, though, he set out in haste for Tlatelolco to fetch a priest, for his uncle was gravely ill. As he had feared, he again encountered the Virgin and had to tell her of the Bishop's demand for more tangible evidence.

Unperturbed, she sent Juan to gather the roses she said he would find growing on the desolate hillside. Then she assured him that there was no need to worry about his uncle, who had recovered his health, and asked Juan to take the roses immediately to the Bishop. When Juan opened his cloak in the prelate's presence, its inner side contained a portrait of the Virgin. Satisfied at last that a miracle had occurred, the Bishop ordered construction of a chapel on Tepeyac Hill; the sacred painting was placed above its altar.

The Virgin of Guadalupe became Mexico's patron saint. Her portrait, in a heavy gold frame, hangs over the altar of the Basilica. Skeptics continue to assail its authenticity, but experts have confirmed that the "canvas" is genuinely of 16th century Mexican manufacture, and that in 1531 there was no one in Mexico capable of painting such a portrait. The paints have so far defied analysis.

In 1787, the Convent of the Capuchin Sisters was built near the Basilica over springs said to have miraculous healing powers. The faithful come here to fill bottles with its water; outside, small bottles are sold to tourists.

Mexico City's Christmas season begins with midnight Mass in the Basilica on December 11, when thousands of the faithful crowd the church and atrium. After an all-night vigil, they sing *Las Mañanitas* (Happy Birthday) to the Virgin at dawn on the 12th.

Teotihuacan

Teotihuacan, 40 km/25 miles northeast of Mexico City via a toll road that takes off from the Laredo highway on the outskirts of the capital, is an archeological site so majestic that the Aztecs, who came upon it several centuries after its abandonment, named it the "City of the Gods." Its urban area covers 23 square km/9 square miles; at the height of its glory (A.D. 200–600), its inhabitants numbered between 100,000 and 200,000. The magnificent ceremonial center and some of the outlying palaces and priestly dwellings have been restored, and the zone is open every day.

The largest and oldest monument is the Pyramid of the Sun. It was constructed in about 100 B.C. over a long, sinuous, sacred cave—the relics found there prove that the site had been populated for 200 years or more before the pyramid was built. Including the sanctuary that once stood on its summit, the pyramid is 230 feet high, the tallest so far discovered on the North American continent.

The broad Avenue of the Dead, 2 km/1.5 miles long, runs precisely parallel to the Pyramid of the Sun. On the north it terminates at the Plaza and Pyramid of the Moon (considerably smaller than the Pyramid of the Sun, and erected some time after the larger building was completed). To the south it passes in front of the huge enclosure erroneously called the Citadel, and there it ends. In reality, the so-called Citadel was a ceremonial complex; the ancient Mexicans worshipped their gods in the open air.

On the eastern side of the square court stands the Temple of Quetzalcoatl (Plumed Serpent), its facade

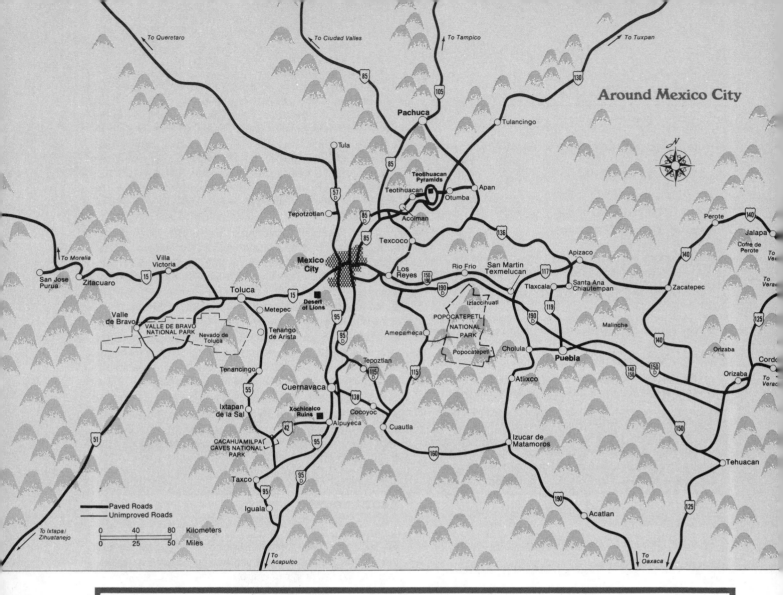

Around Mexico City

Details at a glance

How to get there

Mexico City makes a good base for short forays into the surrounding area. Driving is the best way to reach most of the small villages.

Cars can be hired in the larger towns—Cuernavaca, Taxco, and Puebla. Roads are good to most destinations. Though traffic is terrible in the capital, it's not a problem elsewhere. Government-licensed guides with cars are also available in Mexico City. Ask your hotel for recommendations. To get the most out of your tour, hire a guide who speaks English fluently and knows the areas where you wish to travel.

Tours

If you want to see as much as possible in a short time, package tours are often your best bet. Gray Line Tours (and others) offer a wide variety of excursions.

Accommodations

You'll have your choice of accommodations in most of the towns surrounding Mexico City. Gracious haciendas and charming small hotels with flower-filled gardens await you near Cuernavaca, Taxco, Puebla, and Cholula. Spas provide comfortable lodging at Ixtapan de la Sal, San Jose Purua, and Cuautla. Valle de Bravo offers everything from country clubs to rustic inns. (For more information, see the "Essentials" section on page 155.)

Climate and clothes

"Land of eternal spring" is one name given to the area around Mexico City. Shed your more dressy Mexico City attire; replace it with casual, comfortable clothes to explore surrounding attractions. You'll need flat, rubber-soled shoes for climbing pyramids and Taxco's steep streets.

Cave exploring at Cacahuamilpa

The great caves of the world embody the same characteristics—like mountains and glaciers, they are ageless, yet everchanging. Trickling, seeping water dissolves the rock in such mysterious ways that cave explorers seldom feel sure they've found every passage or palatial chamber.

In their dazzling complexity, the Caves of Cacahuamilpa (Las Grutas de Cacahuamilpa, pronounced ka-ka-wha-*meel*-pa), though not well known outside of Mexico, rank right along with Mammoth Caves in Kentucky and Carlsbad Caverns in New Mexico. The Mexican government has now made them easier than ever to see. As you stroll the 2 km/1¼ miles of concrete walkways, electric lighting illuminates great rooms more than 100 feet high and 200 feet long, and clusters of long stalactites and stalagmites.

Cacahuamilpa is 152 km/95 miles south of Mexico City via Highway 55 from Toluca, or 32 km/20 miles northeast of Taxco on a side road branching off the main highway between that city and Cuernavaca. At 3,360-foot altitude, the caves are close to springs, rivers, and falls. Near the caves are a swimming pool, a parking area, and restaurants.

An Englishman discovered the caves of Cacahuamilpa about 130 years ago, long after the Indians who originally inhabited them had left. Lured on by curiosity, he ventured deep into the caves and never returned; a cross inside is his memorial.

Official national park guides lead scheduled tours daily (10 A.M.–3 P.M. Monday through Saturday, 10 A.M.–4 P.M. Sunday). For larger groups of visitors, special tours at other times can be arranged for a slightly higher admission charge. Tours take about 1½ hours.

Outside the entrance, local people sell canes with forked tops and attractive containers shaped like water birds, all carved from native woods.

---

covered with superbly carved stone heads of feathered serpents and of the rain god Tlaloc.

Facing on the Plaza of the Moon and along both sides of the Avenue of the Dead are numerous small, flat-topped pyramids and temples. At the southwest corner of the plaza stands the Palace of Quetzalpapalotl. Completely reconstructed, it exemplifies the sumptuousness of that era's palaces. On the walls of some chambers are traces of the mural paintings that once covered all pre-Hispanic buildings.

In its heyday, Teotihuacan drew religious pilgrims from as far away as Yucatan and Central America. During that same period, it was also the most important trading center in the Mexican highlands.

Several good restaurants operate in the archeological zone, including one installed more than 50 years ago in a mammoth grotto. There is a small, good museum.

From October to May, every night except Monday, a light-and-sound spectacle in English is presented at 7 P.M. The script incorporates the legends that sprang up with respect to Teotihuacan, place of mystery. Warm clothing and a lap robe are essential. Tickets are available from travel agencies.

Acolman

Just off the toll road, about 9 km/6 miles south of Teotihuacan, is the handsome, fortress-type Church and Monastery of Acolman, established by the Augustinians in 1539. Probably its most interesting feature is its severely simple, beautifully executed plateresque facade — the purest example of that style in Mexico. In the interior of the temple, under many layers of paint, colossal 16th century frescoes in three colors — red, black, and yellow — were discovered during renovation. They resemble those found in more ancient Italian churches. A collection of religious art is exhibited in the monastery.

The route to Texcoco heads across a vast lake bed directly east of Mexico City. The salty soil of the old lake bed, dry during the winter months, is being reconditioned to permit farming and reforestation. Plans call for part of the 169-square-km/66-square-mile area to become a recreational center. All this will not only put an end to the dust storms that plague the capital in the dry months, but will avert the threat of flooding in the rainy season.

It was in Texcoco (then on the eastern shore of the lake) that Cortes, after being ignominiously routed from the Aztec capital in 1520, assembled 13 brigantines for another assault. Timbers were cut in Tlaxcala and carried across the mountains to Texcoco by 8,000 Indian bearers; by April, 1521, the warships were ready for launching. Four months later, the Conquest had been accomplished.

Texcoco now has 70,000 inhabitants. Sunday and Monday are market days, and the market is famous for *barbacoa* (pit-barbecued lamb), ceramics and textiles of distinctive styles and designs, and blown glass.

Chiconcuac is less than 10 minutes north of Texcoco over a narrow dirt road. Before the Conquest, Chiconcuac was also on the lake shore — a tiny village that even then specialized in weaving, delivering its goods to market by canoe. Today it is a town of 11,000, and the volume and variety of its textile products in wool and acrylic fibers are unsurpassed anywhere.

In more than 50 shops along the main street, you'll find blankets, wall hangings, and sarapes; handmade hooked or shag rugs; sweaters in any style or color for men, women, and children; and *jorongos*—sarapes with a slit in the center to put your head through—as well as shawls, overblouses, stoles and *rebozos* (long scarves). For anything knitted or woven, Chiconcuac is the place.

Tepotzotlan

Amid the wealth of religious art and architecture that is Mexico's heritage, the Church of San Francisco Javier in Tepotzotlan is outstanding, a masterpiece of ultrabaroque magnificence. Drive 40 km/25 miles north on the highway to Queretaro; the church tower is visible on your left. The National Museum of Colonial Arts and Handicrafts was installed in the monastery after renovation and restoration in 1959. Church and museum are open from 10 A.M. to 6 P.M.; the museum is closed Monday.

Every year, in a patio to the left of the church, the *pastorela* is presented nightly from December 16 to December 23. It's an ingenuous version of events surrounding the birth of Christ, conceived by Spanish nuns during the Middle Ages. Tickets can be secured from travel agencies, and the cost includes dinner, piñatas, village bands, and a *posada* or reenactment of the Holy Family's search for shelter. Dress warmly!

En route to Tepotzotlan you'll pass several bustling industrial suburbs, one of which houses the Mexican plants of such well-known American firms as Ford, Goodyear, and Monsanto. (When the factories in this area end their day shifts, this highway is crowded with workers returning to the city.)

Tula—former Toltec capital

About 42 km/26 miles north of Tepotzotlan are the remains of the Toltec capital of Tula (built around 935). Distinguished by 15-foot stone idols atop the Temple of the Morning Star, the ruins are extremely photogenic. Though most of the area's best sculptures have been moved to Mexico City's Museum of Anthropology, a small museum in Tula contains finds from the site.

West to Toluca to market

Friday is market day in Toluca. The drive from the capital is well worthwhile, even if you only absorb the local color; the countryside is beautiful, and you can enjoy the surrounding baths, spas, and resorts by venturing only a little farther.

One way to get to Toluca is to go through the Desert of Lions (neither a desert nor filled with lions), a national monument and park, via Highway 15. Discover ruins, secret passages, and cool pine forests in which to picnic.

Toluca—brisk city by a huge volcano

Nestled in the center of the green Valley of Toluca is the bustling commercial city of Toluca, an hour's drive from Mexico City. The invigorating, brisk weather typical of this flat valley is an inevitable result of its high altitude (almost 9,000 feet). Nevado de Toluca, an extinct, sometimes snow-shrouded volcano, towers over the city. Within its walls, the crater of the 15,000-foot volcano holds two lakes filled with rainbow trout—for the warm-blooded angler. Views are spectacular on the road into Nevado de Toluca's crater.

Most visitors spend hours at the market in Toluca. The old market downtown is no longer; the new modern market, opened in 1973 south of the city just off the peripheral highway, operates every day. Friday is the day when merchandise floods the adjoining plaza. The popular arts section is installed in one of the permanent buildings.

Also worth a visit are the Museum of Popular Arts on Highway 15 at the eastern entrance to Toluca, and the Museum of Charreria (horsemanship) downtown. Archeological pieces from the Toluca area and the entire state of Mexico now reside at the Museum of Teotenango, 18 km/11 miles south of Toluca on Highway 55.

Just west of the city stands the Church of Our Lady of Tecajic, a popular Indian shrine with a much venerated image. Uetepec, a few kilometers south of Toluca, is a charming old town with buildings the color of its fine pottery. Plan to visit the Monday market.

Linger in a spa in Ixtapan de la Sal

This popular spa and resort, noted for its luxurious mineral baths, lies south of Toluca on Highway 55. The busiest season is winter, when tourists from colder climes flock here for relaxing sessions at the thermal baths.

There are two towns—the old town, purely Mexican, rustic, and bright with tropical vegetation; and Nuevo Ixtapan, beautifully landscaped, with a huge luxury hotel as well as more modest establishments. A public bathhouse, five outdoor pools, and individual "Roman" baths adjacent to the big hotel serve all visitors, for a fee. A little train tours the grounds.

San Jose Purua—baths and bubbly streams

West of Toluca on the road to Morelia is the turnoff to San Jose Purua, one of Mexico's most celebrated spas. (Don't attempt to take a trailer down the steep road.) Here you'll find Balneario San Jose Purua perched on the edge of a canyon in a lush, tropical setting of flowering trees, bubbling streams, waterfalls, and quiet ponds. The hotel has several thermal spring swimming pools, and some of the rooms have private mineral baths. Reservations are an absolute must. The area is mountainous, interspersed with arid plains.

Sarapes from Saltillo *brighten market stall. Mexico City area is good place to buy goods from all over country.*

Valle de Bravo—weekend resort

Roughly 128 km/80 miles southwest of Toluca or 2½ hours from Mexico City, Valle de Bravo is reached on a mountainous, paved road. The town slopes down to the shores of an artificial lake constructed as a huge hydroelectric project to benefit the surrounding region.

The area of Valle de Bravo, including the lake, has become an increasingly popular resort. On weekends, Valle de Bravo comes alive. Hordes of visitors from Mexico City come for picnics near the two waterfalls (the Molino River and Velo de Novia), walks into the shady, verdant woods, fishing for the abundant trout, water-skiing, and yacht racing. There is an outstanding golf course and the accommodations are good.

French, Americans, and Canadians, as well as the wealthier Mexicans, escape into the modern-colonial vacation and retirement homes neatly arranged around the lake. Both local inhabitants and weekend visitors revel in the resort's romantic, restful attitude. Valle de Bravo is an arts and crafts center noted for its pottery.

Country clubs and rustic inns provide lodging and entertainment in this resort of orchids and butterflies. Strict government building codes have been established to maintain the still unexploited atmosphere of the area.

The return from Valle de Bravo to Highway 15 can be made by an alternate paved route — unfortunately, it's somewhat deteriorated. No airport has yet been constructed and the helicopter pad is strictly for the use of government officials.

The Golden Triangle

Mexico City-Cuernavaca-Taxco is one of the most popular package tours sold in the U.S. From Taxco you can continue on to Acapulco (see page 43) on the fast superhighway and return to the capital by air. The toll road between Mexico City and Acapulco bypasses Taxco, but you can turn off to reach this intriguing colonial town. Or you can reach Taxco by taking the older, more winding Highway 95 all the way from Mexico City. Maintained as a toll-free road, it is about 32 km/20 miles longer than the toll road and much slower. The two routes join near Iguala.

Taxco is a popular overnight stop. Since most tourists going to Acapulco include this stopover on their itinerary, you'd be wise to have confirmed reservations. (See the "Essentials" section on page 155 for hotel information.) Cuernavaca also has excellent accommodations and is likely to be less crowded.

(Continued on page 98)

Poinsettias add color *to courtyard of Cuernavaca cathedral. Often called Mexico's garden spot, city is popular with visitors for its springlike weather, luxuriant walled gardens, fine hotels and restaurants.*

Taxco's tangled buildings *cling to mountainside halfway between Mexico City and Acapulco. Former silver mining center is now national colonial monument.*

Milkman *makes deliveries on mule. Sure-footed animal must climb steps and plod up and down steep, slippery cobbled streets.*

Hilltop Cholula church *was constructed over old Indian pyramid. Restoration is still underway.*

Tiled dome *of Sanctuary of Los Remedios sparkles in sunlight. Cholula is a city of churches.*

Cuernavaca—a top garden spot

Capital of the state of Morelos, Cuernavaca impresses visitors more with its lush, gardenlike personality than with its bustling, metropolitan character. Travelers who don't have much time to spend in the various regions of Mexico will appreciate the colorful town of Cuernavaca — it's a mixture of all the best Mexico has to offer. But you'll have to look behind the walls to discover its charm; on the surface, it appears to be a community in need of cleaning and repair.

Balmy Cuernavaca provides a large number of Americans and residents of Mexico City with a popular weekend and holiday retreat. Shimmering pink blossoms, rainbows of flowering vines, an intoxicating mélange of scents drifting over the walls of hidden gardens, and trees bedecked with splashes of reds, oranges, blues, and yellows — all create the experience that awaits the visitor to Cuernavaca.

The Borda Gardens on Avenida Morelos were once the epitome of the town's elegance and tropical atmosphere. Here, you'll find a grand old mansion, a mirror pool, fountains, and the exotic but somewhat neglected gardens. The mansion, which was the summer home of Maximilian and Carlotta from 1864 to 1867, now houses an arts and crafts shop, an art gallery, and a small museum. The simple Church of Guadalupe, once the Borda family chapel, adjoins the gardens; the cathedral is across the street. A stunning Festival of Flowers takes place in the gardens in April.

The Cathedral of Cuernavaca has a beautifully restored, modern interior; the exterior reflects the bold architectural style of the palace. During colonial years, missionaries used the cathedral (then a monastery) as a departure point for their missionary work in Asia. For a special treat, attend the Mass on Sunday and absorb the unique, spine-tingling experience of hearing inspirational music played by a mariachi band.

Museo Cuahnahuac, in the Cortes Palace, houses the exposed Tlahuican pyramid and Diego Rivera's famous mural, "Conquest of Mexico." In the palace museum, visitors can review the history of the states of Guerrero and Morelos. Artisans display their wares in the adjoining plazas.

Shopping is not at its best in Cuernavaca; however, the shop in the Cathedral courtyard does stock some fine handcrafted metal items. You'll also discover other downtown stores with pottery, shoes and huaraches, silver, and handblocked and handloomed fabrics.

Dining, possibly the best reason for visiting Cuernavaca, is one experience you won't want to miss. Las Mañanitas is *numero uno* in Mexico, and four or five other restaurants are also outstanding.

Little hotels, hidden behind the walls, are all excellent bases from which to visit the nearby attractions — the Caves of Cacahuamilpa (page 93), Lake Tequesquitengo, and the ruins at Xochicalco.

Around Cuernavaca

You'll discover some of Mexico's most interesting sightseeing around Cuernavaca. Restored haciendas, old Indian villages, and pre-Columbian remains can be investigated on drives of less than an hour.

Tequesquitengo and Vista Hermosa. Tequesquitengo lies about 40 km/25 miles south of Cuernavaca (right turn at Alpuyeca), on the eastern edge of a crater lake popular with Mexican youth for a variety of water sports. During a visit to the nearby visually delightful Vista Hermosa, once part of Cortes' vast estates, you can lunch in an attractive dining area and swim in a truly unique pool.

Xochicalco. Located south of Cuernavaca, the Xochicalco ruins resemble the Toltec capital of Tula. Once an important stop on 9th and 10th century trading routes, these ruins command a spectacular view of the valley of Morelos. You'll need a flashlight if you wish to enter the cave leading to the observatory.

Tepoztlan. Snuggled against some spectacular cliffs just north of the junctions of Highways 115D and 138 is Tepoztlan: an Indian village just beginning to be discovered by travelers. Nahuatl is still as widely spoken here as Spanish. The town's fortresslike structure is a Dominican convent, built between 1559 and 1588. On the steep, rocky hill above, a pre-Columbian pyramid rises—it was erected in honor of the god of *pulque* (a drink made from maguey cactus). Tourists should plan to visit Tepoztlan during the markets on Wednesday and Sunday.

Cocoyoc. One of the country's top vacation spots lies only 19 km/12 miles from Tepoztlan. Once part of a sugar plantation, restored Hacienda Cocoyoc looks like a green oasis in the surrounding brown countryside. Though little known outside of Mexico, the resort is crowded during the weekends with visitors from Mexico City; plan your visit during the week to take advantage of uncrowded golf courses, tennis courts, and swimming pools, and to enjoy horseback riding, restaurants, and nightclubs. The hacienda and chapel sit on lush grounds that were once part of Cortes' botanical gardens.

Cuautla. At Cuautla, 45 minutes east of Cuernavaca, you'll discover a relaxed hot springs resort that's been popular with vacationers for many years. It's a good place to have lunch during a drive around the area.

Taxco—tied to its silver heritage

With twisting streets and red-tiled roofs, Taxco hangs on a steep mountainside as if someone had planned it as a movie set of an Old World village. It is one of Mexico's most colorful towns, and a favorite subject for artists and photographers. The Mexican government has designated Taxco as a national colonial monument.

Taxco is immersed in its silver heritage. Representing the center of Mexico's silversmith trade, the city has been molded by silver mines, silver barons, and the silver industry of modern times. Silver was first discovered in the area by Cortes in 1522, paving the way for the arrival of a French miner, Jose de la Borda, who created his own silver empire in the 18th century. A few crumbling, ghostly mines testify to his good fortune and subsequent wealth. The silver industry evolved to its present status over 50 years ago after being revitalized by an American, the late William Spratling. Today, you'll find silver showrooms and workshops all over town—though little silver is actually mined around Taxco any more.

Taxco's streets, hills, buildings, and shops are best explored on foot. (One suggestion—wear tennis shoes to avoid slipping.) Taxco is another of those towns whose streets are mostly one way and change names frequently. Cobblestone streets and narrow passageways lend a feeling of authenticity to the colonial atmosphere established by the town's architecture.

Sights. In Taxco, as in most Mexican towns, the zocalo is the center of activity. Shaded by tall trees and graced with a bandstand and benches, it's a good place to sit, listen to music, and watch life swirl around you.

Lovely Santa Prisca church's graceful twin towers and tiled dome are a photographer's delight. The church is considered an outstanding museum of ecclesiastical art. Behind the church, the William Spratling Museum contains an impressive collection of pre-Columbian antiquities and silver items. The Casa Borda, once the Borda residence, also houses a fine silver collection. From the rooftop garden of Felipe Zamora's four-story shop, you'll get a breathtaking view of the church.

Shopping. Silver shopping is fun; but be sure to shop carefully, since a great quantity of cheaply produced merchandise is mixed in with some fine handcrafted pieces. Taxco is also the location of the Tissot ceramics factory.

Shops center around the plaza, the old shopping streets radiating from it, and north around Posada de la Mision. Most shops close Sunday, or open only until 1 or 2 P.M.; but if shops are closed, you can browse at the flower and Indian markets.

Hotels. Taxco's hotels, for the most part, cling to the hills around town, providing spectacular views of the nightly fireworks in the square below. The local tourist office (at the town's entrance on Highway 95) provides general information and a map of the town.

The Olmec, Mexico's mother culture

Thirty years ago considerable mystery surrounded the Olmecs. Today, though, archeologists agree that these people were the initiators of all that became known as "high culture" in pre-Columbian Mexico, and that their homeland was on the Gulf Coast, in the jungles of the present states of Veracruz and Tabasco.

Their name comes from the Indian word *ulli*, or rubber, and means "inhabitants of the country of rubber." Their civilization had its beginnings around 2000 B.C.

Stone was scarce in the Olmecs' jungle home, and that prevented them from developing a lasting architecture. Structures found at La Venta, San Lorenzo, and Tres Zapotes are earthen— temple bases arranged around plazas, forming ceremonial centers. The stone they were able to bring into the area was used for carving colossal figures, notably the so-called "baby-face" heads.

Though their architecture wasn't sophisticated, the Olmecs possessed impressive intellectual and artistic skills. They developed a numbering system, hieroglyphic writing, and a calendar— the Maya calendar, the most exact ever devised, was based on the original Olmec invention. The Olmecs were also masters at carving stone and jade. Particularly notable in their culture was the deification of the jaguar; feline motifs in pottery, figurines, and masks all signal Olmec influence.

As an ethnic entity, the Olmecs had disappeared by about the beginning of the Christian era. Groups of them wandered and merged with other peoples, spreading Olmec achievements throughout Mexican territory—into Oaxaca, the central highlands, as far north and west as Colima and Guerrero on the Pacific coast—and even to Guatemala and El Salvador.

La Venta, Tabasco, close to the mouth of the Tonala River, is one of the few Olmec sites that can be visited easily. Earth mounds can still be seen, as well as a few stone monuments, but most of the sculptures unearthed have been removed for display at La Venta Park, in Villahermosa, Tabasco.

East of Mexico City

Every long-distance traveler who gets caught in a frantic sightseeing schedule develops a desperate thirst for a refreshing change of pace, and that's what you'll get on the trip from Mexico City to Veracruz. This adventure can be approached as a loop drive — down by way of Puebla, Orizaba, and Cordoba, and back by way of Jalapa, Perote, Apizaco, and Texcoco. The loop starts from a region overflowing with churches, pyramids, and other monuments so typical of central Mexico. Slowly, the emphasis of the trip shifts to a seductive, tropical atmosphere that lulls even the most hardened traveler into a relaxed mood — even one who, anywhere else, would want to see "everything" in as little time as possible. The drive will submerge you in a rich variety of landscapes and climates — green valleys and desert on the plateau, pine forests, subtropics, and tropics. Though you can visit Puebla and Cholula in 1 day or drive the loop in 2 days, you should really take more time. Though the roads are off the heavily traveled tourist track, they're nevertheless paved all the way. One very rewarding feature of this loop drive is the opportunity to see five of Mexico's most famous mountains — Popocatepetl, Iztaccihuatl, Malinche, Pico de Orizaba, and Cofre de Perote.

November through February is the dry season, though you might get caught by a *norte* (overcast sky and a cold wind blowing sand from the dunes around Veracruz); the rest of the year, it's hot in the morning with showers in the afternoon, but the land is at its greenest. The toll road that connects Mexico City with Cordoba is a high-speed but highly scenic highway. If visibility is good, you'll see 17,893-foot Popocatepetl and 17,591-foot Iztaccihuatl — both majestic and snowcapped all year. Once over the crest (which, incidentally, is the Continental Divide), you slowly descend into a green, fertile valley.

Tlaxcala—Cortes and his Indians

Capital of Mexico's smallest state, Tlaxcala is set in the hills of an area steeped in history. A crossroads of Indian trade routes and cultures, this region reveals the influence of highly cultured groups from the beginning of the Christian era. Most famous of these were the Tlaxcaltecas, for whom city and state were named. Allies of Hernando Cortes in confronting their common enemy, the Aztecs, the Tlaxcaltecas gave him their constant support—particularly during the battle of Lake Texcoco in 1521, when the final Spanish victory over the Aztec empire was achieved.

Weaving is an important craft in this region; vibrantly colored sarapes and woolen fabrics are produced here. The area around Tlaxcala and nearby Santa Ana Chiautempan is one of Mexico's most prolific wool centers. Top quality tweeds, handwoven sarapes, and rugs are sold in San Martin Texmelucan, Huejotzingo, and also at a government market along the toll road at Rio Frio.

Cholula—Christian churches in an Indian city

Cholula, just off Highway 190 about 29 km/18 miles beyond San Martin Texmelucan, is a town of churches. Here, as elsewhere, the Spaniards built churches over structures sacred to the Indians. You can visit some 39 chapels in close proximity, and many more are not far away. Most notable is the Sanctuary of Los Remedios (a climb of some 200 steps); it was built atop Cholula's main pyramid, a mile in circumference at its base. In fact, this building wasn't a true pyramid, but a citadel composed of numerous structures; it was fashioned over a period of several centuries, beginning about A.D. 100. Tunnels allow you to explore some sections.

The ancient city has been under study and restoration for many years. A museum at the excavation site houses a collection of fabulous Cholulteca pottery, a polychrome lacquer-type ware decorated with intricate designs.

Cholula is also the location of an impressive new campus of the University of the Americas, moved here from its outgrown facility on the western edge of Mexico City.

In nearby Huamantla a running of the bulls (said to predate Pamplona) takes place in August on the Sunday following the Feast Day of the Assumption. You watch the 4-hour event from city rooftops.

Puebla—Talavera tile from a Spanish town

Puebla is one Mexican city that has retained much of its Spanish heritage. Its modern architecture contrasts sharply with the many colonial buildings, some of which are among the oldest on the North American continent.

The city's plazas, especially the main plaza, are ideal vantage points from which to absorb the beauty of the polychromatic tilework used on a number of the town's buildings.

Sights. A profusion of ornate and intricately decorated churches are located in Puebla. Two that you shouldn't miss are the cathedral, with its carved marble doorways, 14 chapels, and two large bell towers; and the elaborately gilded Chapel of the Rosary in the Church of Santo Domingo, at 5 de Mayo and Avenida 4 Pomente.

Visit the Puebla Regional Museum in the ornate 17th century Casa de Alfenique at Avenida 4 Oriente and Calle 6 Norte. Open all day during the week, the museum closes on Saturday and Sunday afternoons. The Secret Convent of Santa Monica, Avenida 18 Poniente 103, has a fascinating history of intrigue: you'll enter a secret passageway from a house to discover a maze of rooms, cell-blocks, and winding staircases.

For a fine view of the city, tour the Forts of Guadalupe and Loreto, 3 km/2 miles northeast of the zocalo. The latter fort has a historical museum commemorating the May 5, 1862 Battle of Puebla against the French. A 15-minute drive south of Puebla brings you to Africam Safaris, a 200-acre game preserve.

Shops. Puebla has always been an important ceramics center. Even before the Spaniards arrived in Mexico, Indians of the area were accomplished potters, utilizing the nearby clay deposits for the manufacture of earthen kitchenware. After the Conquest, potters from Toledo, Spain, brought their famous Talavera pottery techniques to the newly founded city of Puebla.

Talavera ceramics of varying quality are still available. The best Puebla pottery and dinnerware, artfully designed and beautifully glazed, feature bold geometric designs against a milky white background. Bright blue or yellow appear most frequently in the principal design, often accentuated with secondary patterns in contrasting tones of green, red, or brown. Colored designs applied thickly after glazing give the finished product a somewhat irregular, bas-relief effect that emphasizes its handcrafted appearance.

Most of the ceramic manufacturers maintain their own display and salesrooms at or near the place of manufacture. A single family usually operates the small-scale *fabrica* (work area) in a courtyard; the display or salesroom is often located within the family home. The three best-known tile factories are La Purisima, La Trinidad, and Uriarte, but you'll discover other good shops around town.

Another Puebla product is onyx. At the Barrio de los Artistas market, stalls are filled with onyx fruit, ash trays, paperweights, centerpieces, and other attractive items, all appealing to tourists.

Food. If you have a sweet tooth, try Puebla's regional specialty: *camote*, made from sweet potatoes. This is also the city that invented *mole* sauce: a mixture of chocolate, chili, tomato, avocado, nuts, butter, and spices, served over meat or tortillas. Puebla has some fine restaurants, a few connected with hotels, where you can taste Puebla cooking.

A thirst-quenching stop in Tehuacan

Though the toll road bypasses Tehuacan, you might want to make a side trip to this mineral springs resort nestled at 5,500 feet. Tehuacan's invigorating, refreshing climate and the nearby natural springs have made it a popular resort. This area is also the source of much of Mexico's bottled water. The bottling plants of two well-known companies are near town and offer tours for visitors, as well as all the refreshing spring water you can comfortably consume.

Tehuacan's pastoral, luxuriant atmosphere is enhanced by jacaranda, bougainvillea, *casahuate* trees, and myriad birds whose chattering awakes you with the rising sun.

On the road to Tehuacan, you'll see Mt. Malinche off to your left just beyond Puebla. Unlike Popocatepetl and Iztaccihuatl, Malinche is snowless all year. It was named for Cortes' Indian mistress.

Southern Mexico

An Indian Culture

(For "Facts at Your Fingertips," see page 156)

Southern Mexico encompasses an area unknown to many visitors; most tourists arriving in Mexico City, Puerto Vallarta, and Acapulco never penetrate the southern states. Yet these states offer rewarding experiences that are missed by those who prefer metropolitan areas to the more primitive regions. Here you'll find modern seaports, small fishing villages, historically interesting cities, many of Mexico's greatest archeological sites, and even an active volcano surrounded by its own devastated landscape; You'll see wide, sandy beaches, exotic birds, and groves of tropical fruits—bananas, pineapples, papayas, mangoes, avocados, coconuts, and oranges.

Southern Mexico is an area vital to the understanding of ancient Mexico; nowhere else in the country can you see Indians who have retained their cultural characteristics in such pristine form as the Zapotecs, Lacandons, Chamulas, and Zinacantecos. The archeological sites of Palenque, Mitla, La Venta, Monte Alban, and El Tajin leave you with lasting impressions of this region's early civilizations. Anthropologists in search of the earliest Mexican culture focus on this region, studying Olmec artifacts.

You'll find travel in the southern area enjoyable all year because of the mild winters and warm summers. (A few places, such as the isthmus area, become extremely humid and hot during the summer.) Vegetation, especially from Tampico southward, is tropical: dense and lush. Among the area's fauna are some unusual species; *quetzals* (Guatemala's national bird, and a Maya religious symbol), egrets, jaguars, and tapirs all roam here.

Along the Coast

Motorists have a choice of two routes to the southern coast —Highway 180 from Tampico or Highway 105–127 through Panuco and Tempoal.

The short route is down the coast on Highway 180, but you'll have to cross the wide Panuco River on a car ferry, which is big and businesslike. The long line-up of cars and trucks waiting their turn to board the ferry can be a bit discouraging, though—and the steady pounding of huge Pemex oil field equipment has ruined the road in places.

The older route across the bridge over the Panuco River at Panuco has been rebuilt from Panuco to Tempoal, and you drive through ranching and sugar cane country and pleasant, rolling foothills. Beyond Tempoal the road is uneven and hilly. At Alazan Junction the two highways meet and go on into Tuxpan on a blacktop road.

South of Tuxpan at Poza Rica the road splits; the right fork is Highway 130, which winds through beautiful mountain country to Pachuca on Highway 85 — one route to Mexico City. Take the left fork in the road to continue on Highway 180 down the coast to Veracruz.

Tuxpan—fishing for tarpon is great!

Tuxpan is known as a quiet paradise for tarpon fishermen. Tarpon can be caught from the river at any time, but June is the peak season. The most important activity of this port town, though, is the shipping of cattle and petroleum.

(Continued on page 104)

Overwhelming vastness dazzles visitors exploring Monte Alban ruins and gazing down to Oaxaca valley.

Snow-shrouded *Mount Orizaba, Mexico's highest peak, shows face briefly amid clouds.*

. . . Continued from page 102

To the east of Tuxpan lies the Gulf of Mexico and a beautiful beach. Delicious tiny shrimp, taken from the nearby lagoons and served with *salsa picante* (a hot sauce), are a specialty of local restaurants. An attractive, divided riverside drive adds to the charm of this tidy fishing port.

A land of oil and Indians

Southwest of Tuxpan is one of Mexico's leading oil towns, Poza Rica, or "Rich Hole." This booming town has one industry—a huge Pemex oil refinery.

Poza Rica has grown quickly in recent years; most buildings were erected hastily — and look it. Oil is king here, and if you happen to forget for a moment, the penetrating stench of petroleum will soon remind you.

The ruins of El Tajin, a site rivaling any of the other major archeological zones in Mexico, are 16 km/10 miles south of Poza Rica on an alternate highway to Papantla.

The Totonacs settled here around A.D. 800, but the site was inhabited as early as the 5th or 6th century. The buildings were erected over six centuries.

The seven-story Pyramid of the Niches certainly reigns as the most important building. The pyramid has a total of 365 niches: 364 in its exterior walls, with the door to the temple on top counting as the final "niche." The number of niches probably represents the days of the solar year. In front of the pyramid is a tall steel pole around which the *voladores*—the famed Flying Pole Dancers from Papantla—perform on special occasions. Today, Papantla is the main trading and cultural center of the Totonac Indians.

A major industry around Papantla and the nearby town of Gutierrez Zamora is the growing and processing of vanilla beans. In June, you'll see the voladores perform as part of a week-long fiesta; the whole town celebrates the sale of last year's vanilla harvest and prays for rain for this year's crop.

Prickly poppy　　　　　　　*Flame vine*

Bougainvillea

On to Veracruz

At Gutierrez Zamora a bridge over the placid Tecolutla River replaces the former ferry. The highway then proceeds alongside the gulf for about 32 km/20 miles, past sandy dunes and beaches, through Brahma ranching country and magnificent groves of coconut palms.

At an old lighthouse junction called El Faro, you have a choice of two routes to Veracruz. Highway 180 continues down the coast; on the other highways you wind inland by way of Teziutlan, Perote, and Jalapa.

Zempoala, the last capital of the Totonacs, lies 112 km/70 miles south and 3 km/2 miles west of Nautla. The ruins—not as impressive as those of El Tajin—have been partially restored and reconstructed; among them are the extensive Temples of the Sun, Moon, and Goddess of Death. Zempoala's cemeteries are worthy of note: tombs are miniature temples about 4 feet high.

Veracruz—the untourist town

Lighthearted Veracruz is different from other Mexican cities, and the difference quickly becomes apparent. Spanish forts, trolleys, old churches, and colonial buildings mingle with modern architecture and bustling docks. The palm-thatched shack is never far from the palatial townhouse, and everyone from *peon* (laborer) to *presidente* gathers under the arcades at the plaza.

Marimba bands wander through indoor-outdoor cafes playing an assortment of Caribbean, American, and Mexican tunes. After the April rains come, the heat is almost palpable; one experience with it helps you understand the paradoxical combination of vivacity and indolence you sense in tropical people.

Above all, you'll notice that Veracruz has not made the special preparations and provisions for tourists found in most cities in Mexico: Veracruz is for itself.

(Continued on next page)

. . .Continued from page 105

But most striking of all is the brilliant light, the glare of the tropical sun. Rain, salt air, and the relentless sun quickly make new walls look old; soon, they blend with ancient walls, adding an atmospheric unity to the city's architecture.

The importance of Veracruz as the main port of entry on Mexico's east coast is evident today in numerous reminders of the ocean and ships throughout town: the Chapel of Christ of the Safe Voyage, forts, lighthouses, shipyards, and an abundance of the freshest and most delicious seafood you've ever tasted. Cortes landed in Veracruz' harbor and founded the city in 1519, before beginning his westward march to conquer the Aztecs. Almost all mail and commerce went through Veracruz during the colonial era. Its harbor has seen invasions by the United States, France, and Spain.

What to do. Stroll through the palm-studded and arcaded *Zocalo* (the Plaza de Armas). The nearby church of Santo Cristo del Buen Viaje is rumored to be the oldest church on the American continents. At Museo de Arte y Historia Veracruzana, you'll see collections of art and artifacts from the Totonac, Olmec, and Huaxtec cultures. Drive out to the 16th century, lichen-covered fortress-prison of San Juan de Ulua, one of the city's most interesting sights. When you tire of sitting in an outdoor cafe or on a gaily tiled park bench, visit the marine curio shops near the docks. You can hire a boat for tarpon or deep-sea fishing; inquire at your hotel or along the malecon. To visit the good beaches on the Island of Sacrifice, catch the boat from the dock in front of Hotel Emporio. Boats leave hourly, Sundays only; the rest of the week you'll have to hire a private boat.

Shopping. Stores are open from 9 A.M. to 2 P.M. and from 4 to 8 P.M. Independencia is the main shopping street, but you'll see few regional crafts. Best buys are liquor, and cigars made from tobacco grown in the Valle de San Andreas.

Sunlight dapples water *with many tints around sailboat anchored in Veracruz harbor.*

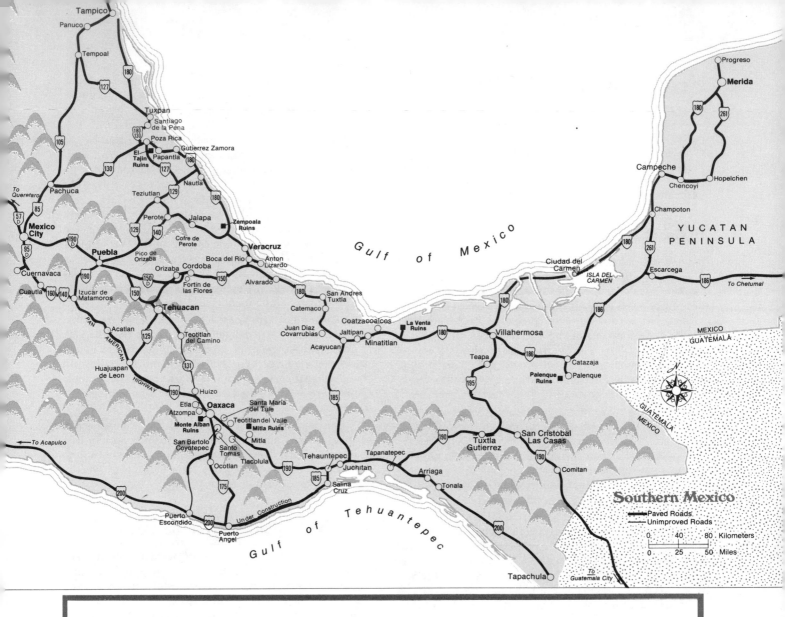

Details at a glance

How to get there

Several daily flights from Mexico City and other major Mexican cities reach Oaxaca, a good base for exploring southern Mexico. Flights from Mexico City also reach Veracruz, Villahermosa, San Cristobal, and other large southern cities.

By air. Air charter services reach smaller villages and towns, as well as many of the ruins.

By car. The best way to tour southern Mexico is by rental car—you'll be able to see as much as possible, and visit all the locations you choose.

By bus. Bus transportation is inexpensive—but if you travel this way, you lose flexibility and may end up viewing the scenic countryside at night.

Accommodations

Simplicity best describes hotels, motels, and campgrounds in southern Mexico. Luxurious hotels are rare and found only in larger cities, but plenty of small, clean accommodations are available throughout the region. (See the "Essentials" section on page 156.)

Climate and clothes

Oaxaca is a popular destination all year. It gets hot during the summer. In San Cristobal you'll need warm outdoor clothing at night or in the early morning. November to April is the best time to visit; winter may be crisp and early spring smoky due to burning of the fields. Nobody would ever say Veracruz is cool; late February or early March is pleasant. Casual attire is appropriate.

From Mexico City to Veracruz

A fast toll road east from Mexico City (Highway 190-D) takes you to Puebla. To continue from Puebla, pick up Highway 150-D, also a toll road. This route from Orizaba passes through rich coffee plantations and flower-garlanded resorts, taking you to the coast and Veracruz.

In the shadow of mighty Orizaba

Beyond the Tehuacan turnoff, Highway 150 climbs to a 7,500-foot summit offering one of the most spectacular views in Mexico — the Valley of Acultzingo. The gradual descent of 4,000 feet is breathtaking — even in the rainy season, when you peer through breaks in the swirling clouds at the patterns of sun and darkness on the blue, green, and yellow patchwork valley below. If you're squeamish about hairpin turns and abrupt drop-offs, though, take the Puebla-Orizaba toll expressway, which misses the Acultzingo descent.

As you approach the city of Orizaba, you'll see magnificent Pico de Orizaba, also called Citlatepetl (the star mountain). This is Mexico's highest mountain—an 18,701-foot peak with perpetual snows on its volcanic cone. The first town of notable size in this warm, lush valley, Orizaba blends industrial claptrap with colonial ambience: textile mills stand next to long rows of tile-roofed dwellings and shops.

Two breweries, coffee and fruit packing companies, and cement plants are central to the city's industrial economy. The Municipal Palace (Palacio Municipal), on the plaza northwest of Castillo Park, was purchased by the city from Belgium. (Originally, the building was part of the Belgian Pavilion in the Paris Exposition in the 19th century.)

Orizaba's orchids and other exotic flowers provide you with an introduction to an area bedecked with tropical blossoms. All kinds of colors and scents will flood your senses and stay with you for weeks after your visit.

Fortin de las Flores — steeped in flowers

Less a town than a flower garden, Fortin de las Flores was a Spanish outpost during the colonial period. Today it's a resort town, noted for exceptionally beautiful gardens filled with gardenias, camellias, and orchids. You can visit the plantation that each day supplies the large resort hotel with the truck-load of gardenias that are floated on its swimming pool. The best of the area's flowers can be appreciated at the annual flower fair in April.

Cordoba — for peacocks and papaya

Cordoba, a little farther down the highway, is a tropical town dominated by pinks and blues. It's a center for rail shipping of the crops you see beside the road — coffee growing in the shade, tobacco drying on racks or in smoke barns, and vast emerald sugar cane fields surrounding sugar mills.

Cordoba's tropical personality is emphasized by the presence of peacocks and other vibrantly plumed creatures, and by the numerous groves of sweet, colorful tropical fruits.

Founded by the Spaniards in 1618, Cordoba has a historically vital heritage. Originally, the Totonacs inhabited this area; the Aztecs, led by Moctezuma, conquered them in 1456. The penultimate scene in the War of Independence in the early 1800s took place in Cordoba. The last Spanish viceroy, arriving in Veracruz after the war was over, met Iturbide in Cordoba in July, 1821, and formally acknowledged Mexico's independence.

Down toward the coast are the fields and groves that make eating here a delight. You'll see ragged banana patches, papaya groves, spreading mango trees, trees that bear enormous avocados, and fields of pineapples. Beyond the cultivated areas, agriculture gives way to rank jungle growth; only a thatched hut in a clearing relieves the monotonous greenery.

You reach the coast at Boca del Rio, a ramshackle, tropical-looking village with coconut palms, pink or buff thatched huts, a weedy plaza, and a tiny church. Stop to watch the townspeople fishing from their boats. Nearby coffee plantations are open for touring.

Jalapa — hillside university town

Returning to Mexico City by way of Jalapa repeats many of the impressions you get on the Cordoba road, but the climb is steadier and you reach pine forests and the plateau sooner. If you're familiar with the history of the Spanish conquest of Mexico, this trip will be much more vivid and absorbing. The road follows the route Cortes followed in 1519, after he scuttled his ships at Veracruz and marched on to the Mexico of Moctezuma.

Jalapa is worth more than just a fleeting stop. This quiet state capital has colorful hillside streets and exuberant vegetation; photographers will be able to get delightful close-ups as well as panoramas. Balconies, wide overhanging eaves, shaped rafter ends, carved wooden doors, and grilled windows will captivate you with their intricate detail.

Another town known for a profusion of blossoms and gardens, Jalapa offers a wide variety of tropical flowers and fruits. Built on a sloping hillside, the city is the home of the University of Veracruz. The university has its own symphony, publishing facilities, and a museum housing a display of archeological artifacts, notably those of the Totonac and Olmec cultures. Parque Juarez, near the massive restored Catedral Metropolitana de Jalapa, contains colossal Olmec heads and pieces of Aztec and Huaxtec work.

You'll appreciate the resolute courage of the conquistadors when you cross the 8,000-foot pass beyond the town

Oaxaca's festive December fiestas

A 3-day fiesta in Oaxaca, beginning December 18, honors the city's patron saint, the Virgin of Solitude. At this time of year, her name seems singularly inappropriate for the festivals held in her honor. Carnival-like activities lasting well into the evening center around the Sanctuario de la Soledad, an ornate baroque church a few blocks west of the zocalo.

As soon as that fiesta is over, the Oaxaqueños begin decorating the town for Christmas. Moss, an essential item for the numerous nativity scenes, is brought from surrounding areas by the Zapotec Indians. Trees and shrubs are adorned with ornaments and gay piñatas, and amusement stands arise overnight around Oaxaca's cathedral at the north side of the zocalo.

With its elegant bandstand and well-kept park, the zocalo is the center of all activities. Restaurants under its surrounding arcades provide the best seats for watching the gaiety. It isn't long before the sarape and rebozo vendors are stopping by your table to show their wares.

By December 23 you smell the buñuelos frying. These light, crispy pancakes, sprinkled with pink sugar and drizzled with syrup, are served from many booths around the plaza. Custom demands that, after eating the buñuelo, you smash the saucer in which it is served. As the evening advances, you may be deep in shards.

That same evening, the radish contest is decided. This yearly competition of imaginative designs created entirely from special elongated, twisted radishes displays some unusual creative skills. The designs typically depict religious scenes, but one year's winner was an Apollo XI display complete with astronauts and spaceships. After the prizes are awarded, the radish figures are sold.

The traditional Christmas Eve parade starts around 9 P.M. Many villages throughout the state participate, each contributing a float and band. People marching ahead of the floats carry colored lanterns and ornaments, little boys shoot firecrackers, and all the bands play different tunes—simultaneously! It all ends with a spectacular fireworks display and midnight services.

---

of Jalapa (near the 14,048-foot peak of the volcano, Cofre de Perote) and see the desolate, windswept highland plains. Maguey and aloe hedgerows define a few Indian fields.

Near the town of Perote you'll see grim Fort San Carlos, built 200 years ago by the Spaniards to accommodate troops protecting Mexico City-Veracruz stagecoaches from attack by bandits. During World War II, the fort served as a prison for aliens; today, it's a rehabilitation center where Mexican inmates produce and sell craft items.

Veracruz to Villahermosa

Just south of Veracruz, a side road leads down the coast to Anton Lizardo, a fishing village.

Not far beyond the turnoff to Anton Lizardo at Paso del Toro Junction, Highway 150 goes west to Cordoba, where it ties into the toll expressway that cuts across the Continental Divide to Puebla and on to Mexico City.

For 96 km/60 miles south of Veracruz, Highway 180 provides glimpses of the gulf—and of shifting sand dunes that sometimes cover parts of the highway.

At Alvarado, you cross the wide mouth of the Papaloapan River over a toll bridge. South of Alvarado, the route goes through rich sugar cane country, then winds along the shore of Lake Catemaco, up into high volcanic hills, and down into the fertile valley of the Hueyapan River. At the small town of Juan Diaz Covarrubias, a sugar refinery, a molasses plant, and an alcohol distillery provide employment for the inhabitants.

At Acayucan, Highway 185 branches south across the Isthmus of Tehuantepec to La Ventosa Junction on the Pacific side.

About 18 km/11 miles beyond Acayucan on Highway 180 is the humble sulfur-mining boom town of Jaltipan. Jaltipan is believed to be the world's greatest sulfur "dome"; millions of tons of this material have already been removed from beneath the town.

Minatitlan, 21 km/13 miles farther, is headquarters for sulfur and oil expeditions into the jungles up the tropical Coatzacoalcos River. Beyond Minatitlan, you drive through about 16 km/10 miles of marshy mud flats to the leading town of the area — the oil and sulfur seaport of Coatzacoalcos. The highway by-passes the town and crosses the Coatzacoalcos River on a toll drawbridge that carries both a railroad track and the highway.

The highway winds through oil fields to the Tonala River, crossed by another bridge. Beyond the bridge a side road to the left leads to the La Venta oil-producing area. In the La Venta swamps, archeologists found giant heads and other stone figures sculpted by the Olmecs; these were later removed for exhibition to Jalapa's Parque Juarez (see page 108).

Visit Villahermosa's outdoor museum

An attractive provincial state capital little known by tourists, Villahermosa is worth visiting even if you do not plan to continue into Yucatan. For many years the city had no road to the outside world; most transportation of both goods and people was by water, on the Grijalva River. This water culture has not appreciably diminished. Villahermosa still has a beautiful riverfront along the placid Grijalva, with an impressive boulevard and flowered plazas.

The archeological museum, Museo Tabasco, contains a good collection of artifacts. The Museo Regional CICOM (Centro de Investigacion de las Culturas Olmeca y Maya), located on the banks of the Grijalva, has a fine collection of pre-Columbian art.

Villahermosa's outdoor archeological museum, Museo Venta, is worth a visit. Located on the western outskirts of town, this unique tropical park reproduces the original site of La Venta (see page 100). Tremendous, heavy Olmec stone heads were transported here from the site of their discovery on the Tabasco-Veracruz border; stone altars and sculpted animals also contribute to the setting's realism. By following the marked paths to the various displays, you can cover the park in under an hour.

Two important routes originate at Villahermosa. The first, Highway 95, heads south to Tuxtla Gutierrez. Now paved for its entire distance, the road has an abundance of curves; allow plenty of time for traveling it. Trailers and most cars should be driven here with extreme caution. The road passes near Teapa, where you can board trains to Merida.

The other route is inland Highway 186, from which a paved side road goes south to the Maya ruins of Palenque. Highway 261 branches off at Escarcega and runs north to Champoton, where it joins coastal route Highway 180 to Campeche. At Chencoyi, 29 km/18 miles east of Campeche, Highway 180 continues north to Merida; Highway 261 runs east 51 km/32 miles to Hopelchen, and then north to Merida. This affords motorists a circle route south of Merida.

Jungle ruins of Palenque

About 120 km/75 miles east of Villahermosa by way of Highway 186, a paved road leads south for 35 km/22 miles to the archeological site of Palenque in the Chiapas jungles. Rental cars are available in Villahermosa; buses also run from there to the ruins. Modest accommodations are available in the small town of Palenque and in the nearby area (see the "Essentials" section for Southern Mexico on page 156).

Considered by many to be the most beautiful pre-Hispanic site in Mexico, Palenque was a Maya center; inhabited even before A.D. 100, the city was at its cultural height from A.D. 600–900. Most of its buildings are gems of light, airy construction. The Temple of Inscriptions contains a Royal Tomb reached by a narrow stairway down into the body of the pyramid, where it opens out into a magnificent burial chamber. Though the central area of the city has been excavated and restored, there is still much to be uncovered. You'll find a small museum at the site.

In April 1982, the eruption of El Chichon, a volcano 120 km/75 miles west of Palenque, covered the site with a heavy layer of ash. Traces of the eruption can still be found here: painted surfaces were "scoured" by the volcanic ash, and lava is embedded deep in the grass surrounding the site.

Mexico City to Oaxaca

Oaxaca has given many travelers some of their warmest, richest memories of Mexico. The city lies 544 kilometers/340 miles southeast of Mexico City, a day's drive by way of Cuautla (a faster route than through Puebla). If you have time, though, Oaxaca is worth a stop on any trip continuing farther south in Mexico or en route to Central America. Oaxaca is about 18 hours from Mexico City by overnight train with Pullman accommodations, 12 hours by first-class bus, and 45 minutes by commercial airline.

Oaxaca—for a relaxing vacation

This far south of the border, you're less conscious of being a *turista* and are treated more as one of Mexico's own people. Even the climate of Oaxaca is friendly; at the 5,068-foot elevation, there are no extremes of heat or cold.

Capital of the state of Oaxaca, Oaxaca City is set in a broad valley, at the center of a constellation of villages. Founded as Antequera in 1522 by a group of Spanish soldiers, the city was named Oaxaca—a corruption of the Indian word *Quauhxyacac* (Place of Trees) — in 1529 by Charles V, who granted the valley to Cortes as his private estate.

The many colonial buildings in the city are noteworthy for their massiveness (this is earthquake country) and the lovely pale green color of the local stone used in their construction. Ambling along the wide one-way streets (one for doctors, one for lawyers) is a pleasure. The streets are immaculate, the people smiling and friendly.

In contrast to Mexico City, Oaxaca's pace is low-key, and its small-town atmosphere is unspoiled. Yet with a population of around 200,000, it's the most important urban center between the capital and the Guatemalan frontier. Descendants of Zapotec and Mixtec builders of Monte Alban comprise two-thirds of the state's population.

Oaxaca is not known for its night life and offers practically none of the tourist amusements available in other parts of Mexico. Instead, its main attractions are its colorfully garbed Indian people and its markets, where popular arts and crafts are displayed in a richness and variety unparalleled elsewhere in Mexico.

Crafts. You won't have to look for handicrafts—they will come to you. Settle back in the shade of the porticos facing the zocalo (the park at the center of town). While you sip a cool drink, vendors parade by with striped sarapes, bright rebozos, and lacy golden necklaces. You can bargain right from your table.

It's an easy walk to craft shops, found mostly in a small area north and east of the zocalo. Here you'll discover the specialties of Oaxaca: pottery, gold and silver jewelry, skirts, blouses, men's shirts, and tablecloths. Oaxaca's knives are famous for the handcarved eagle surmounting the horn grip and for the fine steel blades (often etched with a proverb).

Sights to see. One of the liveliest spots in Oaxaca is the zocalo, where small boys do a brisk trade in shoeshines for idlers sitting on park benches. The cathedral facing the zocalo has a clock donated by a Spanish king.

Five blocks north of the zocalo is the imposing, incredibly beautiful Santo Domingo Church; its interior displays the most gorgeous baroque decoration in all of Mexico. To the left of the atrium is the Regional Museum, where treasures of pre-Hispanic native cultures are displayed. The Tamayo Museum of Hispanic Art has a wonderful collection of Mixtec, Zapotec, and Totonac art and artifacts.

West of the zocalo by the Atoyac River is the market, which explodes with life each Saturday and before important holidays. It's a crowded, fascinating place where you can see the Oaxaqueños and learn about their lives. People from surrounding districts come to barter under billowing canvas sun shades. They may bring flowers, rope, or tin-can mousetraps. There may be a woodcarver who has brought his year's work—a few treasured mythical beasts, painted pink and yellow — or a blousemaker from the Pacific, whose traditional designs are naturally colored from the purple ink of the sea-dwelling *caracol* (snail).

Monte Alban—hilltop monument to its builders

The ruins of Monte Alban, on a hilltop 9 km/6 miles southwest of Oaxaca, are a monument to the master builders of pre-Hispanic Mexico. For the best sense of the past, visit the ruins early in the morning or at sunset. This is probably the country's most impressive site. The hill's summit was leveled and reshaped, and artificial esplanades and structures were raised in harmonious groupings over a period of 17 centuries (700 B.C.–A.D. 1000). The earliest buildings are those found in the inner structure of The Dancers, and the arrowhead-shaped observatory.

In its glory, Monte Alban covered 64 square km/25 square miles. As you see it today, the city is composed of a huge central plaza, limited to the north and south by

(Continued on page 115)

Ceramic bird *is ornate and sprightly traditional handicraft.*

Colorful dyed fiber *creates vividly chromatic chair seats.*

Mitla ruins, *dating from A.D. 500, were once fabled city of gods and Indian burial site.*

Heart of holiday *festivities, Oaxaca's brightly lighted zocalo draws crowds for music and song.*

Tired from dancing, *Chiapas men doze under decorated hats at San Cristobal.*

Natives cross *wide field to reach sugar-cake cemetery in San Cristobal.*

Sightless *serenity charac-terizes stone head in Villaher-mosa outdoor museum.*

114 Southern Mexico

. . . Continued from page 111

acropolis-type platforms and enclosed on the east and west by lower buildings. At a lower level behind the northern platform are several tombs open to the public, among them the famous Tomb 7, where archeologists discovered the magnificent jewelry now on display in the Oaxaca Regional Museum. The many tombs indicate the site's special character as a burial area or necropolis. Mixtec invaders occupied Monte Alban around A.D. 1200, rejuvenating it and burying their rulers in the Zapotec funeral chambers.

A small museum near the entrance contains a collection of artifacts from the ruins.

Mitla's intricate stonework

You drive through tidy Mitla on a paved road to visit the remarkable ruins on the outskirts of town. Mitla is another of the Zapotec-Mixtec ceremonial centers. Intricately carved stone fretwork characterizes the facades of Mitla's temples; arranged in repetitive patterns, the designs are basically geometric. This was the fabled abode of Mictlantecuhtli, Lord of the Underworld, and a sacred city for the burial of Indian kings.

After visiting the ruins, take a look at Mitla, a typical Mexican village: humble, nondescript buildings, pedestrians, perhaps a donkey piled high with fagots or wheat, and a public market. But Mitla has another resource—it's renowned for fine textiles, produced by primitive handweaving methods seldom seen outside the more remote areas of Latin America. The "Mitla design," with a stepped-fret motif, comes from the stone patterns you see on the Mitla ruins.

Much of the weaving is done behind the walls of courtyards at the rear of the room in which handloomed articles are sold. But one establishment, on the left as you enter town from Highway 190, operates in a courtyard where you can see artisans meticulously weaving the threads of a creatively designed piece of cloth.

Villages around Oaxaca

You can drive to most of the villages near Oaxaca; you can also reach all of them by local bus (station on Trujano 3 blocks west of the zocalo) or by taxi (be sure to settle the price before leaving). Some tours include a stop at market towns en route to Monte Alban or Mitla.

Etla, 19 km/12 miles north of Oaxaca, has a Wednesday market; you need not arrive until 11 A.M. or later to see peak activity. The village is noted for its *quesillo,* a cheese boiled into long ribbons and then rolled into a ball.

Atzompa produces pottery—pots with a green glaze and small figures of animals playing musical instruments. The road off Highway 190 is not recommended for the family car. The trip by bus takes about an hour; this is the typical second or third-class bus on which the Indians bring chickens and other goods to or from market. English is rarely spoken in the village.

Culiapan, 12 km/7 miles south of Oaxaca, contains a church and one of Mexico's most massive convents. Begun in 1555, the building was never finished. One of the rooms served as a prison cell for Vicente Guerrero, a deposed Mexican president. After being confined by his enemies, he was shot outside his cell window in 1831.

San Bartolo Coyotepec, about 9 km/6 miles south of Oaxaca along Highway 175, is easily reached by automobile. (In fact, you'll encounter two Coyotepecs on the highway; San Bartolo is the second.) Black, unglazed pottery, made without the use of a potter's wheel, is a trademark of Oaxaca and the surrounding areas. Almost everyone in this village makes pottery. For the best selection, visit the showroom of Dona Rosa's students.

Santo Tomas, beyond Coyotepec, specializes in *fajas* (sashes) woven in the ancient manner, using the backstrap loom—one end tied around a tree and the other to a strap around the waist of the weaver.

Ocotlan, 19 km/12 miles beyond Coyotepec, has a colorful, bustling Friday market; it's also unusually clean. Occasionally, an Indian girl brings in a beautifully embroidered and pleated blouse to sell. Tall stacks of baskets in all sizes and shapes are for sale, and there's a lively market in goats. Be sure to leave the main plaza and walk down the street to see the chicken merchants and sugar cane dealers. During the early morning hours you may see whole families hauling their wares to market on two-wheeled ox carts.

Santa Maria del Tule, 6 km/4 miles southeast of Oaxaca on Highway 190, is renowned as the home of Mexico's largest tree, a 2,000-year-old cypress growing in front of the colorful little church. A small handicraft market is directly across the street. This is mango country; vendors deftly peel the fruit, intricately carve its flesh, and serve it on a stick.

Tlacochahuaya, a rural pueblo a short distance farther along the highway to Mitla, is noted for its monastery. Indian artists decorated the interior with colorful traditional paintings.

Teotitlan del Valle, beyond Tlacochahuaya about 3 km/2 miles, dates back to pre-Hispanic times. Its center is a 17th century church. Best buys are woolen sarapes.

Beyond this pueblo, a road to the right leads to Dainzú. Excavations show that an ancient civilization occupied this site at about the same time Monte Alban flourished.

Closer to the road is the archeological site of Lambityeco, probably occupied after Monte Alban was abandoned.

Tlacolula, also beyond Tlacochahuaya and about 2 km/1 mile to the right of Highway 190, is the site of a fascinating Sunday market. Bargain with the Indians for good buys on extremely well-made sarapes.

To the Guatemala border

The Pan American Highway, Highway 190, continues south from Oaxaca to the Isthmus of Tehuantepec. It follows the south side of the isthmus through flat country covered with scrubby, thorny brush, then climbs through a series of thickly forested mountains and broad, soft, uncultivated river valleys to Tuxtla Gutierrez and San Cristobal Las Casas. Very few settlements can be found along this road. It's wise to fill up with gasoline before leaving Juchitan; though there is a station at La Ventosa Junction, it may not have unleaded fuel.

At Tapanatepec, you can take an alternate route (Highway 200) to the Guatemala border. This lowland highway, completed in 1964, is now the favored route. It goes through Arriaga, then on to Tapachula.

Both routes from Tapanatepec are paved all the way to the border, but the coast route avoids the dangerous El Tapon stretch of Highway 190 — 37 km/23 miles of road running through a winding canyon where landslides and flash floods sometimes create difficulties and delays. You can rejoin the Pan American Highway at Guatemala's capital, Guatemala City, or by taking a scenic toll road that leaves the coast route near Retalhuleu, Guatemala.

The Pan American Highway extends for 4,800 km/3,000 miles through Mexico and Central America to Panama City. The road is paved all the way except for a few short sections in Costa Rica and Nicaragua.

Tehuantepec—a woman's world

If the day is hot and humid when you arrive on this west side of the Isthmus of Tehuantepec, you may wonder why you've ventured this far south into Mexico. The towns and villages seem lackluster, though civilization is reaching them fast. The countryside is tropical, but not as dramatic or luxuriant as it is in other tropical areas.

You soon become accustomed to a lack of comforts and conveniences, though, and after 2 or 3 days you discover that Tehuantepec's main attractions are the Tehuana women and the Pacific beaches.

The women, tall and graceful, are dark-skinned with smooth features. They wear multicolored costumes which are even more resplendent on Sundays and at the many fiestas and dances. You'll notice them especially at Juchitan, a nearby town about the same size as Tehuantepec with adequate tourist accommodations. In Tehuantepec the women run the marketplace and the men stay home and in the fields. In fact, in this matriarchal society, women are the community's most active members, even in local governmental affairs.

You can swim on a beach inside the breakwater at Salina Cruz, a fast-developing port about 16 km/10 miles from Tehuantepec. Swimming and the general atmosphere are even more delightful about 6 km/4 miles south, at the small fishing village of La Ventosa — accessible only by a rough dirt road. Taxis from Tehuantepec will take you there

for a small charge. Several establishments serve refreshments and rent hammocks; one place (with no facilities) allows campers to park under a small grove of palms.

Juchitan—Tehuana town

Juchitan is 27 km/17 miles east of Tehuantepec in open plain country. Juchitan and Tehuantepec have been rivals over the years. One manifestation of this rivalry is a tacit competition in dress—residents of the two towns strive to outdo each other in the splendor of their traditional costumes. Juchitan is about the same size as Tehuantepec, but more spread out; it has larger squares and the streets are wider and gracefully shaded by trees.

The marketplace overflows out of a high-ceilinged shed into a series of arches or portales on one side of the main square.

Juchitan, like Tehuantepec, has a matriarchal society, and the two towns share a similar fiesta tradition—the *Vela*, literally "vigil," but certainly a much happier affair than the name implies. Velas are usually sponsored by a family, frequently on the same date each year; for example, the Ruiz family will offer its Vela every year on April 20. Held in a temporary shelter near (not in) the home of the host family, Velas may continue for 1, 2, or 3 days and nights. Guests are expected to cooperate with food, drink, or funds; outsiders may be welcomed on the same terms.

Marimba music is favored, and it is here that the famous *sandunga* is danced. In rhythm a waltz (the obligatory turns display the skirted Tehuana costume to swirling advantage), the sandunga is usually minor in tone, slow in tempo, and haunting in effect.

Getting across the Isthmus

At La Ventosa Junction you can drive north across the Isthmus of Tehuantepec on a good road: paved Highway 185. In less than 320 km/200 miles, it stretches from the Pacific Ocean to the Gulf of Mexico across land that never rises more than 700 feet above sea level, following the rail route closely most of the way. Near the Gulf, at Acayucan, the road joins Highway 180; here, you can either turn north to Mexico City by way of Veracruz, or southeast to Villahermosa and the Yucatan Peninsula

San Cristobal Las Casas—pure Indian

Five driving hours—256 km/160 miles—separate Juchitan from Tuxtla Gutierrez, capital of the state of Chiapas. Tuxtla Gutierrez is a prosperous, modern commercial center that serves the coffee plantations scattered throughout the surrounding hills. It also has a booming frontier-town atmosphere, because construction workers from nearby dam projects flood the town on weekends and holidays.

San Cristobal Las Casas, clean and quiet, is set 7,000 feet above sea level, in a fertile basin ringed with green mountains. One of these mountains — El Chichon, 80

The colorful Chiapas Indians

Living deep in the jungles of remote Chiapas, the Lacandon Indians have a peaceful, primitive culture. The Lacandons number only around 300, and are being "civilized" at an ever-increasing rate. Paying silent homage to their Maya heritage, they paddle roughly hewn dugout canoes up and down the jungle rivers of Chiapas, perhaps on their way to Yaxchilan, a difficult-to-reach Maya ruin where they worship the ancient Maya gods believed to inhabit the site.

The faces of today's Lacandons so closely resemble the Maya faces depicted in carved temple reliefs that they're sometimes referred to as "living reliefs."

Some are so completely isolated from modern innovations that they still rely on such primitive tools and implements as wooden knives and bows and arrows. The comfort of a warm blanket is a luxury unknown to these people; they sleep in hammocks at night, and are kept warm by the embers of a fire built close to their beds.

If the Lacandons are the recluses of Chiapas, the Chamulas are the area's most overtly progressive and aggressive Indians. In the mid-19th century they rose in open warfare against the "white" town of San Cristobal Las Casas; today, their aggressiveness takes the form of hard trading in the marketplace. Chamula men can be distinguished by their black, or sometimes white, tunics: the decorative colors used and the unique woven pattern of the tunic indicate the village from which each man comes. The women wear black huipiles with red tassels.

The Zinacanteco Indians of Chiapas provide local color. Their handwoven straw hats with wide brims are profusely decorated with brightly colored ribbons. The Zinacantecos' basic attire consists of white cotton shirts and trousers, tunics, colorful sarapes, and kerchiefs worn around the neck. On their feet are traditional Mexican huaraches, with heelguards reminiscent of ancient Indian footwear.

---

km/50 miles northwest of San Cristobal Las Casas erupted April 8, 1982, covering the town with a layer of ash. Geologists studying the volcano predict a 70 percent chance of another eruption in the future. For now, though, clean-up has been completed, and you'll encounter no problem getting in and out of the town.

San Cristobal's charm lies in its setting and solid colonial architecture, and in the comings and goings of the many Indian groups who live in the region. This is truly a photographer's paradise. Visit the cathedral on the plaza; it hides a magnificent interior behind an ordinary facade. The plaza itself is charming, with a lacy ironwork bandstand surrounded by shrubs and brilliant flowering plants. The Church of Santo Domingo, a few blocks away, is not only impressive on the inside, but also has an extremely ornate facade. The archeological and ethnological museum and library in the Na-Bolom guest house is worth a visit.

Calle Guadalupe is the street of the shops — not the curio shops of tourist centers but *tiendas* (stores) that sell to the Indians. For several blocks north of the plaza, you look through unmarked doorways at stacks of sombreros, huge quantities of leather shoulder bags, and dozens of sarapes and rebozos in vivid colors and interesting weaves and designs.

San Cristobal is roughly organized into districts, each occupied by the urbanized descendants of a particular Indian tribe all working at the same trade. Thus in one area you can watch the weavers, in another area the dollmakers, in another the makers of fireworks, and in another the candlestick makers, hanging their products in colorful clusters.

The market — a fairly new one on the eastern edge of town — is of interest because, like all Mexican markets, it mirrors the area's economic life.

San Cristobal is now the departure point for several exciting trips, especially if you enjoy horseback riding. Pack expeditions can be arranged into the tropical highland forests, for a look at half-buried Maya sites and a visit to Lacandon Indian villages.

Nearby caves attract speleologists, and the beautiful Montebello Lakes are a day-long excursion by car. If you're a hardy soul, take a 2½-hour jeep trip to the Indian town of Tenanapa, where two rivers meet and then plunge downward in two waterfalls that rush underground. (Tenanapa's bustling Sunday market is worth a visit, too.)

North & East

To the Gulf

(For "Facts at Your Fingertips," see page 157)

Travelers from the east coast of the United States can use any of several highways to reach Mexico City or some of the pleasant towns along the Gulf of Mexico. Even west coast drivers often take the interior route, Highway 45, to the country's capital.

The northcentral and northeastern sections of Mexico are not exactly filled with tourist destinations, but a few highlights deserve mention. In this chapter, we'll follow the four main routes south, calling attention to some of the attractions along the way.

Along Highway 45

Some consider the northcentral area of Mexico, traversed by Highway 45, dull and monotonous. Part of it is. For at least half the way — between Ciudad Juarez (where the road crosses into Mexico from El Paso) and Durango—the country is flat and semiarid, with practically no variation in the open stretches between towns and villages.

At times the unrelenting sameness of the road gives way to a narrow village street that threads past old buildings, tree-shaded plazas, and roadside vendors selling melons or rebozos; then, you see something of the northcentral Mexico you expect as you drive the first 960 km/600 miles or more through the cattle country below the border.

Mexicans call the southern portion of the highway (between Guanajuato and Mexico City) "La Ruta de la Independencia" (The Route of Independence): Father Miguel Hidalgo, revered as the "Father of Mexico's Inde-

pendence," marched along this route with his ragged army to overthrow the Spaniards. Hidalgo was executed in Chihuahua on July 30, 1811.

Highway 45 never drops below the 3,752-foot elevation at Cuidad Juarez, where it begins. The road climbs gradually, though; for much of the way, the uphill grade is so moderate as to be imperceptible, making this route a good one for trailers. You may enounter dust storms in the northern reaches between February and April, and occasional winter snows around Chihuahua. You'll find good accommodations at major cities along the route.

You can cut east toward the coast by taking Highway 49 at Ciudad Jimenez. This route bypasses Hidalgo del Parral and Durango, taking you through Torreon and Rio Grande and then to Fresnillo, where you pick up Highway 45 again. Highway 49 is a good paved road. Fill your gas tank at Ciudad Jimenez; the next town, Gomez Palacio, is 277 km/145 miles away.

Chihuahua

One of the largest cities in all of northcentral Mexico, Chihuahua owes its beginnings to the rich silver strikes that were made in the nearby mountains in the 18th century.

Parts of the city are quite modern, but the older sections of town contain some fine examples of colonial architecture. Among them are the State Capitol (Palacio de Gobierno) on Hidalgo Plaza (Father Hidalgo was executed here in 1811, during the War for Mexican Independence);

(Continued on page 121)

Stone-walled village is surrounded by expanses of stark scenery typical of northeastern Mexico.

Tarahumara Indian *hunkers down for a brief rest during infrequent visit to Chihuahua.*

Pink sandstone buildings *and sloping setting add to Zacatecas' charm.*

Mexican shorthorns *lie placidly beside highway in Durango state.*

...Continued from page 118

the Federal Palace (Palacio Federal), also on Hidalgo Plaza, where Hidalgo was held prisoner while awaiting execution; and the immense cathedral facing the zocalo (Plaza de la Constitucion).

La Quinta Luz, the home of Pancho Villa's widow, Señora Luz Corral, is open to the public. It houses a collection of weapons and personal effects of Mexico's 20th century guerilla-revolutionist. Combination villain and benefactor — a sort of Mexican Robin Hood — Villa and his band of terrorists ranged across the northern states, ostensibly serving the cause of *La Revolucion*.

From Chihuahua you can take a spectacular rail trip through the mountains and canyons of the Sierra Madre Occidental to the town of Los Mochis on Highway 15 (see page 125).

Ciudad Camargo— in the heart of cattle country

Ciudad Camargo is an old but progressive Mexican town. Operating from a modern headquarters building, the cattlemen's association is central to the town's activities. A large meat-packing plant, located at the southern edge of town, refrigerates and ships meat throughout Mexico and the United States. It also sends hides to Leon and utilizes the rest of the animal in making fertilizer. Other industries in the area include a textile plant, a flour mill, and several cotton gins.

In this bustling and businesslike town, the highlight of the year is the fiesta for its patron saint, Santa Rosalia.

Starting early in September, the 8 days of celebration include dances, horse races, cockfights, and other entertainment. An 18th century, mission-style parish church named after Santa Rosalia is 4 blocks east of the highway.

Many sportsmen visit Camargo for the black bass fishing at nearby Boquilla Dam. The Boquilla Dam blocks the Conchos River to create an irregular body of water some 64 km/40 miles in length. Water from the dam turns the turbines of the big hydroelectric plant that furnishes part of the power for cities as far distant as Juarez. This body of water was stocked with fish from Canada.

Spring months are considered best for fishing. During July and August the lake is closed to fishermen; strong winds in February and March often make the water too rough for small boats. Many sportsmen bring their own boats, which can be easily launched from the sloping shore. Boats may also be rented by the day. The best fishing spots are several miles up the lake from the dam.

Primitive mining town of Hidalgo del Parral

Virtually cut off from the world until Highway 45 was completed, Hidalgo del Parral has remained an isolated, primitive town. Until the highway was built, the town had few visitors other than miners. (Most travelers still tend to use Highway 49 to Fresnillo via Gomez Palacio, rather than Highway 45.) Rich metallic ores were first discovered around here in the middle of the 16th century — and the mines are still producing.

(Continued on next page)

North & East   121

Intricately *carved cathedral tower is Saltillo landmark.*

...Continued from page 121

Six churches are scattered throughout the town—all of them with bullet holes in their stone walls. A large 18th century church on the plaza, La Parroquia, has a richly embellished interior and gilded altar screens.

The general store at one end of Plaza San Juan de Dios was originally a house; Pancho Villa lived here before his assassination. His grave holds a headless corpse, a morbid reminder of a grave robbery several years after his burial.

Durango—Hollywood's favorite backdrop

Durango reflects an openness of design and a provincial atmosphere that are atypical for a city of its size. The streets are wide and paved; the zocalo is gracious and still well kept. One of the most pleasant cities on Highway 45, Durango has several large parks, a few smaller parks, and a riverside promenade. The massive cathedral has a yellow façade and magnificent vaulted ceilings. Inside the Government Palace (Durango is the capital of the state of Durango), the walls of an entire inner courtyard are decorated with murals.

Located about halfway between El Paso and Mexico City, Durango is becoming more popular with tourists. It has served as the location for many western movies, hosts an International Film Festival every October in its multi-million dollar Cinema Center, and boasts a good airport and country club. Drive atop Remedios mountain for a breathtaking view of the countryside.

From Durango, one of Mexico's most scenic roads—Highway 40—winds up and over the Sierra Madre Occidental to meet Highway 15 just south of Mazatlan. A good paved road for its entire length (about 320 km/200 miles), Highway 40 is not a particularly fast route. It takes about 6 hours to reach Mazatlan.

Before you leave Durango, get picnic provisions and fill your gas tank. Eating places along the road are few. Gasoline pumps are located at El Salto, El Palmito, Concordia, and at the junction of Highways 40 and 15. Because of the frequent sharp curves and steep grades, this route to Mazatlan is not recommended for tourists driving trailers and motor homes.

Nombre de Dios—Spanish ghost town

About 56 km/35 miles south of Durango on Highway 45 is the humble old farm settlement of Nombre de Dios, the first Spanish settlement in the state of Durango. Today, only ghostly shadows inhabit this 400-year-old farm, though sometimes an occasional visitor can still be seen lingering amidst the crumbling walls.

Past the detour a dusty road sign informs you that you're crossing the Tropic of Cancer. Some 16 km/10 miles south, Highway 45 reaches La Chicharrona Junction near Fresnillo, where it merges with Highway 49. The road by-passes Fresnillo, a flat, dusty city with gigantic slag piles of tailings from silver mining.

Ruins of La Quemada

About 43 km/27 miles past its intersection with Highway 49, Highway 45 combines with Highway 54 from Saltillo. Six kilometers/4 miles beyond is a traffic circle and a monument commemorating the construction of the highways in this area. The junction with Highway 54 to Guadalajara is another 6 km/4 miles south. From the junction, it's an easy 45-km/28-mile side trip on Highway 54 to the ruins of La Quemada. These are the remains of the Chicomozloc culture—a civilization much older than that of the Aztecs. Ruins on the hillside include remnants of a few columns, a temple, a palace, and a public square with steps. Known by the natives as Cerro de los Edificios, the site is always open; you pay a few pesos to visit it.

Zacatecas—the pink city

This sloping townsite is 8,200 feet above sea level. Parts of town are so steep that stone steps—not streets—climb the canyon walls. The whole town has a faint pinkish cast—a result of the local sandstone used in most of the buildings. Zacatecas has a magnificent cathedral whose huge façade is intricately carved; its vaulted interior is supported with stalwart stone columns.

An early silver mine invites visitors, as does the Museum of Huichol Art's display of elaborately ornamented embroideries. Another favorite attraction in Zacatecas is the intriguing summit of Cerro de la Bufa, a mountain northeast of the city. A blacktop road has been built to the top of "La Bufa," where there's an ancient chapel (built in 1728) and a demure plaza. From atop "La Bufa," you'll see a panorama of the countryside.

Music boxes in Guadalupe

Another small town on Highway 49 is Guadalupe, and it's worth taking time out of your driving schedule to meander through its narrow, quiet streets. The focus of your wanderings will be the old Convent of Guadalupe, housing numerous works of art and handprinted books. The buildings are open to visitors for a minimal admission charge.

At the southern end of Guadalupe is an unusual factory where music boxes are made (and sold), along with an assortment of other beautifully inlaid articles. Items are not cheap.

You're in hot water in Aguascalientes

South from Guadalupe on Highway 45 is the state of Aguascalientes. The colonial city and state capital, also called Aguascalientes, is a railroad center for this area. Industry and crafts (especially sarapes, linen work, and hand-embroidered cotton) contribute greatly to the livelihood of this modern city. Wine making and brandy distillation are other important industries in this grape-growing area.

The town's name refers to its location near thermal springs. These springs provide an opportunity for visitors to indulge themselves in a languorous afternoon of mineral baths and swimming.

For many years the townsite was a small outpost in Chichimeca Indian territory; the Chichimecas were hostile and warlike, making the conquest of the area by Pedro Alvarado nearly impossible. Only after many futile attempts and frustrating defeats was he successful. Don't miss the Government Palace, a 17th century mansion which belonged to the Marquis de Guadalupe.

San Marcos Fair, the spring festival of Aguascalientes, is celebrated for about 2 weeks in late April. An occasion in honor of the city's patron saint, the San Marcos Fair features dancing, fireworks, cockfighting, and bullfighting.

Through the Northeast

Three routes take you through northeastern Mexico from the border: Highway 57, Highway 85, and Highway 180. These highways are all in reasonably good condition.

A faster route to Mexico City than the Pan American Highway (Highway 85), Highway 57 is the alternate route to the interior of Mexico from the east coast of the United States. Driving is easier, since the highway doesn't climb and wind through mountainous regions as the Pan American Highway does. The road is very good—paved all the way. Driving time from the border to Mexico City is about 18 hours.

(Continued on next page)

Details at a glance

How to get there

This large stretch of territory is best traveled by car, though commuter plane service links Mexico City and the larger cities—notably Monterrey and Tampico.

By air. Frequent flights link larger cities to Mexico City. Commuter traffic to small towns is less frequent; you'll usually find just one flight per day.

By car. Highways in northeastern Mexico are paved and clearly marked, making driving the best way to get to—and tour—this area.

Accommodations

Pace yourself to reach a fairly large town for overnight stops. Not much is plush, but clean rooms are available (see the "Essentials" section on page 157).

Climate and clothes

If possible, plan trips for spring or fall. The northern section is desertlike and can be quite hot, while the gulf side may be very humid. Plan your wardrobe for comfort.

...Continued from page 123

From the border towns of Piedras Negras and Cuidad Acuna, just across the Rio Grande from Eagle Pass and Del Rio respectively, it's a pleasant drive over gently rolling countryside to Monclova, where Mexico's largest steel mill is located. At Monclova, Highway 30 to the southwest goes to Torreon and is an excellent short cut for motorists heading for Mazatlan on the west coast of Mexico.

Just beyond the small mining town of Castanos, Highway 53 runs southeast to Monterrey.

Sarapes in Saltillo

Covering a vast plain at a mile-high elevation, Saltillo reaches to the low hills, offering views of higher mountains in every direction. Saltillo is the prosperous capital of the state of Coahuila — a popular stopping place in summer because of its relatively cool climate.

Founded in 1555, Saltillo retains much of its Spanish colonial character. "Downtown" runs chiefly along the two one-way streets of Victoria and Aldama, from the central plaza west for about half a dozen blocks to the shady Alameda. The State Capitol building (Palacio de Gobierno) faces on the plaza; across from it is the Cathedral of Santiago with its 200-foot tower and richly carved facade.

In several small factories you can watch weavers at work on the brightly colored sarapes characteristic of Saltillo. Skilled craftsmen fashion articles of silver, tin, brass, and copper. You'll also find craftwork and souvenirs from many other parts of Mexico.

You have to look carefully so you won't miss the market on Allende; like a normal business block, the street is lined with small shops. The main part of the market is inside a tall, barnlike building and has three levels. This is Saltillo's all-purpose department store: here, you can buy food, clothing, hardware, and all the types of handicrafts sold in town, as well as more utilitarian items such as pottery for use as cookware.

The Interamerican University (La Universidad Interamericana), just a few blocks from the Alameda, attracts many students from the United States, especially in the summer. The state also maintains a university and a technological institute in Saltillo; a school of agriculture is located a short distance to the southwest.

Wine and the Battle of Buena Vista

Highway 40 runs east from Saltillo to Monterrey on a fine divided expressway (eliminating many of the wicked curves that formerly marked this well-traveled route), and west from Saltillo to Torreon through large expanses of desert. About midway between Saltillo and Torreon, a few miles south of an oasis junction called Paila, is the winemaking town of Parras de la Fuente. Nearby is a popular resort named Rincon del Montero. Numerous springs give this small area a verdant appearance—in marked contrast to the desolate countryside around it.

Southwest of Saltillo, Highway 54 heads for the desert past the old mining town of Concepcion del Oro to Zacatecas, beyond which you can continue to Guadalajara. Just southwest of Saltillo, along Highway 54, is the almost forgotten site of one of the confrontations of the U.S.-Mexican War — the Battle of Buena Vista. (The Mexicans call it the Battle of Angostura — the name of a village nearby.) About 10 minutes from Saltillo, a small, weather-beaten shaft marks the rocky spot where the battle took place on February 23, 1847.

The captivating ghost town of El Catorce

West of Matehuala is the tranquil ghost town of El Catorce, once a prosperous silver mining community that boasted a population of 40,000 in its heyday. Now, only a handful of residents remain, and the attractive churches, public buildings, and residences are slowly crumbling.

The town's name is said to have come from a band of 14 (catorce) bandits, who continually raided the trains transporting silver from the mines. The Mint Building (Casa de Moneda) stands as a ghostly reminder of the high volume of silver ($3 million annually in silver ore) produced by the mines in the region near El Catorce.

Several events bring El Catorce to life briefly: On October 14, pilgrims arrive from all over Mexico to honor the town's patron saint, San Francisco de Assisi; a fiesta on December 28 includes Indian dancers and fireworks; and a fair takes place on January 6. Auto or bus tours are available from Matehuala.

For ixtle, visit the Matehuala region

In the desert around Matehuala there are veritable forests of several species of agave and yucca which are the source of various fibers, all generically known as ixtle; these are the basis of Matehuala's all-important industry. Finer quality fibers are used mainly for sacking and for decorative pieces such as place mats and wall hangings. Coarser fiber is made into packing material, brush bristles, and door mats. Ixtle is also used for upholstery filling. Once pounded and shredded, it is wound into hanks that are tied in knots, soaked in water, allowed to dry, and then untied. The resulting curled segments provide the necessary resiliency for the filling.

Food, lodging, and gasoline are available here. You can ride a slightly antiquated bus up to El Catorce.

South of Matehuala, you'll start seeing the nopal or tuna cactus, the fruit of which is quite delicious. Natives gather the fruits and sell them along the highway. The fruit is also used to make a regional sweet—queso de tuna or tuna "cheese."

About 80 km/50 miles south of Matehuala, at an unassuming place called Huizache Junction, Highway 80 from Antiguo Morelos (on the Pan American Highway) joins Highway 57, and the two routes continue as one to San Luis Potosi.

Into Copper Canyon by rail

Most scenic of all Mexico rail trips is the Copper Canyon run along the Chihuahua-Pacific Railway. Originating at Ojinaga, a border town opposite Presidio, Texas, the trip takes you south to Chihuahua, then southwest to Los Mochis. Once past Chihuahua you're swept deep into spectacular Sierra Madre country, where your adventure begins.

Rumbling across bridges, the train snakes through tunnels and passes by deep ravines. Waterfalls slip over rims of red rock where palms and ferns grow in the shade and bush poppies tumble over the sunlit slopes.

Yet all is not wild in the Sierra Madre. Juxtaposed against the forested ridges and simple huts of the Tarahumara Indians are busy towns and small adobe villages. Perhaps you'll decide to stop at Creel, Divisadero, or Cerocahui, welcome breaks in the 14-hour ride from Chihuahua to Los Mochis. All offer hotels and exciting side trips into once inaccessible canyon territory. Explore the Urique and Copper canyons by horseback; hike along canyon rims, or go shopping in town for crafts made by the Tarahumaras.

Pullman trains make two round trips weekly between Ojinaga and Los Mochis via Chihuahua. The Autovias train, a diesel coach with reserved, reclining seats, offers five round trips between Los Mochis and Chihuahua; separate service also connects Chihuahua and Ojinaga.

In addition to the above service, the line operates streamlined vistadome Italian Fiat coaches between Ojinaga and Los Mochis. These coaches run only during the day; you stop over in Chihuahua, where you'll find several good hotels, and resume the trip early the next morning.

For information or reservations you can write directly to the Chihuahua-Pacific Railway, c/o Traffic Agent, Box 46, Chihuahua, Chih., Mexico. Or you can arrange for a package tour through any number of U.S. operators; consult a travel agent.

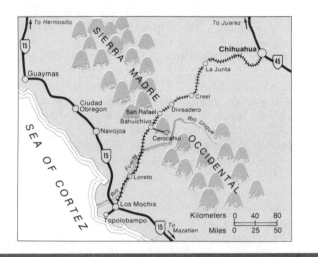

San Luis Potosi— historical and industrial

The largest city along Highway 57 is San Luis Potosi, capital of the state of the same name. The main highway by-passes the city by a mile or so; if you make the side trip into town, you'll consider your time well spent.

A rich mining center since the 1600s, San Luis Potosi is also a modern industrial city and a major rail center. Here, too, is the Mexican plant of another well-known U.S. firm — Allis Chalmers.

The local bazaar, Hidalgo Market, offers good buys in rebozos, locally made pottery, and regional handicrafts. The Chamber of Commerce displays an interesting selection of crafts from the state — and it's all for sale. You'll probably have a chance to sample prickly pear or tuna cheese here.

Of interest, also, are the cathedral, the Church of Our Lady of Carmen, the Potosi Regional Museum, and the famous Caja de Agua — the small, round wellhouse designed by Tresguerras which serves as the hub of the city's water system.

South to rebozos and fighting bulls

About 48 km/29 miles south of San Luis Potosi is the tidy town of Santa Maria del Rio, on the banks of the languorous Santa Maria River. This community is known throughout Mexico for its rebozos. For generations its women have been weaving beautiful silken "Santa Maria rebozos" — highly prized by the ladies of Mexico. Recently, because the Mexican government became concerned that the art of weaving "Santa Maria rebozos" might die out as the older women of the town passed away, a special school was established to teach young girls the art. Tourists are invited to visit the school on the main plaza; you can purchase rebozos and other colorful handicrafts.

Just beyond Santa Maria del Rio is the Rancho Santo Domingo, where for three generations the Labastida family has bred fine fighting bulls. These big, beautiful black animals are in great demand by the largest bullrings of Mexico. Tourists are welcome to visit the old hacienda and the rancho's own little chapel. Señor Javier Labastida, the American-educated grandson of the founder, is sometimes on hand to act as guide.

Monterrey—beer and buildings

You can reach Monterrey from many directions, but if you're driving south from the U.S. you'll probably take Highway 85 from Laredo. The first 72 km/45 miles south of the border are monotonous. South of Vallecillo, though, the road climbs gradually into the foothills of the Sierra Madre, then drops down into the industrial city of Monterrey — capital of the state of Nuevo Leon, and probably Mexico's leading manufacturing center.

Bustling, increasingly modern Monterrey retains much of its colonial charm. Historical landmarks are scattered throughout the city as reminders of its original 17th century settlers.

Interesting buildings deserve a visit, and you should plan to spend some time at the cathedral on Zaragoza Plaza, built between 1790 and 1840; the Municipal Palace (Palacio Municipal), a 17th century colonial-style city hall; the ultramodern Purisima Church with impressionistic statues of the Apostles; and El Obispado (the Bishop's Palace), located on the west side of the city and now a regional museum. Built in 1785, the palace served for years as a residence for church dignitaries. During the U.S.-Mexican War, it functioned as a fort where Mexicans resisted American troops; it was also occupied by Pancho Villa during the Revolution of 1910.

Monterrey bullfights are held in the ring at domed Plaza Monumental. The best season is from November to March, but during the summer, bullfights are sometimes staged on Saturday nights under the lights.

Monterrey is the heart of Mexico's beer industry. The country's largest brewery, Cuauhtemoc Brewery on the outskirts of town, offers guided tours for visitors during the week. Tourists are served free samples of the brewery's products — Carta Blanca and Bohemia beers.

Nearby areas to visit include the Garcia Caves and La Boca Dam. The Garcia Caves are about 48 km/30 miles northwest of Monterrey. A labyrinth of spectacular limestone caverns, the caves are open daily to visitors. A little funicular railway makes hourly trips daily from an excursion depot 8 km/5 miles northeast of the village of Villa de Garcia to the entrance of the caves. The State Tourist Department operates the tram and conducts tours of the caverns. The funicular round trip and tour take about 2 hours.

La Boca Dam can be reached by taking Highway 85 south for about 40 km/25 miles. Here you can refresh yourself by enjoying one of several available water sports: swimming, boating, and water-skiing.

Picnic at Horsetail Falls

Highway 85 enters Huajuco canyon south of Monterrey and follows the canyon for about 32 km/20 miles. The area is one of the most lush and fertile in all of Mexico.

Some 38 km/24 miles south of Monterrey is a short but rewarding detour off the main highway to a very popular resort area; its main attraction is an idyllic waterfall called Cola de Caballo ("Horsetail") which spills in delicate ribbons for 225 feet down a mossy, fern-draped precipice.

You leave the main highway at the south end of the village of El Cercado and follow a paved, privately owned toll road for 6 km/4 miles through orange groves and sugar cane fields into the forested foothills of the Sierra Madre. At the end of the drive is the resort complex of cottages, dining room, and swimming pool. Here you'll be greeted by the resident company of guides, who will take you (for a reasonable fee) to the falls by burro, saddle horse, or horse-drawn cart—or, if you prefer to go without a guide, you can walk the path from the resort to the falls in under half an hour.

The scent of orange blossoms in Montemorelos

Montemorelos, just off the highway about 50 miles south of Monterrey, is Mexico's largest orange-growing district. Fresh oranges and glasses of thick, pulpy orange juice are sold along the road. At Montemorelos the highway is joined by Route 89 from China (pronounced *Chee-nah)*, a popular short-cut road to Mexico from the border cities of McAllen (Texas) and Reynosa (Mexico).

Linares—a scenic by-pass

The largest town between Monterrey and Ciudad Victoria, Linares is the center of an extensive farming, ranching, and citrus-growing area. Linares was founded in 1712 as the Bishopric of San Felipe de Linares. There are two large churches, the Church of Senor de la Misercordia and the Parochial Church, each facing its own plaza.

At Linares, Highway 60 takes off to the west. After winding through scenic Santa Rosa Canyon, it climbs up and over the majestic Sierra Madre to a junction with Highway 57 about midway between Saltillo and Matehuala. A popular short-cut route for motorists from southern Texas gateways, the highway enables you to reach Highway 57 without going through the metropolitan cities of Monterrey and Saltillo.

Ciudad Victoria—a junction

Ciudad Victoria is the capital of the state of Tamaulipas, one of Mexico's most industrialized states, which extends in a narrow strip along the Rio Grande and then follows the Gulf of Mexico south as far as the coastal town of Tampico.

Natural fibers are an important crop in this region, and are used both for industrial purposes and to make the colorful hammocks and other decorative objects sold on the streets and in the markets.

Highway 85 is joined at Ciudad Victoria by Highway 101 from the Texas towns of McAllen and Brownsville. An extension of Highway 101 is open from Ciudad Victoria to the southwest over the Sierra Madre, offering some spectacular scenery before straightening out on the high mesa.

South to the tropics

South of Ciudad Victoria, the highway descends sharply and the country becomes increasingly lush and tropical. You cross the Tropic of Cancer 38 km/24 miles south of the city. Vegetation becomes more dense: masses of colorful vines; thick, tangled forests; and groves of mango, banana, and avocado trees. Fragrant flowers bloom profusely everywhere. The beautifully brilliant *flamboyant* (royal poinciana) trees are scattered among the vegetation, brightening the greenness with vibrant splashes of red.

Ciudad Valles— agricultural shipping center

Until Highway 85 came to Ciudad Valles, the place was just a sleepy little village. One of the oldest cities in the state, Ciudad Valles was founded as a Spanish outpost in 1533. Located near the Sierra, it provides an ideal shipping point for the products of the region: cattle, sugar cane, citrus fruits, and coffee. Most of the products are distributed by rail to other cities within Mexico.

Highway 70 leads east from Ciudad Valles to Tampico. Just off this road, about 16 km/10 miles east of Ciudad Valles, is the well-known resort of Taninul, a popular spa for many years. Not far away are the ruins of important Huastecan archeological sites.

Tamazunchale—Huastec country

One of the most scenic sections of Highway 85 is between Ciudad Valles and Tamazunchale. Exotic tropical vegetation grows luxuriantly along the highway. The quaint old town of Tamazunchale lies at the foot of the Sierra Madre Oriental on the south side of the Montezuma River. Butterflies and birds are the town's most colorful inhabitants; tourists, especially those who enjoy bird watching, may see the unusual species of the area. Don't miss the 16th century church and the unusual market offering tantalizing tropical novelties. Tamazunchale is generally considered the capital city of the somewhat isolated Huasteca Indians, who live for the most part in the nearby mountains.

Some of the most spectacular views to be seen along Highway 85 are from points between Tamazunchale and Jacala, a mountain mining town.

Zimapan, south of Jacala, is a colonial mining town established when lead and silver deposits were discovered after the Conquest. It's still active. South from Zimapan is Ixmiquilpan, where you can enjoy a rest stop and visit one of Mexico's oldest and grandest churches and convents, built by the Augustinians in 1550.

The highest point on the Pan American Highway is reached just north of Colonia Junction, near the old mining city of Pachuca, where you'll reach an elevation of 8,209 feet at a community called Hacienda de la Concepcion. The Americans living in Mexico City have erected a monument here, as a "good neighbor" gesture to the Mexicans.

Lush canyon *near Monterrey cradles Horsetail Falls, good stop for hiking and picnicking.*

Tampico—on the Gulf of Mexico

You'll have your first glimpse of the Gulf of Mexico at Tampico, one of Mexico's biggest and most dynamic seaports. The port itself is inland on the Panuco River, and the city has grown up on half a dozen hills, amid freshwater lagoons.

The river is heavily commercially fished; its banks are peppered with refineries and oil tanks. One of the largest Pemex refineries is at Ciudad Madero, a suburb to the north of Tampico near the mouth of the river.

Today, Tampico is appreciated by tourists who come to fish the coastal waters for tarpon, snook, snapper, and yellowfish. Hunting is also a popular sport for visitors; duck, quail, and turkey can be taken. Make arrangements for fishing charters through your hotel; or a tour operator can also arrange hunting trips.

Akumal resort overlooks palm-fringed Caribbean beach popular with swimmers, snorkelers, and fishers.

Yucatan

Ruins of a Civilization

(For "Facts at Your Fingertips," see page 158)

The Yucatan peninsula — that immense thrust of land dividing the Gulf of Mexico from the Caribbean — is so flat that the landscape takes on a uniformity approaching monotony. But beneath that deceiving cloak of sameness exist a warm, vital people, and a land with an inexhaustible wealth of archeological treasures. Images that will linger in your mind: the smooth bronze faces of Maya Indians, with sparkling eyes and spontaneous smiles; the charm of Merida; the *huipiles*, sandals, and pleated shirts worn by the Yucatecans; and the gemlike brilliance of the Caribbean.

Three islands—Isla Mujeres, Cancun, and Cozumel—lie close to the mainland just off the northeast tip of the peninsula; all are accessible by boat or air. A causeway also reaches Cancun.

The peninsula is divided into the states of Yucatan, Campeche, and Quintana Roo—all once within the land of the Maya. For years, the Maya sites of Chichen Itza, Uxmal, Kabah, Tulum, and others less well known to the casual traveler have lured archeologists and adventurers to this remote part of Mexico. The Yucatan would be interesting even without its ruins, but they make the peninsula one of the world's most fascinating tourist areas. As time and restoration funds allow, more ruins are becoming easily accessible to travelers.

Aside from its Maya ruins, Yucatan is famous for *henequen* (sisal) rope and twine. Until the end of World War II, Yucatan supplied most of the world's high-grade sisal. Since then, synthetic fibers have cut sharply into the henequen market, bringing difficult times to the industry.

Villahermosa to Campeche

Highway 180 has four ferry crossings en route to Campeche. Try to get an early start from Villahermosa so you can catch all four in one day, beginning with the ferry to Frontera. (It's best not to use the ferries if you're driving a trailer, though — the undercarriage has a good chance of being severely damaged. Instead, make the trip on inland Highway 186.)

This first ferry crosses the Grijalva River 72 km/45 miles from Villahermosa, at a community called San Roman; the town of Frontera is on the other side. The ferry runs from early in the morning until late at night. The crossing takes 15 to 20 minutes, and there's a small toll for cars and trailers.

The next ferry, 24 km/15 miles farther down Highway 180, crosses the San Pedro River. The ferry runs throughout the day; cars and trailers must pay tolls. The trip takes just 10 minutes.

The third ferry leaves from Zacatal, just beyond the lighthouse community of Xicalango. It runs to Ciudad del Carmen on the tip of Isla del Carmen, an island separated from the mainland by Laguna de Terminos. This crossing takes longer than the first two—about 30 minutes.

Ciudad del Carmen is 6 km/4 miles long. Beyond the town, the island stretches for 35 km/22 miles to Puerto Real, where you take the fourth (and longest) ferry ride. The crossing from Puerto Real to the mainland takes the

Mountains of Panamas *line shelves in small store.*
Shopping is good around Campeche.

better part of an hour, and ferries run more or less continuously throughout the day. If you miss the last ferry and are stranded for the night on the island, you'll find fairly good motel and adequate hotel accommodations.

After taking the fourth ferry, you proceed along palm-lined Highway 180 for 104 km/65 miles to the seaside shipbuilding town of Champoton and the junction with Highway 261 (the alternate route to Merida). Highway 186, the inland route from Villahermosa, is more monotonous—you won't see much tropical vegetation for most of the way—but you won't have to depend on the ferries. Highway 186 turns east at Escarcega to Chetumal on the Caribbean, thus traversing the peninsula at its base. If you want to go on to Merida, take Highway 261 north from Escarcega to Champoton.

From Champoton, you drive about 64 km/40 miles to Campeche; the road alternates between straight stretches along beaches and winding stretches through hills.

Campeche—pirates and Panama hats

Campeche is the progressive, increasingly modern capital of the state of Campeche. It was the first permanent Spanish settlement on the peninsula, founded shortly after the Spanish Crown granted the area to Francisco de Montejo in 1526. A fascinating old seaport, Campeche has a wall topped by forts originally built in the 17th century as protection against pirates. The waters aren't troubled by marauders now, though, and the new section of the city has risen along the beach. You'll find a fine seashore drive, a freeform Municipal Palace, and a six-story air-conditioned bayside hotel.

Campeche is an important shrimp-fishing center. Along the waterfront south of town, you'll see craftsmen building shrimp boats—all the fittings are made by hand, using fine hardwoods from the nearby forests. Venture a little farther—about 6 km/4 miles from town—to a pier where most of the shrimping activity centers. You can wander along the pier and watch the shrimp being unloaded. North along the waterfront, you'll see thatched huts among the palms that grow to the water's edge. Here, fishers work on their boats or dry and mend nets.

The Campeche area produces some good buys for shoppers, including finely woven Panama-type hats (*jipijapa*), hammocks, and wood specialties.

You can visit the old wall and ancient forts, either on your own or with an English-speaking guide who will drive you there in a carriage with fringe on top. The Arms Museum and the Archeology Museum are both worth a visit; artifacts create a vivid picture of local history.

Visitors view *Hacienda Yaxcopoil,*
200-year-old French henequen farm.

On to Maya ruins

About 24 km/15 miles east of Campeche, Highway 180 branches off north from Highway 261 at Chencoyi. This is an interesting route to Merida, passing through Maya villages that have changed little over the centuries. At Hecelchakan, there's a museum with artifacts discovered on the island of Jaina—the site of a pre-Hispanic Maya cemetery.

To see splendid Maya ruins, continue east on Highway 261. About 14 km/9 miles past Chencoyi, an 18-km/11-mile paved turnoff to the right leads to the ruins of Edzna. This site is remarkable for its five-story structures, unusual in Maya architecture. Back on Highway 261, drive another 38 km/24 miles to Hopelchen; from here, the route

turns north to Merida. Kabah, the first major site explored by archeologists, is 72 km/54 miles away.

The curled noses of Kabah

The archeological site of Kabah is located 104 km/65 miles south of Merida. The outstanding building is the Codz Poop (Rolled Mat), the facades of which are completely covered by masks of the long-nosed rain god, Chac. Twenty years ago the upturned noses were all intact; today, many are missing — taken as souvenirs by thoughtless sightseers. A large corbeled arch at Kabah signals the beginning of the *sacbe* (white road) that once carried Maya religious processions to Uxmal, 19 km/12 miles away.

Secluded sites—Labna, Xlabpak, Sayil

To visit the three lesser-known Maya sites of Labna, Xlabpak (not on map), and Sayil, reserve a jeep and guide at Kabah. The trip lasts a full day, taking you over rough road into the towering Yucatecan bush—a thick, tangled growth of plants and trees that's neither jungle nor forest. Labna, Xlabpak, and Sayil are remarkable cities that have barely been explored; unfortunately, sufficient funds are simply not available for restoration of all Mexico's archeological sites. Highlights include the monumental arch of Labna, which once connected two groups of buildings now in ruins; the Temple of Chac in Xlabpak, a restrained design treatment of Chac's notable feature—his long nose; and the elegant three-story Palace of Sayil (partially restored). From the palace ruins, you'll get a panoramic view of the distant Campeche hills.

Uxmal—the sublimity of Maya architecture

One of the most successful architectural achievements of Maya civilization, the ancient city of Uxmal is noted for the symmetry and proportions of its buildings, constructed in the Puuc style of veneer masonry. Uxmal reached its peak in the last half of the Classic period (A.D. 600–900). From the 10th century on, it was ruled by a family of Mexican origin, and suffered a gradual decline under its foreign conquerors—as did all centers of Maya culture.

Main attractions. As you enter the site, the first structure you'll see is the oval pyramid of the Temple of the Magician. A heavy chain stretched along the almost vertical stairway aids height-wary visitors in making the trip (120 steps) to the top.

Just west of the Magician is the Quadrangle of the Nuns, a great patio flanked by long rows of chambers; the facades are richly ornamented at roof level in typical Puuc stone mosaic style. Among the many elements in the friezes are representations in stone of Maya huts identical to those of present-day Yucatan. A spectacular light-and-sound show is presented here nightly at 9 P.M.

Through an arch in the center of the building on the south side, you can see the majestic Palace of the Governor in the distance beyond the Ball Court. The main facade of the 325-foot-long palace is entirely covered with a stone frieze composed of many thousands of tiny pieces fitted together to form serpents, latticework, thrones, huts, and columns. The palace is similarly, but less lavishly, decorated on the other three sides.

On the same great platform that gives added importance to the Palace of the Governor is the elegantly simple, comparatively small, House of the Turtles — in total yet harmonious contrast.

The front of the Great Pyramid, to the southwest, has been reconstructed. This is a good spot for taking photos of the entire complex. West of the pyramid is an impressive quadrangle known as the House of the Pigeons.

Visiting the site. Uxmal, 80 km/50 miles from Merida, is easily reached by car or bus, or by organized tours that often include Chichen Itza. If you wish to spend some time exploring the Uxmal ruins, stay in one of the several hotels nearby (see the "Essentials" section on page 158). Reservations are advisable, especially in the winter season.

Merida to the Caribbean

From Uxmal, it's only an hour's drive on Highway 261 to Merida. You'll pass through Muna, where Highway 184 takes off southeast to Chetumal, capital of Quintana Roo. At Uman, 18 km/11 miles south of Merida, Highways 180 and 261 merge to enter the city from the south, passing the airport.

Merida—Yucatan's capital city

Charming, hospitable Merida is a blend of large old colonial buildings downtown, modern homes on the outskirts, and thatched Indian huts on the streets in between. The town has a large, open market, well-kept parks and boulevards, good hotels, and excellent restaurants.

Merida was founded in 1542 on the site of the Maya city of T'Ho, but its Spanish heritage is predominant. The Yucatan was long isolated from the rest of Mexico and, for a few years, even politically independent; during its isolation, it cultivated European markets and manners instead of Mexican ones. Now the largest city on the peninsula and linked by highway, rail, and air to central Mexico, Merida plays a vital role as the processing and distribution center for local products.

The people. Merida's people are friendly and very cordial to foreigners. They consider themselves Yucatecans, distinct and apart from Mexicans. Often you'll see faces that closely resemble those on the stone carvings in Uxmal or Chichen Itza. The dress of many of the women is the huipil, a long white overblouse, embroidered at neck and hem; it extends below the knees, and may be worn with or without a lacy petticoat.

In other parts of Mexico, homes are closed and surrounded by high walls; but in Merida, doors and windows are open to the street. In the evening, people sit in chairs on their front stoops and chat with passers-by, friends and strangers alike.

Highlights. Many visitors remark on the beauty and tranquility of Merida's main plaza with its S-shaped benches. Two buildings that face on the plaza are of particular historic interest: the fortress-type cathedral and the Montejo mansion, both built in the mid-16th century by the Spanish conqueror and founder of the city, Francisco de Montejo. Notice the statues of armored soldiers standing on the heads of Indians on the mansion's beautifully carved facade. The facade is lighted at night, and is truly an incredible sight.

(Continued on page 134)

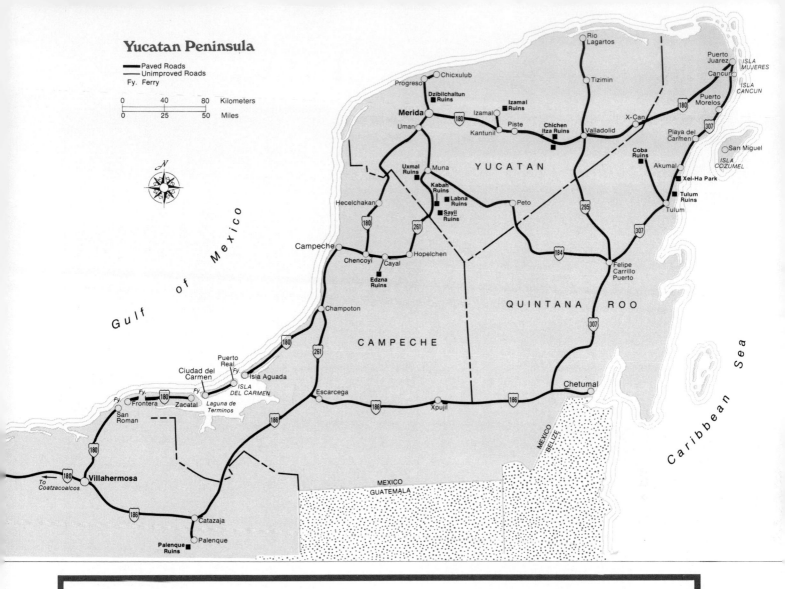

Yucatan Peninsula

Paved Roads
Unimproved Roads
Fy. Ferry

Details at a glance

How to get there

Paved highways make this area easily accessible to motorists, but it's a long, dull drive through Yucatan scrub, with great empty stretches between villages and points of interest.

By air. Merida and Cancun have jet airports and offer direct and nonstop flights to and from major U.S. and Mexican cities.

By car. The easiest and most flexible way to tour the Yucatan is to fly into a major city, rent an air-conditioned car, and explore on your own.

Tours

Package tours from Merida or Cancun stop at the major ruins of Chichen Itza, Uxmal, and Tulum; but you won't have much time at each site (see the "Essentials" section on page 158).

Accommodations

Interesting colonial hotels (many with pools) make Merida a good base for exploring the Yucatan.

Cancun has accommodations ranging from condominiums and villas to deluxe hotels; more are on the way. Cozumel offers a variety of glamorous resorts, some surprisingly inexpensive. You'll also find simple hotels in other cities and some comfortable accommodations at Uxmal and Chichen Itza (see the "Essentials" section on page 158).

Climate and clothes

Usually humid, weather is best from October to March, with clear sunny days and cool evenings. Expect brief tropical downpours in summer.

Dress for heat, bring your bathing suit for the beautiful water, and wear comfortable clothes and rubber soled shoes for climbing around ruins.

Chichen Itza's *immense ball court, once scene of Maya games, retains side wall hoop.*

...Continued from page 132

The newly restored Palacio Canton, former home of governors, now houses the Archeological Museum within its marble-floored and chandeliered interior.

The city. It's easy to find your way around Merida on foot, though it is somewhat tricky to drive within the city. As in most older Mexican towns, streets are one way and very narrow. All the streets running north to south are even-numbered; those running east to west are odd-numbered. You can tour all of Merida for a few pesos in a little horse-drawn cab. On the Paseo Montejo you'll pass buildings painted in pastel blues, yellows, and pinks — some Victorian or French in style. Many of the large mansions were formerly townhouses of henequen barons.

Food. Don't miss savoring the delicious food of Yucatan; it's a cuisine different from any other in Mexico. *Cochinita pibil* (*pib* means "barbecue pit" in Maya) is pork baked in banana leaves and flavored with *achiote* (red seeds ground into a paste whose flavor combines beautifully with meat and fish). Another specialty is *queso relleno* — an Edam cheese hollowed out and stuffed with ground meat, raisins, nuts, and spices.

Shopping. Most shops are found on Calle 57 between Calles 60 and 68. You'll find a variety of henequen items, ranging from bags to mats to hammocks. Straw hats are popular buys, as are tortoise shell and inlaid coral jewelry.

The Municipal Market, 4 blocks southeast of the plaza, offers a good range of authentic articles; nearby Garcia Rejon Market sells a variety of handicrafts.

Entertainment. The Panamericana Hotel's evening dinner show features Yucatecan folkloric dancing. Thursday evenings at 9, you can enjoy a Serenata Yucateca (singing, dancing, music show) at Santa Lucia Park, Calle 60 at Calle 55. If you prefer popular music, join the young people at Heroes Park on Wednesdays at 8 P.M.

Dzibilchaltun — ancient metropolis

North of Merida on the highway to Progreso is a 9-km/6-mile paved turnoff to the right leading to the ruins of Dzibilchaltun, an ancient ceremonial center. The largest known Maya site, it covers almost 52 square km/20 square miles. For the most part the ruins are unrestored, though a major portion of the central area has been cleared. Within this clearing is a *cenote,* a large, deep, natural well into which offerings (including some human victims) were thrown to the water gods, and from which a great many artifacts have been recovered.

Also in the cleared section is the site's most interesting structure, the Temple of the Seven Dolls, where archeologists discovered an offering of seven rubber dolls during excavation. At the entrance to the site is a small but well-organized museum that, for orientation's sake, should be the first stop on your tour.

Progreso—Yucatan's progressive port

Progreso, Yucatan's most important seaport for the fishing and henequen industries, is located on the gulf—about 35 km/22 miles north of Merida. Nearby are Yucalpeten, a huge fish packing plant, and Cordemex, an equally large henequen-processing factory; both are open to visitors. Freighters tie up in deep water at the end of a mile-long concrete pier. To watch the activity, you can drive out to the end of the pier on a two-lane roadway, which is flanked by a railroad track on one side and a pedestrian walkway on the other.

Progreso is also a seaside resort area; both mansions and humble cottages line the beach for 5 km/3 miles to the next resort village of Chicxulub. The area comes alive in July and August, when oppressive heat sends Merida residents scurrying to the cool breezes and gentle surf of Progreso's seashore.

Izamal—Maya holy city

Izamal, the ancient holy city of the Maya, lies 72 km/45 miles east of Merida. To get there, take the turnoff from Highway 180 en route to Puerto Juarez. The ruins, on the outskirts of present-day Izamal, are largely overgrown with vegetation and difficult to see. In the late 1500s, a Franciscan church-monastery was erected over some of the ruined buildings; the monastery and a large central pyramid are now being excavated.

Modern Izamal is a charming town; horse-drawn carriages and the tranquil plaza contribute to the restful, unhurried atmosphere.

Chichen Itza—castles, caves, and cenotes

About 56 km/35 miles beyond Izamal (120 km/75 miles from Merida) on Highway 180, just past the village of Piste, are the ruins of Chichen Itza — the most visited of all Maya cities unearthed to date in the Yucatan.

According to archeologists' theories, construction began in the city about A.D. 450. It was invaded by the Itza early in the 10th century and occupied late in that same century by the Toltecs, who superimposed upon it their architecture and culture.

Acres of henequen *bask in sun prior to baling.*

Toltec ruins. North of the highway is the extensively restored group of structures preferred by sightseers. These buildings reflect the influence of the Toltecs, who occupied the city some time after the close of the Maya Classic period in A.D. 900. The most imposing building is called El Castillo (the castle), and is located in the Great Plaza. It's a pyramid some 75 feet high; each side of its square base is approximately 180 feet long. At certain hours (check at the office or in the official guidebook) you can climb steep stairs up and into an inner temple. Inside is a remarkable spotted stone jaguar, with eyes of a green stone; it may have served as a high priest's throne.

Also on the north side of Chichen Itza are the ruins of a huge ball court and many other buildings; one, the Temple of the Warriors, also has an inner structure that may be visited during certain hours. Like the castle's inner building, this interior structure was the original temple; the pyramid you see today was built over it. Chichen Itza has its cenote, too, into which offerings were thrown to appease the rain god. In 1885 Edward Thompson, then American Consul to Yucatan, bought the area for $75 and spent years exploring the depths of the cenote. Another, more scientific exploration was made in 1968. Many of the objects that have been found—of jade, bone, shell, copper, and gold—were brought from distant areas, indicating that pilgrims came to Chichen Itza from far-flung Maya communities to make offerings at the sacred cenote.

The ruins on the north side of the highway can be covered in 2 to 3 hours, but climbing the steps up the castle and pyramids is hot work and should not be rushed.

(Continued on next page)

Central and Old Chichen ruins. On the south side of the highway are older ruins, less impressive but equally interesting, spread out over a larger area reached by paths cut through the underbrush. El Caracol (the conch) is perhaps the predominant structure. Cylindrical in shape, it may have served as an observatory. El Caracol, the Nunnery complex, the church, and most of the other buildings are pure Maya in style.

Visiting the site. Several hotels are near the archeological zone — one of them built around the manor house of the 400-year-old Hacienda Chichen. Reservations are advisable — especially between Christmas and Easter week, when you'll be likely to find the best weather.

You should take at least 2 days — preferably even longer—to explore all the ruins in the area thoroughly. You can take in the most significant structures in a day. Guides and cars may be secured in Merida; package tours are also available. The archeological zone is open daily.

Cave of Balancanche. The Cave of Balancanche, 5 km/3 miles east of Chichen Itza, is open every day at certain hours. The cave is a labyrinth of passages and chambers containing Maya-Toltec artifacts, including ceremonial vases, jars, and grinding stones. A cenote filled with small, blind fish is located at the end of one passageway.

The cave was discovered by chance 15 years ago when a Yucatecan tourist guide removed some stones piled one upon another near the entrance. Evidently used as a ceremonial center, the cave contains the largest collection of Maya-Toltec ceramics found to date.

Valladolid—town built around a cenote

About 40 km/25 miles east of Chichen Itza on Highway 180 enroute to Puerto Juarez is the town of Valladolid, one of Yucatan's larger cities. Near the center of town, an attractive park surrounds a large cenote; a good restaurant is located on its rim. At one time the city's water supply was taken from this cenote. As you drive into town on the main highway, the cenote is a few blocks to your left.

An unusual event takes place in Valladolid during the latter part of January. Known as *Las Candelarias,* the festival features regional folk dances and colorful parades.

If you're driving on to Puerto Juarez, be sure to fill up with gas and buy any necessary supplies; Valladolid is the last town before you reach the coast where you can be sure of finding them.

Along the East Coast

On the highway to Puerto Juarez the vegetation changes from thick bush to jungle—not dense, humid jungle, but the South Sea islands variety, fringing the gleaming white Caribbean beaches. This is the location of Mexico's first computer-planned resort.

Isla Mujeres—island of women

The embarkation point for the boat trip to Isla Mujeres is just north of Puerto Juarez. There's also daily air service from Merida and Cozumel to this small, remote island, and a 20-minute jetfoil from Cancun, but the boat ride shouldn't be missed. It's a photographic bonanza. The 19-km/12-mile round trip by boat can be made in a day if you get to Puerto Juarez early enough; but since the number of hotels on the island is growing, you may want to stay overnight and revel in the tranquility and solitude. Thatch-roofed huts, few cars, and the whisper of palms mingle to create a carefree mañana attitude.

Until recently, Isla Mujeres hadn't changed much since its discovery in 1517. The Conquerors named it—not for the women on the island, as legend would have us believe (*mujeres* is Spanish for women), but rather for the many small terra cotta figurines of women they found among the island's Maya ruins.

Isla Mujeres is only 11 km/7 miles long and less than a mile wide. A popular boating excursion includes a look at a crumbling Maya ruin, a stop for swimming or snorkeling, and a seafood lunch. Sailing, fishing, and water-skiing are other activities you can indulge in — that is, if you can't tolerate the quietude that's really the island's greatest asset.

Rainbow-hued tropical fish flash in the remarkably clear turquoise water along the jetties on the leeward side of the island. You'll want to swim, fish, or skin dive here. On the windward side, the surf pounds the shore.

Cancun—a luxury resort

Just south of Puerto Juarez, a coast-hugging road leads to the posh Mexican resort development called Cancun. Crystal-clear seas and spectacular offshore coral reefs are a few of Cancun's assets. Other attractions include luxury hotels, a golf course, a marina, restaurants, and shops. Once a small village of just 120 inhabitants, Cancun is now considered one of Mexico's most beautiful resort areas; its growth (the population now stands at almost 60,000) reflects its popularity.

The sporting life. Cancun's configuration makes it ideal for every type of water sport. Less than a mile wide and 14 km/9 miles long, the resort is bounded to the east by the Caribbean, and on the mainland side by Nichupte Lagoon (a body of water covering 77 square km/30 square miles). Cancun's southern tip, famous for its beautiful coral outcropping, is popular with scuba divers. The crystalline turquoise water is also ideal for skin diving, snorkeling, swimming, water-skiing, and wind surfing; or you can go sailing, power boating, or fishing.

The island's causeway bisects the Pok-ta-Pok Golf Club; the course here was designed by Robert Trent Jones. At the club and at island hotels, tennis buffs will find lighted courts. A 9 km/6 mile moped path, bordered by flowering plants and palms, parallels the north beach; you can rent mopeds at most hotels.

Inside entertainment. Good shopping can be found at hotel stores, in the Convention Center Mall, and in the El Parian and Place Vendome shopping centers. Regional handicrafts can also be purchased at the Ki-Huic Market in Cancun City.

During the winter season you can enjoy the Ballet Folklorico at the Convention Center four nights a week or watch the exciting performances of the famous Flying Pole Dancers at the El Presidente Hotel. Many other hotels offer discos.

Akumal and Xel-Ha—tropical paradise

A 45-minute trip south of Cancun brings you to a gorgeous stretch of beach perfect for snorkeling, deep sea fishing, or just plain relaxing. Once a Maya center, it's now Club Akumal Caribe, a private resort on a beautiful sand area backed by waving palms.

To the south lies Xel-Ha lagoon, a national park for divers and snorkelers. For a small fee, you can rent a mask, snorkel, and fins—and plunge into another world. You'll see colorful tropical fish and interesting coral outcroppings in the clear water. A cave within one coral reef contains an altar stone used long ago as a Maya shrine.

Tulum—a coastal ruin

If you haven't had time to explore Chichen Itza or Uxmal, a trip to Tulum, 27 km/17 miles south of Akumal, will be rewarding. Tulum's dominant structure, El Castillo, perches atop a 40-foot cliff above the Caribbean. This is a different type of Maya ruin. Once one of the fortress cities that were strung along the Caribbean coast, Tulum was among the last bulwarks of the Maya culture, constructed and in use from the 11th century until just before the Spanish Conquest. Long stretches of the wall that once enclosed Tulum on its three land sides are still standing.

The center itself was laid out on an urban plan closely resembling that of most U.S. cities — straight streets bordered by buildings, rather than the groupings of buildings around plazas favored in most Maya cities. In the Temple of Frescoes, traces of mural paintings still remain. The site is only partially excavated; an hour is enough time to explore.

Coba

From the village of Tulum, a paved road heads north 40 km/25 miles to the ruins of Coba. This immense site is now being explored jointly by Mexican archeologists and the

The green gold of Yucatan

Yucatan's wealth is stored in its green gold— henequen. All over the peninsula, for as far as the eye can see, vast expanses of the henequen-producing agave plant (agave fourcroydes) form a gray green, prickly carpet. Razor-sharp, sword-like leaves, similar in appearance to those of a yucca, grow from the plant's core. The climate of the Yucatan peninsula provides ideal conditions for cultivation: adequate rainfall and porous limestone soil.

Henequen is also known as sisal or hemp. The name "sisal" comes from a port near Merida that was once the leading port of the peninsula, shipping henequen to all parts of the world. The henequen fibers are made into twine, rope, hammocks, table mats, sandals, and a variety of other woven articles.

The henequen industry got its greatest economic boost in the early 1900s, when the invention of the self-binding harvester created a need for twine and rope to tie bales of cotton, wheat, and other harvested crops on farms. Synthetic substitutes for henequen were discovered and manufactured by the mid-1900s, damaging Yucatan's

importance as the world's foremost fiber producer. Despite competition and the industry's gradual decline, henequen still reigns as the most important industry on the Yucatan peninsula.

Henequen harvesting and processing is simple, but meticulously carried out. Large haciendas cultivate thousands of agave plants in rows about 5 feet apart. The plant is left alone to grow for 6 or 7 years before being harvested for its fiber. The old, outer leaves are cut off the plant with machetes and taken to the defibering plant, often transported the traditional way—in a small wooden cart pulled by donkeys along narrow-gauge railroad tracks.

The cut plants continue to produce spiky leaves that are harvested every year for another 10 to 15 years. The entire field is then cut and burned over.

At the defibering plant (desfibradora), the leaves are crushed and the fiber extracted by a large, noisy machine. The henequen is then dried in the sun and baled for shipment. In some plants, henequen is woven into rugs or made into sacks or twine.

With minimum splash *and maximum wing-spread, band of flamingos takes to the sky near Gulf of Mexico.*

U.S. National Geographic Society. Coba, founded around A.D. 600, was apparently a very important Maya center; it's at the hub of a network of *sacbes*—those wide, level Maya thoroughfares that led traders and pilgrims from town to town. From Coba, the sacbes stretched west to Chichen Itza, south to Tulum, and north and east to other Maya centers. Five lakes found among the ruins explain Coba's Maya meaning, "water agitated by wind."

Chetumal

South of Tulum, the scenery along Highway 307 takes on a new look: the road passes through humid, hardwood jungle, wending its way 192 km/120 miles to Chetumal, capital of Quintana Roo. This port town has a large, busy harbor that ships peninsula products such as chicle, tobacco, bananas, and precious hardwoods.

If shopping is your idea of good sport, you've come to the right place—Chetumal is a free port, so all imports are low priced. You'll find European and American wares as well as Mexican handicrafts.

Though Chetumal is a frequent target of hurricanes, its modern storm warning systems and extrasturdy building construction allow the city to carry on its busy economic life almost unaffected by the weather. Modest accommodations and good restaurants are available (see the "Essentials" section, page 158).

West of Chetumal on Highway 186, another Maya ruin (Kojunlich) is being restored. Though few of the buildings have been uncovered, it appears that this 4th century city contained at least 200 structures. Several buildings around the plaza have been excavated, along with a ball court and an intriguing temple—called Temple of the Masks for the eight red masks decorating the facade.

East of this Maya center is Laguna de Bacalar (also called Lagoon of Seven Colors); the water's color varies from deep blue to pale green. Nearby is the deep Cenote de Azul (Blue Well).

For those who wish to learn more about Yucatan, the best travel book ever written about the area is still John L. Stephens's *Incidents of Travel in the Yucatan*. First published in 1841, the book has recently been reissued in paperback.

Cancun's hotels *line Caribbean coastline. Computer-planned resort features crystalline turquoise waters, talcum powder-soft sand.*

Wide river *at Chetumal divides Mexico and Belize.*

Know Before You Go

Facts at Your Fingertips

Planning a trip is not only part of the fun — it's essential for a smooth stay. Fortunately, going to Mexico, North America's nearest "foreign" country, is extremely easy. Because it's close, transportation is frequent and convenient—and you don't need a visa.

The paperwork

The basic documents that you should have handy at all times are a tourist card and proof of citizenship (see below). If you're planning to take a car, trailer, camper, boat, or any other vehicle into Mexico, you'll have to get the necessary permits, licenses, and insurance before going. Arrange for any vaccinations and medications well ahead of time.

Tourist cards

All U.S. citizens visiting Mexico for less than 180 days must have tourist cards. These cards are available at Mexican consulates, Mexican government tourist offices, some auto clubs and Mexican insurance agencies, offices of airlines, cruise ships, and bus companies serving Mexico, and travel agents.

When you apply for your tourist card, be sure to have with you your proof of citizenship: a birth certificate, passport, notarized affidavit, or voter's registration slip. Naturalized citizens must carry naturalization papers or a U.S. passport. Canadian citizens are also required to submit a birth certificate, passport, or naturalization papers when applying for a tourist card.

Single-entry tourist cards are free of charge and valid for 6 months. Multiple-entry permits are also free, but for these you must provide three passport-type photographs. Multiple-entry permits enable you to enter Mexico more than one time during the card's 6-month validity.

If you're staying anywhere north of Maneadero (a few miles south of Ensenada) for less than 72 hours, you needn't have any formal travel documentation except for some kind of personal identification and proof of citizenship. A minor traveling alone, accompanied by only one parent, or with someone other than a parent, must present written, notarized authorization from parents or guardian. Children under 15 years of age may be included on a parent's single-entry card.

Aliens residing in the United States are subject to special requirements. They should contact their nearest Mexican consulate well in advance of departure date.

Vaccinations

A smallpox vaccination certificate is no longer necessary when you're entering Mexico from the United States — or when you're reentering the U.S. from Mexico, as long as you traveled only within Mexico. If you're entering Mexico from Central or South America, you must have evidence of a smallpox vaccination given within the last 3 years.

Though not required by either Mexican or United States quarantine officers, antityphoid injections may be a wise precaution, particularly if you plan to spend much time in tropical areas or remote sections of the country. Consult your physician for other immunizations.

Automobile papers

Automobile permits, required for entry into Mexico, are good for 6 months and may be obtained free of charge from the customs office at the border. Permits are not required for visits to Mexican border towns for periods of less than 72 hours (this includes Ensenada in Baja California and Puerto Penasco in Sonora). In Baja California only, you may use your vehicle for the length of time that your tourist card is valid without an automobile permit. You must, however, obtain a permit if you plan to take a ferry to the mainland from Baja.

To obtain an automobile permit, you'll need proof of ownership: a license registration, a "pink slip" or legal title, or a notarized bill of sale. If you don't own the car, you'll need a notarized statement from the legal owner giving you authority to drive the car into Mexico. You should carry the ownership papers with you at all times. If the vehicle is rented or leased, you'll be asked to produce the notarized statement from the owner or a copy of the formal rental or lease agreement.

Your car must return with you; it cannot be sold in Mexico. If it's impossible to return your car to the U.S. before the permit expires, a bond must be posted with the Mexican customs department to cover duties.

Your valid U.S. driver's license is also valid in Mexico, but your U.S. automobile insurance is not. Mexican insur-ance company agents at the border issue short-term policies at reasonable daily rates that are standard on either side of the border.

Automobile accidents in Mexico are handled from a criminal rather than a civil standpoint. This means that drivers are liable to jail sentences in cases where fatal injury results, and even in minor accidents drivers may be held pending proof of innocence. Because of this arrangement, it's very important that you take out Mexican insurance.

It is customary

Clothing and other personal items within reason may be taken into Mexico duty free. Each adult tourist may take into Mexico one kilogram of tobacco (about two cartons of cigarettes or one box of cigars). Three bottles of wine or liquor and up to 500 grams of perfume may be taken into the country. Going through at the Mexico City airport doesn't take long; you'll be on your way after just a few brief questions.

When you return to the U.S., your bags will be inspected at the point of entry in compliance with customs regulations. To expedite the inspection and to avoid having anything confiscated by the customs officials, make sure you know the limits and restrictions on objects you can take out of the country.

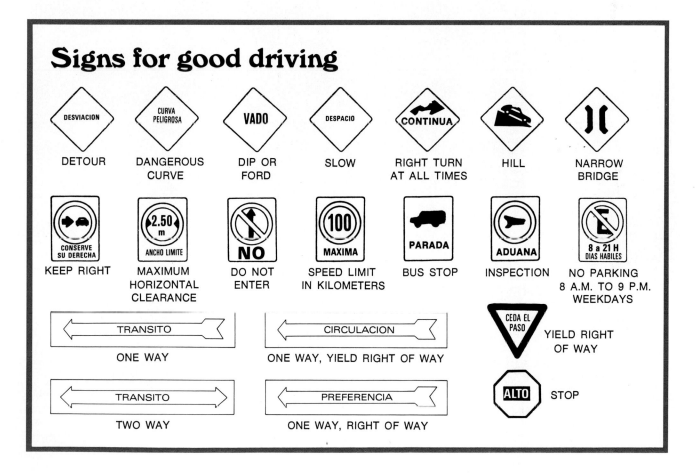

Signs for good driving

DETOUR — DANGEROUS CURVE — DIP OR FORD — SLOW — RIGHT TURN AT ALL TIMES — HILL — NARROW BRIDGE

KEEP RIGHT — MAXIMUM HORIZONTAL CLEARANCE — DO NOT ENTER — SPEED LIMIT IN KILOMETERS — BUS STOP — INSPECTION — NO PARKING 8 A.M. TO 9 P.M. WEEKDAYS

ONE WAY — ONE WAY, YIELD RIGHT OF WAY — YIELD RIGHT OF WAY

TWO WAY — ONE WAY, RIGHT OF WAY — STOP

Tiny Tarascan girl *weaves bright sashes using a belt loom.*

Basic baggage

Residents of the United States returning from Mexico are permitted to bring back up to $400 worth (retail value; be sure to keep your sales slips) of articles duty free within any 30-day period. There is no time restriction for tourists returning through an Arizona, California, New Mexico, or Texas port; however, at least a 48-hour stay in Mexico is required at all other ports to obtain the exemption.

Know Before You Go, a booklet published by U.S. Customs, is available at local offices for a slight charge. The list of items which you cannot bring back to the U.S. from Mexico includes most fruits and vegetables, plants, livestock, poultry, meats, uncured hides, Cuban imports, gold coins, medals (except special awards), bullion, lottery tickets, Decca and Columbia records, and articles made from animals on the endangered species list.

If you are at least 21 years old and return to the United States from Mexico by private automobile, plane, or boat, you may bring in one quart of liquor duty free. For liquor in excess of one quart, you must pay federal tax plus duty. Since customs regulations and taxes are subject to change, be sure to read up-to-date state regulations.

Canadian citizens can bring back duty-free items totaling $250 per year: $150 for a one-time return, plus two quarterly returns of $50 each. They may bring back one bottle of liquor and one carton of cigarettes. Purchases shipped to homes are not included in the exemption.

Driving *in Mexico allows for flexible scheduling, requires some prior planning.*

Taking your pet?

Dogs and other pets may be taken into Mexico (very few hotels will allow them, but most motels will), provided you present a veterinarian's certificate stating that they are in good health. Rodent poison is often placed in seaport rooms; check carefully before letting pets roam. You'll also need a certificate, issued by a veterinarian and visaed by a Mexican Consul, certifying that the animal has been inoculated for rabies within the last 6 months. If your pet is out of the U.S. for more than 30 days, you'll need inoculation certificates to reenter the U.S. Dogs can be left at kennels on the border in Texas, California, and Arizona.

Guns and fishing tackle

Special restrictions apply to firearms taken into the country. Check with your nearest Mexican Consulate regarding gun permits and regulations.

Any reasonable amount of fishing tackle may be brought into Mexico duty free. You may pick up fishing licenses at the border or from local fish and game wardens. A fishing license is good in any state in Mexico.

For the photographer

Each tourist is permitted one still camera and one movie camera (8mm or Super-8mm), with eight rolls of film for each. For anything more sophisticated, you must obtain a permit.

(Continued on next page)

Sleek cruise ships *ply east and west coasts, making shore stops at major resort cities.*

. . . Continued from page 143

Don't forget to register foreign-made cameras at your point of departure, so that you can prove your camera wasn't purchased in Mexico.

Film is available in most cities. Photographic supply stores in Mexico can process black-and-white film, and Eastman Kodak has color processing plants in Mexico City and Guadalajara. It's best, though, to get your film developed in the United States.

When photographing throughout Mexico, remember that you're a guest. Respect the Mexicans' privacy; they are a proud and sensitive people. Professional photographers are not allowed to shoot in archeological zones or museums, or at colonial monuments, without special permission from the National Institute of Anthropology in Mexico City.

Gift shipping

If you intend to have purchases sent home for you, choose well-established shops that enjoy a good reputation among tourists. Factories and shops that sell frequently to tourists are usually very experienced at arranging for merchandise shipment and will handle all details for you.

Merchandise shipped from Mexico to your home cannot be included as part of the $400 exemption. Any article that you ship will be taxed on its appraised value at the applicable rate of duty.

You may send gifts valued at less than $25 to people in the United States without including them on your declaration, provided the addressee does not receive packages totaling more than the $25 limit in a single day. The word "gift" and the retail value of the contents must be written clearly on the outside of the package. Perfumes, alcoholic beverages, and tobacco may not be sent as gifts.

How to get there— and back

Whether you enjoy flying, driving, sailing, or taking a train, choosing a means of transportation for your trip to Mexico can be the most crucial decision in planning of your trip. When you're deciding, keep in mind the length of your stay; distance to be covered; budget allowance for transportation; number of people in your party; and goals or purpose of your trip. Weigh these considerations carefully; then make a choice that lets you get the most out of where you are, and frees you from worry about how you're going to reach your next destination.

Each chapter contains a special feature on ways to get to that specific area — by car, plane, or other means of transportation.

Driving in Mexico

In general, the main highways are good and well marked. Some driving precautions, though, should be observed.

Highways are often unfenced, and animals are apt to wander onto the road. For this reason, driving at night is not recommended. As one popular Mexico guidebook says: "Burros don't wear taillights."

Only one brand of gasoline is sold in Mexico—Pemex, which gets its name from the words "Petroleos Mexicanos," the government-owned oil company. There are two grades of this gasoline: Pemex Extra and Pemex Nova. Pemex Nova (in blue pumps) has the lower octane rating. Pemex Extra (in the silver pumps) is lead free, has a higher octane rating, and is recommended for high-compression engines. The red tanks contain diesel fuel. Service stations sell Pemex oils, lubricants, and additives. U.S. brands of oil are sometimes obtainable in independent repair shops and stores. (Your U.S. oil company credit card will not be good in Mexico, so be prepared to pay in pesos; traveler's checks are usually not accepted.

Gasoline is sold in *litros* (liters). One liter equals about one quart. Consequently, if you order *diez*, you will get about 10 quarts instead of the 10 gallons you would get in the United States. Forty liters equals about 10 gallons.

Camping and trailering—for the adventurous

Attitudes about camping in Mexico are sharply divided. Some travelers recommend camping as the only way to get away from the tourist crowds, to mingle with the people of Mexico, and to explore some out-of-the-way places. Others, though experienced campers north of the border, wouldn't attempt to camp in Mexico.

Members of the first group of tourists—avid campers —are usually adaptable souls willing to adjust their normal camping routines to meet the special health problems of food and water in Mexico.

The second group — the doubters and disclaimers — sometimes tends to think of Mexico as a land of roadside bandits. But more often, these tourists are simply people who decide that camping loses its appeal when they must cope with the health precautions and campground improvisations necessary in Mexico.

Beaches can serve as primitive campsites if you can find a suitable access road; all beaches in Mexico are public. Camping or RV facilities are extremely primitive at the *presas* (dams) and *lagos* (lakes), but you can use them for overnight campsites. When trailering, go with a caravan; it's not wise for a single car or camper to park overnight along highways or to stop at length in a lonely spot.

The American Automobile Association lists recommended trailer parks in its guidebook to Mexico (available free to members). Another excellent source of information on Mexican highways, accommodations, and trailer parks is the series of bulletins and road logs published by Sanborn's Mexican Insurance Service, McAllen, Texas 78501. The Mexican Trailer Park Association also publishes a directory. Send $3 to ANAPARM, A.C., Zacatecas 229-411, Mexico 7, D.F. The directory also offers information on renting and servicing RVs.

(Continued on page 146)

Fiestas—Mexico's colorful celebrations

Fireworks, snapping fingers and swirling skirts, the aroma of cooking food, music and dancing—it's fiesta time in Mexico! Just about any event, happy or sad, becomes an excuse for a celebration. So many events crowd the calendar that the Mexican tourist council's recently published book *Fiestas in Mexico* required nearly 200 pages.

Below is a list of the more popular events to enjoy during your visit to this festive country.

January 1: New Year's Day celebrations much like those in the U.S. A carnival-like atmosphere with games, events, and fireworks throughout Mexico.

January 6: Three Kings Day (Santos Reyes). Throughout Mexico children set out shoes to be filled with gifts.

January 17: San Antonio Abad and Blessing of the Animals. All over Mexico household pets and barnyard animals are taken to the churches for priestly blessings.

February 2: Dia de la Candelaria (Feast of the Candles). A colorful celebration with dances, bullfights, and processions along decorated streets.

February 5: This national holiday commemorates Mexico's present government, the Constitutions of 1857 and 1917.

March 21: Birthday of Benito Juarez, the "Abraham Lincoln of Mexico."

March–April (Holy Week): Variable date. An especially intense and passionate religious celebration observed throughout Mexico; particularly inspiring in Taxco, Patzcuaro, and San Cristobal Las Casas.

On Saturday before Easter, papier-mâché figures representing Judas are burned. This holiday is referred to as Judas Day.

April 15–May 5: Feria de San Marcos (Fair of St. Mark). One of the most important festivals in Mexico features native dances and bullfights.

May 1: Mexico's Labor Day is celebrated with parades, dances, and civic exercises.

May 5: Cinco de Mayo celebrates liberation from the French.

May–June: Corpus Christi Day. Variable date. In Mexico City, children and babies are dressed in native costumes and taken to the cathedral to be blessed.

July 7–15: Festival of St. Fermin. Also known as the Festival of Lights because offerings of candles are placed in and around the church.

July 15–31: In honor of Our Lady of Carmen. A festive celebration with fireworks and bullfights.

September 6–9: Festival of Our Lady of the Remedies. Native dances are featured in the atrium atop the largest pyramid in the world, located in Cholula.

September 16: Independence Day. Begins the night of September 15 when the "grito"—Father Hildalgo's original cry for independence—is shouted by public officials. Impressive celebrations are held at the Zocalo (plaza) in Mexico City and in Dolores Hidalgo.

September 30: Festival in Morelos commemorates birth of Mexican Independence hero Jose Maria Morelos and the lifting of the siege of Cuautla.

October 4: Day of St. Francis brings particularly good celebrations to Pachuca, Uruapan, and Puebla.

October 12: Columbus Day in Mexico. A national holiday commemorating Mexico's discovery by Christopher Columbus.

November 1–2: All Souls' Day and Day of the Dead. All-night candlelit vigils at cemeteries. (See page 59.)

November 20: Anniversary of the Mexican Revolution of 1910.

December 12: Dia de Guadalupe (Day of Our Lady of Guadalupe). Celebrations of Mexico's patroness saint take place throughout Mexico.

December 16–25: Christmas Season. Especially colorful and festive time of year with celebrations all over Mexico.

December 28: All Fools' Day. Like April Fools' Day in U.S.

...Continued from page 144

Check with your insurance broker to find out just how well your U.S. automobile policy protects your trailer. Some companies include trailer protection with the policy for the automobile, at least to the extent of physical damage to the trailer itself, others require a separate policy for the trailer.

When pulling a trailer, stay on the main highways. Unusually high centers, sharp curves, and narrow bridges are sometimes encountered on secondary roads. If you plan to make a side trip to a small town that interests you, check first with local gas station attendants or other tourists with trailers; find out if the road is suitable for travel with a trailer and if you can pull one into the town. Many small towns in Mexico have steep, narrow streets through which it would be difficult to pull a trailer.

Bus touring—an insight to the offbeat

If you're young and/or hardy, traveling throughout Mexico by bus can be a great way to see the Mexican countryside and offbeat villages, as well as the big population centers and favorite tourist destinations.

Mexico City can be reached inexpensively and comfortably by bus from border cities such as Tijuana, Nogales, El Paso, Eagle Pass, Laredo, and Brownsville. The best bus lines between these points and the capital compare favorably in equipment, safety, and speed with bus lines operating north of the border. Fares are low, and you won't need to pay extra government taxes.

Take only first-class or deluxe buses. Fares are higher, but so is your level of comfort. Reserved seats (standard or first-class buses) are of the reclining type and well upholstered.

Package tours, which include all arrangements, are offered by Greyhound and Continental Trailways, as well as by some excellent smaller operators. Tours will take you anywhere from the dry deserts of Chihuahua (where you can visit Pancho Villa's home) to the high mountains in the interior to the colorful resorts down the west coast. Most tours return via the west coast—inland through Sonora, then on to the border.

Drawbacks to bus travel in Mexico are the too infrequent rest stops and the inadequate rest room facilities and lunch counters at many of the smaller stops. One must be prepared to travel 4 (and sometimes more) hours without a stop on some routes. The bus traveler will always do well to follow a common Mexican practice and take along a box lunch.

To get there fast, fly

Travel by air is the fastest and easiest way to reach your destination in Mexico. Airlines fly into Mexico from all parts of the world. Even if you're going to some out-of-the-way spot, you can usually fly to an airport not too far from it and take local transportation from there, saving yourself tedious and sometimes rugged driving.

Airlines offering service to Mexico from points within the United States include Aeromexico, Air Cortez (to Baja), American, Continental, Eastern, Frontier, Mexicana, Pan American, United, and Western. These lines serve principal cities along the tourist routes. Other, smaller Mexican carriers reach spots off the tourist track. A travel agent can help you to work out the air routing that is best for you.

The two leading Mexican airlines (Aeromexico and Mexicana) also operate flights from Mexican border towns such as Tijuana, Mexicali, Juarez, Nuevo Laredo, Reynosa, and Matamoros—usually to Mexico City. These flights are less expensive than those from U.S. cities.

If you enter Mexico by private plane you will, like any other traveler, need a tourist card; and you'll be required to pass through customs and immigration inspection at the airport of entry. Take with you proof of ownership and registration of the airplane.

Your first landing in Mexico must be at a Mexican port of entry. Airports that are ports of entry are shown on U.S. Air Force World Aeronautical Charts and in the International Flights Information Manual (CAA).

Gasoline costs slightly less than it does in the United States. You may not always be able to get the kind of oil you want, so if possible take along enough to last the length of your stay.

One important caution: Remember that all of central Mexico, including Mexico City, is at a high altitude; you must have a plane that will perform adequately at altitudes of from 7,000 to 13,000 feet. Another caution: Runways are sometimes unpaved, especially in Baja California.

When you return to the United States, you must land at a U.S. port of entry for customs and immigration inspection. Notify the field of your expected time of arrival in advance. You can do this by telephoning the field from the Mexican side of the border or by calling a United States CAA communications station by radio.

Railroading in Mexico

Being gently rocked to sleep aboard a Mexican train can be a pleasurable experience, and the cost is minimal. Main lines operate with diesel engines, and offer Pullman cars on overnight runs plus dining and club cars. Even though food isn't gourmet quality, it's tasty and inexpensive. One-way fares include multiple stop-over privileges; return fare must be purchased (and Pullman reservations made) at the point from which you intend to return.

Rail tours are offered by a number of U.S. operators. Several use private Pullman cars to ensure good accommodations and food. The basic tour is along the west coast, from Mexicali or Nogales to Mazatlan, Guadalajara, Mexico City, and the Yucatan. Many tours include Copper Canyon; others go to Copper Canyon only.

Three main rail routes connect U.S. border points of entry with major interior cities. They roughly parallel the Pan American, Central, and West Coast highways.

Tequila—the spirit of Mexico

The process of making tequila can be a far lengthier one than most imbibers of the Mexican national drink realize. The magic liquid used in producing this renowned drink comes from the *agave tequilana* plant. Also known as the maguey plant, it's related to the century plant common in the southwestern United States.

How do you make tequila? It involves several time-honored steps. First, the spiky leaves of the maguey plant are cut off, leaving only the heart—called a *piña* because of its resemblance to a huge pineapple. The maguey hearts (some weighing as much as 150 pounds) are then harvested, put into trucks, and taken to the factory. Here, they're cut up and loaded into giant steam ovens, then roasted until they're soft enough to be shredded easily. After shredding, the pulp is pressed to extract the juice.

The juice is poured into large vats; sugars are added, and the mixture ferments. After 4 days, the distillation process begins; two distillations are required before the tequila is drinkable. Tequila can be ready to market within a week after the maguey hearts are harvested; but for a fine, full-bodied tequila of good quality, much more time is needed. Longer aging means better—and more expensive—tequila; the highest grade spends up to 7 years in wooden casks, achieving a mellow golden color and velvety texture.

The town of Tequila, about 56 km/35 miles northwest of Guadalajara, is the center of the tequila industry and the best place to see Mexico's national drink in the making.

Tequila was founded in 1530 by a Spanish captain, Cristobal de Onate. In 1873 Don Cenobio Sauza founded the tequila industry, using mules to drag the stones that crushed the agave hearts. Today the Sauza family and several other large growers are producing many millions of liters a year for sale to more than 40 countries.

Tours are available if you wish to see the various steps involved in the tequila-making process. To tour the Sauza distillery, make reservations at the Sauza bottling plant at 3273 Avenida Vallarta in Guadalajara. Even if you don't have reservations, you can often join morning tours of the distillery (Calle Nuñez No. 80). The Sauza family estate, located across from the distillery, is also open to visitors.

• **West coast route** from Nogales to Guadalajara includes stops at Hermosillo, Empalme (for Guaymas), Ciudad Obregon, Navojoa, Culiacan, Mazatlan, and Tepic with connections at Benjamin Hill for the Sonora-Baja California Railway from Mexicali. From Guadalajara, *El Tapatio* (fast overnight train) runs to Mexico City.

• **Central route** from Ciudad Juarez to Mexico City stops at Chihuahua, Jimenez, Torreon, Zacatecas, Aguascalientes, Leon, Irapuato, Celaya, and Queretaro.

• **Eastern route** from Nuevo Laredo to Mexico City, with through service on the *Aguila Azteca* (Aztec Eagle), stops at Monterrey, Saltillo, Vanegas, and San Luis Potosi.

There's also a fast overnight Pullman, *El Regiomontano*, between Monterrey and Mexico City.

Private yachts and public liners

More and more people are becoming intrigued with the possibilities of sailing their own craft down to Mexico. As yet, information regarding procedures and problems isn't readily available. But, by getting in touch with people who have sailed to Mexico, you probably can gather the most reliable and up-to-date information. Another source of information is the Mexican Consulate.

Several cruise lines offer schedules to Mexico from U.S. ports (see page 45). Since space is limited, you'd be wise to make reservations well in advance. For details on any of the sailings, see your travel agent.

Prepare yourself for...

To assure yourself an enjoyable experience in Mexico, you should learn something about conditions in Mexico, and about the attitudes and culture of the Mexicans.

A new climate

The climate throughout Mexico varies more according to altitude than according to season. Coastal areas and low sections of the interior are usually very warm, though there are occasional cool days in coastal areas during the winter months. At altitudes of 3,000 to 6,000 feet, the climate is temperate; the cool zone extends upward from 7,000 feet.

The rainy season in Mexico is generally from May to October. Rains usually occur late in the afternoon and don't greatly inconvenience the tourist. Though the rainy season may not be the most popular tourist season, the countryside is at its greenest during that time.

Dress in Mexico City as you would in large U.S. cities; weather is mild and bracing all year (winter months are nippy). You'll need a raincoat and boots during summer's rainy season. Bring slacks and rubber-soled shoes for archeological zones. Women should have a scarf handy for entering churches.

At the casual coastal resorts it's always warm (hot and humid during the summer). Men won't need to wear a jacket, even for evenings.

A new language

Though a knowledge of Spanish isn't essential, it does make a visit to Mexico more enjoyable. You'll naturally learn a great deal more about the country if you are able to converse with its people. You can get along surprisingly well with sign language, though, and it's almost always possible to find someone who speaks a little English. Most personnel involved in serving tourists speak good English.

Different time zones

Mexico is divided into four time zones: Pacific Standard in Baja California Norte (Daylight Savings Time from late April to late October); Mountain Standard in Baja California Sur, Sonora, and Sinaloa; Eastern Standard in the Yucatan; and Central Standard in the rest of the country.

Different health conditions

Regardless of the stories you've heard, there are no serious health hazards involved in traveling in Mexico. It's wise, though, to take certain precautions.

Most hotels throughout Mexico provide bottles of purified water in the rooms. If you're ever in doubt about the water, ask for *agua mineral* or *agua purificada*. Stick to good restaurants; don't buy from vendors along the street. Two good habits: Don't eat uncooked fruit or vegetables unless you can peel them, and avoid anything that can turn bad from improper refrigeration.

If you do run into the "turista" problem, be prepared. At the first symptoms of stomach upset, take drugs prescribed in advance by your personal physician.

Using or buying drugs illegally is a criminal offense punishable by imprisonment. If medical attention is necessary, competent physicians and surgeons are in all the large cities and towns in Mexico. In case of serious illness or other emergencies, contact the American Embassy in Mexico City or the American Consulate in any of the following Mexican cities: Ciudad Juarez, Guadalajara, Guaymas, Matamoros, Mazatlan, Merida, Mexicali, Monterrey, Hermosillo, Nuevo Laredo, Chihuahua, San Luis Potosi, and Tijuana.

Pesos, centavos, and dollars

United States traveler's checks and currency in any denomination may be taken into Mexico. Traveler's checks can be cashed in most cities, and it's advisable to carry the bulk of your money this way. Purchase most of your traveler's checks in small denominations ($10 and $20); Mexican establishments may not be able to cash checks for larger amounts. Personal checks drawn on United States banks are virtually impossible to cash, but credit cards are accepted in most parts of the country.

At 1983 press time, tourists are not required to declare the amount of money they're carrying into the country.

Upon departure, excess pesos are refunded for foreign currency (up to $250 U.S.).

After 27 years of stable currency, the Mexican peso is currently fluctuating; for latest official rates, check with local banks, money exchange firms, or Mexican tourism offices and consulates. Best exchange rates in Mexico are from local banks. Banking hours are 9 A.M. to 1:30 P.M. weekdays.

The dining & drinking scene

Mexico's best restaurants rank among the finest in the world, and the service is equally impeccable. Unless you choose to dine alone, it's wise to note the customs of the country: breakfast is at about the same time as in the U.S.; the day's main meal usually starts around 2 P.M.; in the evening, it's fashionable to dine after 9 or 10.

As a rule, dining well is less expensive in Mexico than in the U.S. However, in the capital and in some of the major resort areas, you can easily spend as much for dinner as you do at home. A 10 percent Value Added Tax (IVA) is added to restaurant, bar, and nightclub checks.

Fresh seafood, fruits, and baked goods are among the country's specialties. Freshly squeezed orange juice and fine sauces such as *mole* get rave reviews.

Locally distilled liquors (Kahlua, tequila, rum, gin, brandy, vodka, beer) are good and usually inexpensive. Wine is costly unless you drink Mexican brands. Wines from Baja California are generally the best.

Tipping tips

In hotels, restaurants, and bars, tip the same percentage as you would at home. Normally, service charges are not included in your bills.

Tipping elsewhere depends on service. You should plan to tip maids, porters, bellhops, doormen, gas station attendants, and the person who watches your parked car. You do not need to tip taxi drivers unless they give extra service. On tours, guides should receive 20 percent of the tour price.

Essentials of your trip

On the following pages we list some of the first-class and deluxe hotels in each region, provide an overview of how to get around particular cities and areas, and list some of the tours you can take to get more from your trip.

Since it's not possible to keep a book absolutely up to date in regard to hotels, we haven't attempted to list all of them in this publication. However, hotel lists may be obtained from AAA, insurance companies serving Mexico, and Mexican tourist offices. Travel agents will make suggestions and reservations for accommodations when planning a trip.

Essentials/Baja California

Accommodations

Only in Baja's larger cities or south along the Cape resort area will travelers find much choice in accommodations. En route along Mexico 1 the chain of government-owned El Presidente hotels is your best bet for an overnight stay in San Quintin, Santa Ines (Cataviña), Guerrero Negro, and San Ignacio. These hotels are also among the choices in Tijuana, Ensenada, Loreto, La Paz, and San Jose del Cabo. Most hotel chains have reservation offices in the U.S.; check with your travel agent for additional information on location, rates, and types of rooms.

Campers find sites at paradors at San Quintin, Santa Ines (Cataviña), the turn-off to Bahia de los Angeles, and San Ignacio. Other campgrounds are available at San Felipe, Guerrero Negro, Bahia de los Angeles, Mulege, Loreto, La Paz, and the Cape.

Bahia de los Angeles. Hotels: Casa Diaz (on beach), Villa Veta (trailer park adjoins).

Cabo San Lucas. Deluxe resorts include Cabo Baja, Finisterra, Hacienda, Hotel Cabo San Lucas, Las Cruces Palmilla, Solmar, and Twin Dolphin. Mar de Cortez is a modest motor inn.

Ensenada. Most hotels are motels; El Cid, Estero Beach Resort, La Pinta (government owned), San Nicolas, and TraveLodge are among the best.

La Paz. First-class hotels around town: Castel Palmira (near Pichilingue ferry terminal), El Presidente, Gran Hotel Baja (best), La Posada, Los Arcos (old favorite). Trailer parks with hookups: El Cardon, El Rey Sol, Villa Lorena.

Fishing resorts south of La Paz: Buena Vista, Las Arenas, Palmas de Cortes, Punta Colorado, Punta Pescadero. Most resorts have airstrips.

Mexicali. First-class hotels: Holiday Inn, Lucerna (attractive grounds).

San Felipe. Castel San Felipe has rooms overlooking the Gulf of California, a pool, and one tennis court. Others: El Cortez (on beach), Riviera, Villa del Mar (on bluff).

San Jose del Cabo. El Presidente is the first of the deluxe accommodations scheduled for this small town. Amenities include pools, tennis courts, and snorkeling facilities. Hotel Costa Aquamarina (under construction at press time) will offer two pools and a variety of water sports facilities. The new San Jose del Cabo Golf Course will be located near this hotel.

Getting around

Distances are great between Baja California cities. If you don't drive to Baja, your activities may be limited to one destination unless you choose to use air taxi, rental car (available from only a few larger towns), or cab. You can hail a cab in most border towns, in La Paz, and at Cape resorts. Boat rentals, available at most larger towns, are the best way to explore the islands and waters of the Gulf of California.

Border area. Taxis are plentiful in Ensenada, Mexicali, and Tijuana. You can charter a boat for sport fishing at Ensenada's marina.

Cape resorts. Resorts at Cabo San Lucas and San Jose del Cabo often make arrangements for guest transportation. Boats can be rented through your hotel or at the Cabo San Lucas airport.

La Paz. Cruising taxis are easy to find in town. From the ferry terminals, you can cross the Sea of Cortez to mainland Mexico. Small planes offer service to Loreto, Mulege, the Cape, and Guaymas; car rentals and bus transportation are available to the Cape. Fishing boats can be chartered at the harbor.

Tours

Baja California cities offer little in the way of area sightseeing; fishing is the primary reason for Baja's popularity. Ensenada tours visit the wine country and Punta Banda. Cabo San Lucas boat trips go out to the photogenic offshore rocks. From Loreto you can get a car and guide for a full-day trip to San Javier, or take a boat trip out to Isla Carmen. Whale-watching tours are the major attraction on Scammon's Lagoon at Guerrero Negro.

Many U.S. companies specialize in Baja California expeditions. Check with your travel agent for trip details.

Entertainment

Sophisticated entertainment is available only along the border; you'll find nightclubs in Tijuana, Ensenada, and Mexicali. Otherwise, Baja nightlife is usually limited to your hotel.

Essentials/West Coast

Accommodations

Accommodations along the west coast run the gamut price-wise. Listed below are hotels that fall into the deluxe and first-class categories. Air conditioning, restaurants, tennis, golf, and swimming facilities are generally included in the price. Rates tend to drop between May and October (off season), though hotel policies may differ in different areas.

Most hotel chains have reservation offices in the U.S.; check with your travel agent for additional information on location, prices, and types of rooms.

Acapulco. Acapulco's hotels get bigger, better, and more flamboyant each year. Newest of the deluxe offerings is the Acapulco Plaza (near the Acapulco Center). Two towers offering 500 suites only (no single rooms), one pool, and two restaurants were completed at press time. The main pyramid-shaped building (open this year) will make the hotel Acapulco's largest. The new Princess tower is also open, adding new pools, restaurants, and bars to the attractive complex. Also polished to perfection are Las Brisas (new pink casitas and jeeps), the two Hyatt facilities (Continental Hyatt and Hyatt Regency), and hideaway Villa Vera. Other first-class to deluxe hotels: Acapulco Malibu, Castel la Palapa, Condesa del Mar, El Presidente, Holiday Inn, Paraiso Marriott, Pierre Marques, Ritz, Romano Palace.

Guaymas. First-class to deluxe hotels: La Posada de San Carlos, Las Playitas, Playa de Cortes.

Ixtapa. First-class to deluxe hotels: Aqua Marina, Aristos Ixtapa, Camino Real, Dorado Pacifico, El Presidente, Holiday Inn, Krystal Ixtapa, Marriott, Quality Inn, Riviera del Sol, Sheraton Ixtapa.

Manzanillo. First-class to deluxe hotels: Club Santiago, La Posada, Las Hadas, Roca del Mar, Vida del Mar.

Mazatlan. First-class to deluxe hotels: Balboa Club, El Camino Real, El Cid, Hacienda Mazatlan, Holiday Inn, Oceano Palace, Playa Mazatlan, Posada de Don Pelayo.

Puerto Vallarta. First-class to deluxe hotels: Buganvilias Sheraton, Camino Real, Costa Vida, Fiesta Americana, Garza Blanca, Holiday Inn, Las Palmas, Los Tules, Posada Vallarta.

Zihuatanejo. First-class to deluxe hotels: Catalina, Villa del Sol, Sotavento.

Getting around

Rental car companies have offices throughout the west coast, at airports, in towns, and at assorted hotels.

If you're hiring a car or taxi, agree on the price beforehand. Public transportation is worth investigating—it can be an efficient and inexpensive way to travel.

Acapulco. Yachts are popular for cruising Acapulco Bay; several are available daily, each with a different theme. Some hotels include a car or jeep with the room, and inexpensive green buses run along the waterfront.

Guaymas. Ferry service departs for Santa Rosalia three times weekly; check schedules upon arrival. Boats, ranging from small craft to large cruisers, can be rented by the hour or day. A train and buses are available for travel to nearby San Carlos.

Ixtapa/Zihuatanejo. Boats are available for rent; shop around for the best price. Water taxis provide transportation from pier to beaches.

Mazatlan. To get around the beaches, you can hire a *pulmonia* (an open-air three-passenger taxi). Ferry service departs for La Paz; check schedules upon arrival. Limousines and economy buses transport visitors from the airport to town; public buses offer service to beach hotels from other parts of town.

Fishing boats can be chartered; be sure to shop around for the best price.

Puerto Vallarta. Yachts are a popular means of transportation, along with speedboats and trimarans. Ferry service connects Puerto Vallarta with La Paz and Cabo San Lucas; check schedules upon arrival.

Tours

Larger resort areas offer an assortment of guided tours worth investigating. Smaller areas are best seen on your own—by rental car or on foot. You can hire guides for explorations into the surrounding countryside.

Acapulco. The city tour picks you up at your hotel and covers the major attractions around town in just over 3 hours; a full-day tour explores the area around the city. For an introduction to Acapulco's famous night life, consider the night tour; it departs from major hotels at 9 P.M. and takes in Acapulco's hot night spots.

A glass-bottomed boat tours Roqueta Island, Acapulco Bay, and views the underwater Shrine of Our Lady of Guadalupe.

Ixtapa/Zihuatanejo. A "day on the ranch" tour jeeps you to a ranch to watch *vaqueros* (Mexican cowboys) in action. Boat tours include trips to Ixtapa Island (where *Robinson Crusoe* was filmed) and uninhabited Isla Grande—a tropical island abounding with bird life and lush greenery.

A Sunday tour of Agua de Correa Market gives you a look at local crafts; tours of Cabritero anthropological ruins and the ruins at Cocolmeca provide an introduction to Mexico's past. You'll also find tours to isolated bays for swimming and snorkeling.

Manzanillo. The city tour covers the town of Manzanillo and takes you past the exclusive resort of Las Hadas.

Mazatlan. Take a city tour, or see the town on your own in an *arana* (horse-drawn carriage). A full-day tour takes you to San Blas, a remote seaside town (see page 37). Boat tours explore the bay and Deer Island.

Puerto Vallarta. A city tour is offered twice daily; it lasts about 3 hours. You can also visit Mismaloya beach, a jungle hideaway; the original set of *Night of the Iguana* is located here. A nightclub tour departs from major hotels at 10 P.M. and introduces visitors to night life in Puerto Vallarta.

Entertainment

Mexico's west coast offers the most entertainment—and largest variety—in all of Mexico. The resorts know what you come to the west coast for, and are geared to keeping you happy and busy. So take advantage of it, and experience all the activities for which you have the time and energy.

Acapulco. Described by many as Mexico's "playground," Acapulco can keep you entertained 24 hours a day. The famous *Voladores de Papantla* (Flying Pole Dancers of Papantla) put on one show nightly; check with your hotel for locations. The La Quebrada divers perform once at noon and three times during the evening. Bullfights take place every Sunday during the winter months.

Parachute riding is popular; tennis, golf and swimming facilities can be found at most hotels. Acapulco offers numerous discos and nightclubs (many in hotels).

Guaymas. The International Deep-Sea Fishing Rodeo is every July; the Fiesta de la Pesca is in May. If you don't like to fish, you can go riding, snorkeling, or water-skiing.

Beautiful stretches of beach beckon the visitor; the water is ideal for swimming, the sand perfect for relaxing or playing on. Golf and tennis can be arranged through your hotel; fees are reasonable.

Ixtapa/Zihuatanejo. Parachute riding is popular; there's also sailing and snorkeling. Golfers will enjoy the golf course (designed by Robert Trent Jones). Discos and occasional live entertainment are evening diversions.

Ixtapa has several lighted tennis courts for the aficionado. Sailboats and water-ski boats can be rented, usually in front of the larger hotels. Charter a fishing boat in either Ixtapa or Zihuatanejo. Shell collecting is also a popular and productive pastime.

Manzanillo. Water sports are excellent. There's good deep-sea fishing from October through June, and Manzanillo hosts an annual International Sailfish Tournament in November.

El Palmar is a nicely laid-out 18-hole golf course located along the edge of lagoons and canals. If tennis is your game, you'll find 17 courts in Manzanillo, with more underway.

Mazatlan. Fishing—especially for sailfish and marlin—is good all year. Skin diving, water-skiing, and hunting are excellent. Spectator sports such as baseball and bullfights occur in the winter months. Concerts take place regularly in the main plaza; nightclubs and discos can be found throughout town.

Horseback riding along the beaches is inexpensive; take some binoculars for bird watching, a popular sport. Shell collecting is quite rewarding; magnificent coral pools reveal beautiful one-of-a-kind treasures at low tide.

Puerto Vallarta. Parasailing, golf, and tennis are favorite pastimes. The Annual Deep-Sea Fishing Tournament takes place in the first week of November. During the season, "polo burro" is played on the beach and at the Camino Real. Nightclubs and discos are plentiful in Puerto Vallarta.

Skin-diving equipment is available for rent; lessons are also provided. Snorkeling equipment can be rented either in town or at the beaches, and speedboats can be rented for water-skiing. There's horseback riding—or muleback, whichever you prefer—along the beaches or in the hills.

Accommodations

Accommodations in Guadalajara range from inexpensive to deluxe; first-class and deluxe hotels are listed below. It's wise to make reservations in advance; check with your travel agent for additional information on location, prices, and type of room.

There are four trailer parks in the Guadalajara area—either within the city or just outside it.

Guadalajara. Deluxe hotels: Camino Real (nightclub), Fiesta Americana (three restaurants), Guadalajara Sheraton (once the Marriott), Hyatt Regency Guadalajara (within a mini-city), Lafayette (in heart of Pink Zone). First-class hotels: Best Western Fenix (Mexican decor), Castel Plaza del Sol (bar and disco), Holiday Inn, Hotel de Mendoza (downtown).

Getting around

Guadalajara's streets are clearly laid out; you won't have to worry about getting lost. Many downtown streets are pedestrian malls, perfect for strolling and browsing. Take advantage of them and explore the city on foot. Metered cabs are available around town; make sure the flag has been lowered once you've entered, or agree on the fare beforehand. If you want to drive yourself, you can rent a car—offices are located throughout Guadalajara (many at the major hotels). Bus service is efficient and inexpensive.

Tours

A 4-hour city tour of Guadalajara's highlights includes the village of Tlaquepaque. Bus tours leave from San Francisco Church or Parque Revolucion; check schedules upon arrival. Hotel desks will have all the necessary tour information.

To Tlaquepaque and Tonala. Some tours include visits to these attractive handicraft centers, but it's often best to plan your own itinerary. Check with your hotel for a car and driver, and plan to spend the day. Tlaquepaque contains more than 200 shops, restaurants, and other attractions. Nearby Tonala, an important pottery center, offers colorful markets on Thursdays and Sundays and fine studios and shops.

A tequila tour. Tours are available from Guadalajara to the Sauza tequila distillery. Here you'll see the complete process of making Mexico's national drink, from harvesting the maguey heart through bottling the liquid. The Sauza family estate, across from the distillery, is also open to visitors.

To Lake Chapala. A 6-hour tour from your hotel to Lake Chapala also includes lunch. You'll get a look at the charming residential communities of Ajijic and Jocotepec, and have time for shopping. Handloomed fabrics are good buys.

Other tours. Do-it-yourself tours to Barranca de Oblatos (Monks' Canyon) about 8 km/5 miles east of the city give you a good look at a 2,000-feet scenic gorge, a good place for a picnic.

Interested in opals? Drive out to Magdalena, about an hour northwest of Guadalajara on Highway 15. The San Simon opal mine is still operative. Your best bet for genuine gems is to buy from one of the city stores.

Entertainment

Activity in Guadalajara doesn't end when the sun goes down; there's plenty of night life. Hotel bars have the most action; entertainment ranges from mariachi bands to discos. Many restaurants have musical entertainment (in addition to great food).

Guadalajara is the center for mariachi music; expect to hear the sound everyplace. Plaza de los Mariachis is where the groups congregate. You can hire them for a song—or for an evening.

For a cultural experience. The Degollado Theater schedules opera, symphony, and ballet performances; check schedules upon arrival or with a travel agent before you begin your trip. Folklore productions—traditional music, dancing, and theater—are performed at the University of Guadalajara on Sundays at midday.

Strolling through stores. Shopping is a major form of entertainment in Guadalajara, and every visitor should take advantage of it. Visit the markets, as well as the shopping areas on the west side and in the Pink Zone. You'll find excellent buys in Mexican handicrafts in the villages of Tonala and Tlaquepaque.

Sports for all. Hotels have the usual recreational facilities; you can enjoy tennis, golf, and swimming. Bullfights, baseball, polo, and *futbol* are available for those who prefer spectator sports.

Essentials/The Colonial Circle

Accommodations

Accommodations in the towns within The Colonial Circle are generally first-class, clean, and simple; in many cases, hotels are built in charming colonial style. If you're traveling by car, plan to reach your destination by nightfall. Depending on the time of year, it's wise to make advance reservations; check with your travel agent for additional information on location, prices, and types of rooms.

Campers will find trailer parks outside of Patzcuaro and San Miguel de Allende. A trailer park adjoins the Azteca Hotel in Queretaro.

Guanajuato. First-class hotels: Castillo de Santa Cecilia (looks like a castle), El Presidente (a converted hacienda), Real de Minas (pool and tennis courts).

Morelia. First-class hotels: Posada de la Soledad (originally a colonial monastery), Villa Montana (cliffside), Virrey de Mendoza (originally a colonial residence).

Patzcuaro. First-class hotels: Best Western Posada de Don Vasco (hacienda style), Meson del Cortijo (converted hacienda).

Queretaro. Deluxe: La Mansion Galindo (16th century elegance with 20th century comfort, tennis, golf). First-class hotels: Holiday Inn, Jurica (golf, riding), La Mansion Golf Club (resort), Real de Minas.

San Miguel de Allende. First-class hotels: Casa de Sierra Nevada (bedrooms with fireplaces), Hacienda Taboada (resort with mineral spas), Rancho Hotel El Atascadero (fireplaces and bungalows).

Uruapan. First-class hotels: Mansion del Cupatitzio (next to national park), Motel Pie de la Sierra (terraces and fireplaces).

Getting around

If you really want to capture the flavor of The Colonial Circle, travel by rental car. Rental offices are located in Guadalajara (many in the major hotels). The roadways in the area are well laid out; but roads in the towns themselves can be confusing, so tour on foot here. Stroll the village streets and browse in the shops; this way, you won't miss a thing. In Guanajuato, you can either walk (arm yourself with a good map) or hire a car and driver. Taxis serve San Miguel de Allende.

Tours

You'll find few formal sightseeing tours in The Colonial Circle; these towns were meant for exploring on your own—be sure to wear comfortable shoes.

Guanajuato offers a city tour twice daily; another way to see the town is to hire a car and driver. In Patzcuaro, you'll find information on reliable city guides at the Posada de Don Vasco. San Miguel de Allende has a house and garden tour every Sunday; you'll visit four private colonial homes.

Highlights of some of the towns in The Colonial Circle are listed below.

Guanajuato. See the central plaza, Jardin de la Union, Teatro Juarez, Church of San Diego, Plaza de la Paz, Basilica of Our Lady of Guanajuato, Mercado Hildago, the museum Alhondiga de Granaditas, the Chamber of the Heroes, and the Granary (Spanish fort). Be sure to tour the wealthy residential areas.

Morelia. See the Plaza de los Martires, the Cathedral, the churches of San Agustin and Santa Rosa, and the Sanctuary of Our Lady of Guadalupe. Browse through Plaza Las Americas and Casa de las Artesanias.

Patzcuaro. Visit the Plaza Principal (surrounded by Spanish buildings), the Basilica de Nuestra de la Salud, and Casa Gigante—once the home of the Count of Menozal. Shop at the Plaza Grande market; stop in at the Museo de Arte Popular (lovely Tarascan artifacts).

San Miguel de Allende. Visit the Plaza Insurgentes Allende, the church of La Salud, the lovely chapel of San Miguel Viejo, and the church and convent of San Francisco.

Uruapan. On Sundays, the band still plays on the Plaza Principal; facing it is an excellent museum.

Entertainment

Travelers will find surprisingly good restaurants in The Colonial Circle, especially in San Miguel de Allende. Shopping is another form of entertainment here, and this is one of the best shopping areas in Mexico. You'll also find many facilities for tennis, golf, and horseback riding. Night life is limited; there are no discos or nightclubs. The towns themselves, and the people living there, are the best entertainment—enjoy them.

Accommodations

Hotel accommodations in the capital range from good to great. You'll also find a few motor inns off Paseo de la Reforma, conveniently located for most sightseeing. As in most large cities, trailer parks are located in the suburbs.

Most of the hotels center around three areas: Zocalo, Paseo de la Reforma, and Zona Rosa. Each of the areas has advantages. The listing below covers major first-class and deluxe hotels in these areas. See your travel agent for reservations and for additional information on price, exact location, and type of room.

Zocalo. First-class to deluxe hotels: Alameda, De Cortes, Del Prado, El Mexico Plaza (new Holiday Inn under construction), Gran, Majestic, Metropol, Ritz.

Paseo de la Reforma. First-class to deluxe hotels: Bristol, Camino Real (deluxe; near Chapultepec Park), Casa Blanca, Continental, El Presidente Chapultepec (deluxe; in park), Emporio, Fiesta Palace, Maria Isabel Sheraton (deluxe), Reforma.

Zona Rosa. First-class to deluxe hotels: Aristos, Century, Del Paseo, El Presidente, Galeria Plaza, Geneve, International Havre, Krystal (formerly Holiday Inn), Plaza Florencia.

Getting around

Fixed-price minibuses transport passengers from the airport to most downtown hotels. Don't take the Metro from the airport; no luggage is allowed on the trains.

Driving in Mexico City is nerve-frazzling. Park your car and use local transportation.

Around town, you have a choice of first-class buses, taxis, and cars or limousines with drivers and/or guides. Along the Reforma, you can catch buses or *peseros* (jitneys that travel main city streets). English-speaking guides with private cars cluster around major hotels. Check at the hotel desk for recommendations, and be sure that your guide has a license from the government.

Whenever you engage a driver-operated vehicle, settle the one-way or round trip fare before entering. If you plan to spend a few hours at a location outside the downtown area, be sure you can get transportation back to your hotel before letting your vehicle leave.

Riding the Metro, the city's subway, is an inexpensive experience. Clean, quiet, attractively decorated marble stations (many with archeological treasures) may change your image of underground transportation. Don't attempt the trip during rush hours and keep an eye on your wallet or purse.

Tours

Gray Line Tours and other tour operators offer a number of city excursions covering major points of interest. Local tours last from half a day to all day, depending upon the attractions and events included. Prices for full-day tours usually include lunch. Even if you've been to Mexico City before, a half-day orientation will refresh your memory on location and keep you up to date with changes in the capital.

City tours. A full-day city tour normally covers such destinations as the Zocalo, Reforma attractions, Chapultepec Park (Castle and Anthropology Museum), markets, University City, Pedregal residences, San Angel, and Xochimilco. Saturday tours also include the Bazaar Sabado; Sunday ventures might add the Ballet Folklorico (see below) and the bullfights.

Area tours. The most popular excursion goes to the pyramids of Teotihuacan, the Guadalupe Shrine, the Plaza of Three Cultures, and an Indian market. Tours also go to Cuernavaca and Taxco; Puebla and Cholula; and to Toluca for Friday market.

Entertainment

Mexico City is a lively town; you can find something to do until early in the morning.

Nighttime activity isn't limited to restaurants, hotel lounges, nightclubs, and discos, though you'll find plenty of these. Don't sally forth for cocktail hour until at least 7 P.M. or you'll be all alone. Dinner begins around 9 or later, and evening entertainment goes on until the wee hours of the morning. You can also take an evening excursion to Teotihuacan for the light-and-sound spectacle or visit Garibaldi Plaza to hear the mariachis compete.

The highlight of any trip to Mexico, though, is a visit to the Ballet Folklorico. Nightly presentations (Tuesday and Sunday) are an experience in dance, music, and costuming. (Ballet Folklorico also performs on Sunday mornings.) Get tickets in advance; excursions include reserved seats and transportation to and from your hotel.

Accommodations

The area around Mexico City contains accommodations in a variety found nowhere else in the country. Centuries-old haciendas ring the countryside around the capital. Lush gardens and high walls hide gemlike inns in the hills. Quaint colonial hotels offer a touch of the past. Resort spas add landscaped grounds and beauty regimens. All hotels have restaurants and many other amenities.

Some travelers prefer to pick one site as a base for sheer relaxation; others sample each different area's offerings. A few choices are listed below. For details on these hotels (and for other suggestions), check with your travel agent.

Cholula. First-class hotel: Villa Arqueologica. Others: Campestre, Los Sauces.

Cuernavaca. Deluxe hotels: Cuernavaca Racquet Club (open to the public), Hacienda de Cortes, Hosteria Las Quintas, Posada Las Mañanitas (Mexico's top restaurant is located here). First-class hotels: Arocena Holiday, Casa de Piedra, Posada Jacarandas, Posada San Angelo.

Trailer parks: KOA (pool, tennis courts), San Pablo (en route to Cuautla; pool).

Around Cuernavaca. First-class hotels: Vista Hermosa (between Cuernavaca and Taxco), Hacienda Cocoyoc (pools, tennis courts, riding, restaurants, nightclubs).

Ixtapan de la Sal. Resort: Hotel Ixtapan (full facilities, train). First-class hotel: Bungalows Lolita (dining room).

Puebla. First-class hotels: El Meson del Angel (balconies or terraces, pools), Lastra (grand volcano views from roof garden). Moderate hotels: Del Portal, Royalty, Senorial.

Taxco. First-class hotels: De la Borda, Hacienda del Solar, Holiday Inn, Los Arcos, Posada de la Mision, Posada de los Castillo, Santa Prisca.

Tehuacan. First-class hotels: Mexico, Spa Penafiel (northwest of town; tennis court, nine-hole golf course).

Toluca. First-class hotels: Castel Plaza las Fuentes (new), Del Rey Inn (steam baths, sauna).

Valle de Bravo. First-class hotel: Golf Hotel Avandaro (resort motor inn).

Zitacuaro (San Jose Purua). First-class hotel: Spa San Jose Purua (resort motor inn on canyon brink).

Getting around

This area is best traveled by car; half the delight of visiting the region is the fun of exploring. Rental cars are available in larger towns such as Cuernavaca, Taxco, Puebla, and Toluca. Some areas can be reached by bus from Mexico City; bus transportation to small towns is unreliable, though, and should be avoided by tourists.

Some of the regions are so small they can easily be explored on foot. Guides with cars are available in Cuernavaca and Puebla.

For 2 or 3-day trips, you may prefer to take advantage of guided tours, using Mexico City as a base. Though driving in the capital is not for the timid, touring outside the city is remarkably easy.

Tours

Not many organized tours are available. From Mexico City, tour organizations offer excursions to principal attractions in Cuernavaca, Taxco, Toluca, Puebla, Cholula, and surrounding villages. Good information on Cuernavaca attractions is available through most hotels.

Setting up your own tour from Mexico City through the countryside is relatively easy. Local travel agencies can assist you in hiring a car and driver or guide. They can also arrange advance accommodations for popular spots.

If possible, plan your countryside exploring during the week, when accommodations are easier to locate and traffic is considerably lighter. On weekends, families in the capital leave town for vacations, inundating small resorts. Also avoid popular holiday periods.

Entertainment

Long days in the sun exploring caves or visiting Indian sites; swimming, golf, and tennis; shopping; gazing at waterfalls, lakes, and volcanoes—these are the major attractions around Mexico City. At night, you can dine well at one of the region's excellent restaurants; then enjoy mariachi music or go dancing at a disco.

Your choice of destination determines your activity. Don't expect much in the way of gala entertainment in quiet haciendas or small spas. Best bets for late-night activity might be Cuernavaca, Puebla, or Taxco.

Accommodations

You can be assured of clean, simple, and moderately priced accommodations in southern Mexico. Most visitors to this area are interested in ancient ruins and Mexico's Indian heritage, so the hotels won't be deluxe. If you're touring the area by car, plan to reach your destination by nightfall (your choice of accommodations will be greater in large towns). Check with your travel agent for additional information on location, prices, and types of rooms.

You'll find trailer parks in Oaxaca, Palenque, and Veracruz.

Oaxaca. First-class hotels: El Presidente (originally 16th century Convento de Santa Catalina), Mision Oaxaca (newest), Victoria (overlooks city), Villa Arqueologica.

Palenque. First-class hotels: Chan Kah Cabañas (overlook the river), Mision (pool and golf course), Villa Arqueologica.

San Cristobal Las Casas. First-class hotels: Bonampak (new), Molino de la Alboriada (dude ranch), Posada Diego de Mazariegos (rooms with fireplace), Villa Arqueologica.

Veracruz. First-class hotels: Calinda Quality Inn (on the beach), Colonial (on the plaza), El Presidente (new), Emporio (overlooks harbor), Playa Paraiso (on the beach), Prendes (colonial style), Puerto Bello (pool and entertainment).

Villahermosa. First-class hotels: Cencali (entertainment), El Presidente (pool and tennis courts), Maya Tabasco (modern), Villahermosa Viva (pool and tennis courts).

Getting around

Southern Mexico is best seen on your own in a rental car —you'll avoid set schedules, and be able to spend more time in the areas that interest you most. Rental cars are available in Oaxaca and other larger cities.

Buses serve Oaxaca and offer transportation to and from Monte Alban and Mitla. Cabs are reasonably priced. They'll stop off at the lesser-known towns of Tule and Tlacolula; agree on the fare before entering the cab. Major hotels in the city have minibuses that serve the airport.

Buses commute between San Cristobal Las Casas and Tuxtla Gutierrez several times daily; the fare is reasonable.

Air transport is a popular form of transportation from San Cristobal Las Casas to the surrounding ruins and small villages.

Buses serve Palenque from Villahermosa; check schedules upon arrival. Small (three-passenger) planes fly into Palenque's airport; four passengers can charter a flight to Palenque that includes stops at Bonampak and Lacanja. The plane will wait for up to 3 hours while you tour the ruins. Taxis carry passengers to and from the airport.

Tours

Half and full-day tours cover main attractions in most major cities. If you choose to tour on your own, arm yourself with a good map and comfortable shoes. Take advantage of group tours to the ruins; English-speaking guides are usually quite knowledgeable.

Oaxaca. Travel agents in the area offer half-day tours of the city, as well as tours to Mitla, Tule and Tlacolula, Ocotlan, Coyotepec, Jalietza, and Monte Alban. If your time in Oaxaca is short, hire a car and driver at your hotel for a quick condensed tour. Be sure your driver speaks English; agree on the price in advance.

San Cristobal Las Casas. The city tour lasts 4 hours. Air tours are available to the unrestored ruins of Bonampak and Yaxchilan.

Veracruz. You can take a half-day city tour or see the city on your own.

Villahermosa. Full-day guided bus tours to Palenque depart from your hotel. If you prefer to determine your own schedule, hire a car and driver.

Entertainment

Oaxaca offers the most sophisticated entertainment in the area. Regional dances take place on Saturday at the Monte Alban Hotel on the plaza (get tickets in advance). There are mariachi concerts almost every night; the plaza is the scene for Saturday night concerts. The Victoria Hotel boasts a disco. In Veracruz, the major form of entertainment is people-watching and relaxing around the plaza. There's a disco in town, and a band concert takes place a couple of times a week. For the most part, though, travelers visit southern Mexico to view the ruins and experience a virtually untouched Mexico.

Accommodations

Scattered across central and eastern Mexico are clean, simple, moderately priced hotels. You'll also find some deluxe facilities here and there, usually in the larger cities. If you're traveling by car, plan your trip to reach a town (the larger the better) by nightfall, to ensure a wider choice of accommodations. Hotel amenities usually include a restaurant.

Check with your travel agent for additional information on location, prices, and types of rooms. Trailer hookups can be found in most large cities.

Aguascalientes. First-class hotels: Castel Las Trojes, Medrano (free airport transportation), Paris (country club privileges).

Chihuahua. Deluxe accommodations: El Presidente (great view), Hyatt Chihuahua (newest). First-class hotels: Posada Tierra Blanca (in older section).

Durango. First-class hotels: Campo Mexico Courts (adjoining trailer park), El Presidente.

Monterrey. First-class hotels: Ambassador (rooms with balconies), Gran Hotel Ancira, Holiday Inn (deluxe), Hotel Monterrey (nightclub), Ramada Inn Monterrey (resort), Rio.

San Luis Potosi. First-class hotels/motels: Cactus Motel (trailer park), Hostal de Quixote (new), Hotel Panorama (rooftop restaurant).

Tampico. First-class hotels: Camino Real (rooms, bungalows set in tropical gardens), Inglaterra (rooftop nightclub), Posada de Tampico (putting green, tennis courts).

Zacatecas. First-class hotels: Aristos (view of the city), Quality Inn Calinda Zacatecas (previously Arroyo de la Plata).

Getting around

The best way to see the area is to rent a car and tour the towns and villages on your own. You can take buses to larger cities, but you'll miss trips to the out-of-the-way places that make this area so special.

Car rentals are available in most large cities. One caution: plan your stops carefully; there's often a shortage of good accommodations in smaller towns.

Tours

You'll find half and full-day city tours offered in the larger cities, along with organized excursions to some of the surrounding areas. Arm yourself with a good map and do some exploring on your own.

Aguascalientes. Tour the wine-growing areas and the farms where fighting bulls are bred; your hotel will make arrangements. Highlights of the city are the churches.

Chihuahua. Local travel agents offer city tours. Highlights are the baroque cathedral, the Palacio Federal, Quinta Luz (Pancho Villa's former home), the Palacio Gobierno (where Miguel Hidalgo was executed) and, to the north, the spectacular views from Cumbres de Majalca.

Durango. See the colonial homes (the best is that of Count Kuchil), the Ichnographic Gallery of Bishops, and the cathedral.

Monterrey. Highlights are the 3-hour city tour, Carta Blanca brewery tour (free beer included), a shoppers' tour to Saltillo, an hour burro ride to Horsetail Falls, and a 4 to 5-hour excursion to the spectacular Garcia Caves.

San Luis Potosi. Take a self-guided tour; include the cathedral, the colonial-era Convent of San Francisco, the Governor's Palace, the Plaza de Armas, Our Lady of Carmen Church, the Potosi Regional Museum, the Loreto Chapel, and the Guadalupe Shrine.

Tampico. A half-day city tour includes a boat ride on the Tamesi River. See the Plaza de Armas, the Cathedral, and the Palacio Municipal.

Zacatecas. Visit the lovely baroque cathedral, the Church of San Francisco, Santo Domingo Church, and the Museum of Huichol Art; for something different, tour a silver mine. About 48 km/30 miles to the southwest are the restored ruins of Chicomoztoc.

Entertainment

For the most part, you won't find much night life in east-central Mexico. A few nightclubs and discos may be found in the larger cities, usually in the bigger hotels. The attractions of this area are the people—their traditions, their towns, and their lives. You'll also discover a curiously refreshing lack of tourist-oriented facilities.

Accommodations

Travelers will find the greatest range of accommodations in the resort areas of Cancun and Cozumel, and in the city of Merida. The archeological sites of Chichen Itza, Coba, and Uxmal have Villas Arqueologicas, inns managed by Club Med and geared to explorers (see page 29). You'll find simple and comfortable accommodations scattered throughout the Yucatan. Check with your travel agent for additional information on location, prices, and types of rooms.

Campers will find sites outside Campeche, Merida, and Chichen Itza.

Campeche. First-class hotels: Baluartes (open-air dining), El Presidente.

Cancun. Deluxe hotels: Camino Real (grand renovation), Cancun Caribe (faces ocean), Cancun Sheraton, El Presidente, Fiesta Americana Cancun (new), Hyatt, Krystal Cancun (swim-up bar), Miramar Mision (new), Playasol Cancun (gym and sauna), Villas Tacul (private maid with each villa). First-class hotels: Aristos Cancun, Calinda Quality Inn (on the beach), Carrousel (good swimming), Casa Maya (rooms with kitchens), Club Verano (on beach), Maya Caribe (three pools), Viva Cancun (disco).

Within driving distance of Cancun. First-class hotels: Balam-ha (45 minutes from Cancun), Club Akumal, La Ceiba Beach Hotel (cottages).

Chetumal. Continental (near the market), El Presidente (entertainment).

Chichen Itza. Deluxe hotel: Mayaland (5-minute walk to ruins). First-class hotels: Mision 2.5 km/1.5 miles from ruins), Piramide Inn (2 km/1 mile from ruins), Villa Arqueologica (tennis courts, library, 5 minutes from archeological zone).

Cozumel. Deluxe hotels: Cozumel Caribe (on San Juan Beach), El Cozumeleño (marble baths), El Presidente (good bay swimming), Mayan Plaza (good scuba diving), Sol Caribe-Cozumel (across from Paraiso beach). First-class hotels: La Ceiba Beach Hotel (beachfront), Nuevo Playa Azul.

Merida. Deluxe hotel: Krystal Merida. First-class hotels: Casa del Balam (colonial style), Holiday Inn, Hotel Los Aluxes (international restaurant), Montejo Palace (nightclub), Panamericana (nightly entertainment).

Pez Maya Resort. A small island complete in itself; accessible from Cozumel or Cancun. All-inclusive packages (prices include accommodations and plane fare) are available from Cozumel.

Uxmal. Deluxe hotels: Hacienda Uxmal (luxurious), Mision (2 km/1 mile from ruins), Posada Uxmal (same grounds as the Hacienda, but smaller rooms), Villa Arqueologica (near ruins).

Getting around

If you plan to explore the ruins, it's a good idea to rent a car. Taxis can be found in Merida; buses serve Cancun and will take you to any part of the island for a low fare. A ferry serves Cozumel from Playa del Carmen on the mainland; hydrofoils connect Cancun and Cozumel.

Tours

In the larger cities, half and full-day city tours are offered. Excursions to the ruins are a must if you're in the vicinity —you can take a tour starting from the city you're staying in, or hire a guide at the entrance.

Campeche. The whole city is worth exploring; be sure to visit the Archeological Museum (Maya artifacts).

Cancun. Full-day trips are offered to Chichen Itza, Uxmal, and Merida; half-day trips are available to Tulum. Go snorkeling or diving at Xel-Ha.

Cozumel. Cruise to one of the beaches (San Francisco or Passion Island) on the Robinson Crusoe tour; or take a day trip to Tulum or a glass-bottomed boat tour.

Merida. A 2-hour city tour covers the city; there's also a 3-hour home and garden tour that takes in four elegant homes. Or take a day trip to Chichen Itza or Uxmal (some tours visit Kabah).

Entertainment

You'll find evening entertainment in the form of discos in Cancun. The Flying Pole Dancers put on shows at the El Presidente, and the Ballet Folklorico performs at the Convention Center. Merida's nightly gala evening at the Panamericana Hotel features Yucatecan folk dancing. The rest of the area offers little in organized entertainment, but you'll find music in most hotels.

Index

Photographers